T0339797

Nation Building

Or Democracy by Other Means

NATION BUILDING

OR DEMOCRACY BY OTHER MEANS

Hamid Karimianpour

Algora Publishing
New York

Library of Congress Cataloging-in-Publication Data —

Karimianpour, Hamid, 1968-
  Nation Building, Or Democracy by Other Means / Hamid Karimianpour.
     p. cm.
  Includes bibliographical references and index.
     ISBN 978-0-87586-843-1 (soft cover: alk. paper) — ISBN 978-0-87586-844-8 (hard
cover: alk. paper) — ISBN 978-0-87586-845-5 (ebook) 1. Democratization. 2. Liberty—
History. 3. Equality—History. 4. Democracy—Islamic countries. I. Title.
     JC423.K284 2011
     321.8—dc22

                            2011004662

Printed in the United States

To those who stand up for peace

Acknowledgements

Over the years, I have written numerous articles, essays, and short stories, but nothing has given me as much delight as working on this book. Compiling this study took many long hours of meticulous work and many wakeful nights. What has always driven me forward is a longing to be a part of the efforts that make our future brighter than our past, and I hope that the work presented here can serve this endeavor.

In compiling this book, I am much indebted to Nima Ghitani and Mehran Mehrabanpour for their unwavering support and encouragement throughout the whole process, and to Crystal Lantz and Hari Shroff for reading and commenting on parts of my manuscript. I am also thankful to many other friends, colleagues, and my closest family, who in one way or another added a personal touch to this book.

Furthermore, this book benefited from the library resources at the University of Virginia, without whose great collection of books and material this work could not have been possible. For many years, I have made the library my second home.

Finally, I am grateful to the editors at Algora Publishing, who made this book a reality. The editorial comments and critiques have helped immensely to sharpen the language and the effectiveness of the arguments offered in this book.

Hamid Karimianpour

TABLE OF CONTENTS

FOREWORD

On the day of September 11, 2001, I was in the library at the University of Virginia, reading a book, completely unaware of the events of the world outside. I only learned about what had happened hours later when I decided to break and have something to eat. I was at first puzzled to find dozens of students congregating in front of a widescreen TV in the cafeteria, attending to what I at first thought was a science-fiction movie. As I tried to figure out what was happening, a middle-aged woman—whom I assume was a faculty member or a staff, but I never dared to ask—approached me and asked me from which country I was. I answered that I was Iranian. She told me what had happened hours earlier, and said that "what happened this morning was terrible, but it is sad that we will now attack Afghanistan. Many innocent people will die there as well." She impressed me deeply with her compassion. At the very moment when America was announcing that it had been attacked, and many Americans were calling for Al Qaeda to be brought to justice, she was concerned about civilian Afghani lives. That day made many heroes and heroines, and to me she was one of them. I never found out who she was.

A decade has passed and we are still dealing with the aftermath of that tragedy. In the meantime, we have seen two bloody wars and much devastation. Innocent people were killed on that day and many more have been killed since then. The world has become ever more dangerous, with more and more countries involved in wars and conflicts. Sadly, many countries do have long lists of grievances against one another. If we always go the way of vengeance, there will be no peace on Earth.

Aside from geostrategic power struggles at the highest levels, what makes these grievances so hard to overcome at the level of the populace is the lack of an ability to see the world from the opposite side of the cultural divide. We persistently fall into the trap of downplaying our own nations' shortcomings and mistakes while overplaying those of our perceived enemies.

In the wake of the Abu Ghraib prison scandal in 2004 a long-forgotten book by the anthropologist Raphael Patai (1910–96) was reprinted, which some observers then believed had been used by US interrogators as a torture manual for extracting information out of Iraqi detainees. The book is entitled, *The Arab Mind*. In the new reprint's foreword long-time army colonel Norvell B. De Atkine makes the (difficult to qualify) assertion, "While [the Palestinians'] conflict with Israel has been a bloody one over the years, it cannot approach the level of death and destruction incurred in Palestinian wars against the Lebanese, Syrians, and Jordanians. Despite this great violence, the Palestinian–Israeli conflict retains its place as the primary galvanizing issue for the 'Arab street.'"

With these words De Atkine emphasized a double standard which plagues Arab societies. But is the double standard an exclusively Arab problem? Do not Americans react differently when, say, they hear that a foreigner has been killing Americans than when a member of their own society is exposed as a serial killer? Generations of racial profiling seems to suggest an affirmative answer to this question. The Palestinian–Israeli conflict is a more sensitive issue for most Arabs because this conflict more than any other conflicts—including many bloody wars among the Arabs themselves—has divided the world into two poles, where Arabs are put on one side and the West on the other.

De Atkine refers to the "Arabs' tendency to blame others for the problems evident in their political systems, quality of life, and economic power." As an immigrant to the West myself, I have amply witnessed how foreign residents are blamed for all the social and economic problems during times of recession and rising unemployment. Today, Americans blame China for the US trade deficit, as if China created the American consumer culture. It is we who demand Chinese products because we'd rather pay $10 for a Chinese toaster than $100 for one made in America. According to estimates by the CIA World Factbook, the Chinese GDP at purchasing power parity (PPP) per capita in 2009 was just about $6,600, compared to $46,000 in the United States. The average Chinese has just about 15% of the spending money of the average American citizen, meaning that for every dollar, Chinese workers must work up to seven times longer. Still, we have no moral qualms if the Chinese work harder and earn less so that we can indulge in their cheap toasters and yoyos, but we consider it unfair if they buy less from us than we buy from them. We need a scapegoat to blame for our own economic mismanagement, and what better scapegoat than the Chinese?

While the US military was bogged down in two scorching wars in Iraq and Afghanistan with no end in sight, the Bush Administration mounted verbal attacks and threats of invading Iran. This proved a monumental blunder as Iranians began sending arms and money to militants inside Iraq in an attempt to weaken the US military wherever they could reach it. The Bush Administration needed to find a scapegoat to blame for its grave mismanagement of the "war on terror," and who better than the already demonized leadership in Tehran? There are plenty of such examples of double standards and hypocrisy within the United States.

I decided to write this book to bring out a different perspective. I wanted to expose the complexities of cultures and their roles in shaping politics and human societies. I wanted to show that while there are many ways in which various cultures are different, there are more ways in which they are alike. The question is whether we have the courage and willpower to view events from different perspectives, and so far the answer has been in the negative.

De Atkine writes in the same foreword, "In his section on the 'sinister West,' Patai gets to the heart of the burning hatred that seems to drive brutal acts of terrorism against Americans. Despite its lack of a colonial past in the Middle East, America, as the most powerful representative of the 'West,' has inherited primary enemy status, in place of the French and British." The good news in Patai's and De Atkine's insight is that there is an opportunity for the US to normalize its relations with the developing countries just as Britain and France did. This insight reflects the flexibility of Arabs to put past history behind them and move forward, even though the Middle Easterners appear generally more bound than the West by their past. It demonstrates the calamities the US is creating for itself by attempting to take ownership of conflicts around the world. In 1953, the US replaced Britain as the mastermind of a plot that ousted the Iranian government. In 1965, the US replaced France as the main player on the Western side in the Vietnam War. A few years ago, the US took ownership of the Saudi king's fear of Iran's nuclear capability. Today, the US is trying to replace South Korea in the South-North Korean conflict. Washington's desire to take ownership of conflicts across the globe generates anti-American sentiments in the conflict zones, and De Atkine's attribution of this phenomenon to Third World double standards is either cynical propaganda or, at best, it reflects his personal inability to view events outside his own cultural perspectives.

After the 9/11 tragedy, we were encouraged to detest "the terrorists" without questioning why anyone would commit such heinous acts. Bush and Blair were portrayed as men of faith and God had secretly told Bush to go to war. A witch hunt was put in motion by these men and anyone even attempting to study the causes behind terrorism was branded a terrorist sympathizer or a potential terrorist himself. Washington had fought its proxy war against the Soviet Union on Afghani soil, and now it seemed that Washington's own pawns had turned against the US itself. We were told that jealousy towards the West's colossal economic success and a repugnance for our liberal morals underlay the supposed Arab "hatred"; that Arabs only understood the language of humiliation; that terrorism was a disease, but one whose causes we did not need to diagnose. A CNN journalist admitted two years after the Iraq War that she was so intimidated by the Bush war propaganda in 2003 that she did not dare to question the legitimacy of the war.

Ten years have gone by but the pain remains strong. Given the many grievances on all sides of every conflict, we can either fight one another to the brink of extinction or we can strive to understand and respect one another, and make room in the world to live together in peace. I hope this book makes a convincing argument that the second position is a viable one.

PART I.

INTRODUCTION

THE EVOLUTION OF CHANGE

Ever since the end of its colonial power, the West has put pressure on the developing countries in other forms, for one thing by insisting they adopt democracy; the outcome has been little better than chaos.

The West's global democratization projects, which occasionally have included coup d'états, assassinations, and military operations, failed in country after country.

The relationship between the United States and South American countries have been filled with tension for more than 100 years, with the US alternately overthrowing legitimate rulers to install US-friendly strongmen, and blaming its southern neighbors for "not understanding democracy" and the merits of the free market, while southern countries accuse "the Yanquis" of employing the language of democracy as a pretext for extending their imperial reach all over the region. From the 1960s through the 1975, a costly war was fought in Vietnam, only to see the communists quickly gain control over all of Vietnam promptly after the US military withdrawal.

The Middle East and Central Asia are a whole different ball game. The West under the leadership of the United States is coming off badly in its wars in Iraq and Afghanistan. If the vision was to build democracies there, the result has been destruction, death and humiliation for all parties involved. Some form of a multiparty system has been imposed, but the political reality is nowhere near the ideals of democracy. What really happened, and why? What went wrong, or rather, could it have gone right? The proceeding analysis shows that attempts to transform developing countries often go wrong not on account of mistakes made on the battlefield, but because the mission itself is misguided from the outset. A dream cannot be imposed on those who do not dream it.

If the vision was not to build democracies in Iraq and Afghanistan but to build US hegemony around the globe, control the Middle East, or tap into the region's natural resources, then again this book will show how an increasingly intricate world and the increasingly politicized cultures in the Middle East are making these objectives ever harder for the West to achieve by force.

If the vision was to fight Al Qaeda and root out Saddam's assumed WMD program, the proceeding study will show that magnifying these objectives became counterproductive. By militarizing the objectives, neglecting or rejecting diplomacy, and using the language of a "war on terror" and "us versus them," an otherwise limited operation was turned into a near-world war. The last part of the book will question the efficacy of warfare—let alone its legitimacy—in producing intended results in general.

One Globe, Worlds Apart

The relationship between the developed and the developing world has grown tenser with the spread of globalization and modern communication technology, but it has never been easy. Ever since the two worlds crossed paths, their relationship has been affected by misconceptions and cultural disconnection. A millennium ago, the Mongols and Arabs found themselves superior to their European counterparts; then the tide was turned in Europe's favor. Feeling culturally, racially, and militarily stronger, the European powers colonized vast areas in the Third World.

The Second World War changed dramatically the political landscape. The United States of America appeared as a world superpower. By the time the United States asserted its world power, it had already become well rehearsed in democratic ways and was a role model for others. This was no small achievement for an era riddled with strife and bombshells.

With their growing power, many Americans began to entertain the notion of having a responsibility to change the world for the better. They began to think that they were the chosen people to lead the world forward. They felt that it was their destiny to combat injustice anywhere on earth, using either their military or financial strength to effect change. For many average Americans their nation's success story was a source of romanticism and a manifestation of their moral superiority. The United States had succeeded in developing the largest economy and the mightiest army the world had seen in less than two centuries. This achievement naturally gave Americans self-assurance and a sense of unlimited power. If they were capable of building colossal success in a short time with little more than a few shovels and rifles to start with, many Americans thought they would surely be able to move mountains and transform the world.

The American idealism and optimism proved naïve and counterproductive for two reasons. First, in their eagerness to transform the world, Americans ignored the cultural norms and aspirations of the people of other nations. The result was cultural ego-centrism and an addiction to viewing the world only through the American lens. The world turned out to be a harder nut to crack than the American people had initially envisaged. The complexity of societies and the interaction and interconnection between culture and politics meant that they could not change the world on exclusively American terms. Additionally, it made American society look hypocritical. While American missionaries pontificated about democracy and human rights to people elsewhere in the world, civil rights violations were rampant here in the US throughout the twentieth century.[1]

Perhaps one of the most high-profile manifestations of this America-centrism in recent history was the work of the Iraq Study Group in 2006. The Iraq Study Group was a bipartisan panel commissioned by Congress to assess the US military engagement in Iraq and come up with recommendations for alternative courses of actions that could bring peace and stability to that country. As the focus of the study was Iraq, it is natural to expect that an opinion poll should have been conducted in the country to map the wishes and wants of the Iraqi people and then to take those wishes into consideration. Ironically, an opinion poll was the one thing that the study group did not do. The report from the Study Group referred to US interests, the opinions of US generals, and even the interests and roles of Iraq's neighboring countries Iran and Syria, but not the interests of the Iraqis—the aspirations of the people themselves—(the panel only interviewed Iraqi officials that were allies of the US, and the views of the Iraqi population were ignored). The only polling referred to in the report mapped what the Iraqi people thought of the war, but not how they wanted their government to be organized: "Recent polling indicates that only 36 percent of Iraqis feel their country is heading in the right direction, and 79 percent of Iraqis have a 'mostly negative' view of the influence that the United States has in their country. Sixty-one percent of Iraqis approve of attacks on U.S.-led forces."[2] This was the only opinion poll of the Iraqi people.

The fact that this panel was commissioned by Congress is interesting. The Bush Administration had already been criticized harshly for its wars in the Middle East. Congress stepped in, presumably to clear the mess and do what the American people thought was right. When even this Congressional panel failed to conduct so much as a superficial survey of the Iraqi people in regard to the future of their own country, it exposed the chronic ignorance of those very same politicians who would insist that democracy means empowering people.

The Iraq War was marketed to the American people and their allies partially on a platform of liberating the Iraqi people from Saddam Hussein's oppressive regime. (Claims are now commonly heard that other factors, such as gaining control of oil supplies and achieving regional dominance, constituted the real reasons for the war; that is another issue.) Even if we take the platform of "liberation" at face value, there are grave problems with it. Former British Foreign Secretary Jack Straw defended the war in his address to the International Institute for Strategic Studies in February 2003 by claiming that, "The Iraqi people deserve the chance to live fulfilling lives free from the oppression and terror of Saddam... Our first objective will be to secure Iraq's disarmament. But our next priority will be to work with the United Nations to help the Iraqi people recover from years of oppression and tyranny, and allow their country to move towards one that is ruled by law, respects international obligations and provides effective and representative government."[3] The primary reason for invading Iraq would have been legitimate as Straw phrased it, had Saddam indeed possessed WMD. We now know that it was clear he did not. But further, Straw's second stated objective, namely to help Iraqis recover from years of tyranny—without even bothering to consult the Iraqis themselves, demonstrates not only Straw's belief that he could tap into US and British zeal to assist oppressed people in a volatile corner of the world, but also a general complacency in believing that he (we) on his (our) own—not unlike Saddam himself—could determine what was good for Iraq's people.

This eagerness to help, when it truly exists, is commendable, but this obliviousness to the preferences of a nation's own citizens is not.

As the president of the Arab American Institute, James Zogby, stated in his recent book—*Arab Voices: What the Arab World is Saying to Us and Why It Matters*—the animosity in the Arab world is due to the West's inability or unwillingness to listen to the voices of people in the Middle East. Any action, whether at the individual or national level, that fails to take into consideration the wishes and dreams of the people who are affected, is bound to trigger frustration and a sense of enmity.[4]

The second reason why American idealism proved naïve or counterproductive was that the US government hijacked the best intentions of the American people and transformed them into grounds for further exerting its power across the world. The government used its leverage to suppress countries that refused to align with the US interests. The mainstream US media went hand-in-hand with the government to highlight human rights violations in the Third World. The more the American people disliked what they saw on their TV screens, the more Washington could advance its agenda under the banner of "democratizing" other nations. In so doing, the US government violated the democratic ambitions of its own people, let alone the ambitions of the people in other regions.

The critics claim that access to cheap oil, minerals, and markets are among the real reasons why the West wants to get on the ground in Third World countries, and that they only use the veil of democratization to mask their intentions. Some go as far as accusing the US of empire building.

For centuries, European industrialization prompted waves of colonization. The desire for gold and silver and the need for scarce resources fed the rivalry among European powers, who sought spheres of influence where treasures were to be found. Europe's mighty armies poured into continents far from their homelands with the purpose of establishing strongholds. The indigenous people were merely in the way; viewed as primitive or savages, they were suppressed, often violently. The need to justify colonization to themselves and their people led the great powers to designate their mission as one of civilizing the primeval world. Fleets of missionaries were dispatched to Africa, Asia, and the Americas to spread the message of Christianity. Then laws were enforced to regulate the aboriginal societies after Western models; often at gun point. Having co-opted some percentage of the populace into the new belief system and having succeeded in creating the impression that they represented something superior, the Westerners then proceeded to intrude more and more.

If "civilization" of the primitive world was the watchword of the nineteenth century's great colonial powers—by which was meant the cultivation of science, arts, industry, economic growth, law, and order, but not necessarily the rule of people—"democratization" has been the motto since the middle of the last century. Critics believe that the same kind of thirst for resources and access to remote markets for Western products are the real driving forces. A recent controversial remark by Germany's former president Horst Koehler has fueled such suspicions about ulterior motives. As a NATO member and an ally in Western coalition, Germany has sent troops to Afghanistan to participate in the nation-building project. After a short visit to Afghanistan in May 2010, Horst Koehler stated in a radio interview that for an export-oriented country like Germany, it was necessary to send in troops to protect trade routes. Koehler resigned shortly after the interview amidst controversy caused by his comments.[5] Although the function of the German presidential office is primarily ceremonial, his assertion was for many an indication of the prevalent view among hawkish Western policymakers that trading blood for oil and trade routes was justified—a policy known as "gunboat diplomacy."

The recent Wikileaks revelations of the list of strategic infrastructure sites[6] around the world that the US considers significant to its national security certainly reinforces the impression that US authorities are anxious to maintain a presence in various regions and is willing to use the name of "peacekeeping" or "democratization" to justify its doing so. Since 2001, the US has spent over a trillion dollars on two wars in Iraq and Afghanistan in the name of democratizing the region—not even including the opportunity costs and the interests on borrowed money to pay for these wars—while a recent survey revealed that one in seven Americans live in poverty, over ten million Americans do not have health insurance and millions more have insufficient insurance (the numbers may have vastly increased recently, due to rising unemployment), and a million homes were foreclosed on only in 2010.

President after president has insisted that America's wars are grounded on humanitarian considerations. Meanwhile when Hurricane Katrina hit the shores of New Orleans in 2005, no rescue package was rushed from the White House. For those who believe every word coming out of Washington, it appears as though America's love of humanity has put this nation on a suicidal path, bringing democracy to Iraq and Afghanistan and devastation to our own states.

Democratizing the Third World is the official language of Washington today, but Western foreign policies have not always been focused on or in favor of promoting democracy. Western foreign policies have rather aimed at strengthening the hands of puppet governments in the developing countries who were willing to put Western interests in a favorable position. During the Cold War, Western policymakers backed authoritarian rulers around the world, as long as they proved skillful in containing the spread of communism, that is, blocked the interests of the Soviet Union and China.

The last shah of Iran was supported by the United States. In a private conversation with the shah, President Lyndon Johnson said that his administration would understand if the shah saw it necessary to use a heavy hand in dealing with dissent. And not all the dissidents were communists. Many cried out for democracy or for economic betterment for their families. The dissidents were smashed, regardless of their political affiliations. Thousands suffered torture in the country's notorious prison, Evin, while Washington looked the other way and supplied the shah with more sophisticated armaments and financial aid.

Similar occurrences plagued Africa and Latin America. Western support for the ANC's anti-apartheid movement in South Africa gained momentum only after the fall of the Soviet Union towards the end of 1980s. Until that time, a democratic South Africa was not high on the West's agenda. The Mujahideen fighters, the predecessor to Taliban, were supplied with arms and finance during the long struggle against the Soviet invasion of Afghanistan in the 1980s. Thousands of civilians were killed by the Mujahideens during this period, right under the CIA's nose.

Washington has made much noise about Iran's support for Hezbollah and Hamas, calling it state-sponsored terrorism, but few commentators have bothered to point out that the US itself set an example of sponsoring terrorism in Afghanistan and elsewhere as a way of curbing the influence of its rival, the Soviet Union. If it was the fear of communism under the Cold War, fear of terrorism is often cited as the new justification for collaborating with dictators in the developing world—the popularly known policy of making friends with the "bad" in order to ward off the "worst."

The West supported Saddam during the eight year long Iran–Iraq War. When Saddam used deadly chemical weapons against Iranians or when his planes randomly targeted civilians in Iranian cities, no word of condemnation came from the West. But as soon as Saddam attacked Kuwait and threatened to take control of Kuwaiti oil resources, the first Bush Administration intervened to push him back. While in rhetoric the war was sold as an operation to liberate Kuwaitis, critics saw only oil as the motive.

Saddam was again in the spotlight a decade later, when the Bush Administration accused him of harboring a program to create weapons of mass destruction (WMD). His abysmal human rights record was brought forward only in the run-up to the 2003 invasion of Iraq to create support for the war plan. As part of justification for the invasion, the former British Prime Minister and the staunchest ally of the second Bush Administration's war efforts, Tony Blair, warned that "more people [would] die" if the coalition forces did not oust Saddam from power. Critics saw again oil as the motive and fear of WMD or human rights considerations as pretexts. They pointed out worse human rights abuses in the world that received little attention; they took place in locations where the West has little strategic interest. It is hard to paint the war in altruistic and benevolent terms, when the pattern of behavior of the decision-makers in Washington and London shows that they do not act benevolently on other, more acute, occasions.

The chaos after the war made Iraq one of the most acute regions in the world in terms of death and destruction. But in the weeks before the war, Blair had argued that the war would save lives. Meanwhile, for example, AIDS and poverty continued ravaging much of Africa.

For decades, antiwar campaigners have questioned the legitimacy of wars fought under the flag of democracy. Former Pentagon analyst and Vietnam War whistleblower Daniel Ellsberg leaked top secret "Pentagon Papers" revealing that President Lyndon Johnson had lied to both the public and Congress about "a subject of transcendent national interest and significance" in order to keep the war aflame throughout his time in office.[7] The leaked documents showed that Presidents Kennedy, Johnson, and Nixon knew all along that the war was not winnable and that many more casualties were to be expected, if the conflict continued, but they kept it going nonetheless. For one thing, ending the hostilities without a clear US win would humiliate Washington and ruin the presidents' reputation, too. Who knows what else was going on, if the war was part of the effort to stop the "domino effect" of Communist takeovers?

President Hosni Mubarak of Egypt is one of the most recent examples of a US backed dictator, who only now is drawing media's attention. Washington showered Mubarak with billions of dollars for over 30 years (a billion dollars just in 2010), and the CIA collaborated with Mubarak's torture agents, who ensured that democracy would never get a chance in these 30 years. Suddenly, in the wake of the 2011 riots, Washington took an urgent interest in making Egypt a democratic state. As if this popular uprising against one of its key allies has not been enough of a slap in Washington's face, the White House is desperately trying to hijack the event and make it its own doing; so it looks like it is not the Egyptian people, but the President of the US, who is kicking Mubarak out of his seat.[8] There has been talk in the US media that it was President Obama's speech in Cairo in 2009 that mobilized the Egyptian protestors, despite a recent opinion poll which showed that about 82% of Egyptians do not approve of the US Middle East policy. The White House needs a political boost after two years of poor performance here at home as well as Washington is interested in regaining its geopolitical clout by replacing the dictator with another US-friendly dictator, but to look into the Third World for sources and resources for gaining wealth, power, or prestige has always been the well-known policy of the Western leaders. And they have spared no occasion to capitalize on events in the Third World, be it a democracy movement, a dictatorship, or a gold mine. In the case of Egypt, there are indications that the newly appointed Vice President Omar Suleiman is the candidate the White House might be pushing as Mubarak's replacement. Suleiman's reputation as the former chief of the Egyptian intelligence agency has earned him the nickname "the Mubarak's Mubarak" among the Egyptian people, but he has been a dear ally of the CIA during the "war on terror."

All in all, critics complain that policymakers switch between fighting and befriending leaders in the Third World depending on what suits their political and economic interests, with no regard for "democracy." When Western leaders are interested in taking down the so-called "bad guys" in the Third World, they label them rogue dictators (even if they were elected) and call the dissenters "freedom fighters"; when they want to support the leader, they label dissidents in the region "insurgents" or "communists."

Because in the West all government actions ultimately need popular support, the public must be convinced that the policymakers' intentions conform to the beliefs and interests of its people. If the loss of face for Washington is going to sap popular support for the war in Vietnam, critics suggest, "a subject of transcendent national interest and significance" must be officially invoked as the objective of the war; if defending trade routes is not going to rally the German public behind their troops' involvement in Afghanistan, protecting the social status of Afghani women must become the official German goal. According to this theory, rationalizations for military intervention must appeal to emotions associated with fear and self-defense, or values that the populace believe are part of their own self-definition, such as defending human rights, or democracy. The voters must be led to believe that democratization is the goal of intervention, even if it is not.

Of course, there may be a variety of conflicting interests at work, each pulling the string a little towards its side. Some army generals may want war, not for access to oil resources or to spread American hegemony, but to defend the country against a perceived threat (or perhaps even subconsciously for the adrenaline rush?). It is a known fact that the extraordinary level of excitement, heightened awareness, etc., of the war zone, can be highly addictive. The army uses violent videogames for troop recruitment.

Some human rights advocates may genuinely believe that war is an efficient way of breaking loose a suppressed people. Ultra-conservatives may seek war to reverse what they see as the decline of Western power. Financiers, vehicle makers and technology companies can make money. Politicians may win votes by balancing among all these factions. A complex network of players and interests works concurrently to produce the outcome.

Foreign policy requires, however, that the nation speaks with one tongue. Conflicting interests must converge under one banner to promulgate a united front. The banner under which the policy goes must reflect the state of mind of the majority people or it is not rooted in democracy. If fear constitutes the majority attitude, the banner will be self-defense, and fear will be the predominant factor the politicians will play on; if democracy, idealism and a desire to help others is the core attitude in the population, the politicians will play on that. If a military operation is launched in the name of civilizing primitive cultures, it is presumed that self-righteousness and racial prejudice can motivate the voters; in that case the political campaign seeks to intensify the prejudice. Since war must be backed by the people, in a democracy, politicians must present justifications that play on basic instincts common in the population. The fact that American wars are often fought under the banner of democratizing the world shows that playing to an underlying attitude of moral righteousness usually works: Americans believe in the value of democracy and want to share it with other nations.

But the hypocrisy surrounding these wars—such as imposing democracy militarily on others (that is, undemocratically), making allies of the worst despots in a region in order to isolate another country against which a war is being fought, or pouring resources into one region while ignoring worse human rights violations in other regions because they do not possess any strategic value for the US—all this shows that the real reasons for the wars have little to do with "democratization" of developing countries. Further, it demonstrates that the American people are oblivious to what their government is really up to. And thirdly, if they believe that their government would truly be able to install democracy at gunpoint, it shows that the American people do not understand the internal social and cultural mechanisms required for democracy to be implemented successfully. The third point is the focus of this book.

To put it simply, the American people on the whole do not have bad intentions, but greed and power have corrupted the political circles and many faithful Americans are unaware of the extent of this corruption. American optimism, idealism and credulity, partnered with a lack of understanding about the workings of culture in shaping politics, allow the hawks to lead Americans to war.

Americans who support militarized democratization projects around the world fail to understand both the true meaning and the true workings of democracy. They focus too narrowly on their own success story and believe that it can be imposed as a model for change everywhere. They have lost sight of the fact that major transformations in the world almost always need to be endorsed locally; that for change to happen, there must be internal mechanisms in place; that the dynamics for change are intertwined with local aspirations and ambitions; that internal leaders and mobilization from within a culture are essential for any transformation to succeed; that coercive methods from outside will not work because they are not supported by the people in the region; and that a fetus must grow in the mother's womb—not in the Oval Office.

A closer look at successful transformations over the last two hundred centuries reveals very clearly a complex pattern of internal disputes followed by popular mobilization and led by leaders who advocated change yet were loyal to the foundations of their old culture. International pressure and incentives have sometimes played a role in encouraging change, but they have rarely, if ever, by themselves produced the desired outcome. To the extent the international community has succeeded in effecting change, the change has been brought about in partnership with local forces or it has been counterproductive. International pressure to enforce democratic rule in the Democratic Republic of Congo, Kenya, Nigeria, and more recently Iraq and Afghanistan, produced adverse consequences because of a lack of local ambition and mechanisms to make democracy work. In all of these countries democracy was intermingled with chaos and bloodshed. Meaningful transformations cannot succeed unless there is internal willpower, favoring change. Democracy requires unleashing forces that challenge status quo. It cannot be implemented unless people want change. Democracy cannot be dictated. By its very definition it must be built on popular endorsement. As the recent conflicts in the Middle East have demonstrated, if the social, political, and cultural environment in a country is not ripe enough for change, democratization efforts are doomed to fail.

Social change requires cultural evolution. A new vision must be shared by a critical mass of people for a culture to transform itself, and no vision can be dictated by outside forces. The vision must be passionately upheld by the people who entertain it.

THE WORKINGS OF CULTURE: INTERNAL LEADERSHIP AND INTERNAL MOBILIZATION

This book is designed to educate readers about the dynamics and difficulties of social change in general by looking at some concrete historical transformations in the world over the past two centuries. Progressive attitudes have helped America advance fast, but at the cost of losing track of history and the struggle along the way. A recent survey revealed that about a quarter of young Americans between the ages of 19 and 24 do not even know what occasion the 4th of July celebrates, let alone events outside the United States.

Many Americans do not have any concept of how difficult social transformation can be, and how stubbornly cultural obstacles can inhibit change.

Rolling up one's sleeves and building a new life on fresh ground is taken for granted in the United States. The American let's-do-it attitude does not necessarily work elsewhere. Speedy development came to this country owing in part to immigrants who left behind much of their old conflicts and cultural baggage in favor of starting afresh in the promised land. America developed far from the wars and factional infighting that ravaged much of the European continent and, more recently, regions such as Central America. The older and more complex a culture is, the harder it is for change to take place—and the more naïve it is, therefore, to believe that democracy can simply be imposed from outside.

It is beyond the scope of this book to attempt to give a detailed account of how developing countries can or should progress towards more openness and democracy. Authors often fall into advocating radical solutions one way or another, solutions which are imposed prematurely on cultures that are not yet evolved to absorb democracy. Doing this is precisely what this book argues against. This book urges the reader instead to listen to the voices in the Third World. Internal evolution, internal mobilizations, and internal leadership are mechanisms by which sustainable transformations can ensue. Notwithstanding all our well-meaning efforts, for change to succeed, they must evolve from within a culture.

Important Transformations in Modern History

Instead of engaging in a philosophical discussion about why imposing democracy is self-defeating by definition, *The Power to Change* looks at the history of five transformations in the world over the past two centuries to highlight the workings of culture and of the internal mobilization and leadership that made the transformations in question possible. Of course, many societies were transformed by force prior to this period. The spread of imperial power, and often the spread of Christianity and Islam, occurred through violence. But the world has changed, and as President Obama also noted upon taking office; the world population of today is politicized in ways never seen before. In today's world the people of even small nations think for themselves and cannot be pushed around as easily as they could in centuries past.

The language of the book in Part II extends beyond democracy and talks about transformation and the dynamics of change in general.

The discussions will also go beyond the current troubles in the Middle East and Africa. We will focus on social change in a broader perspective and not only consider democracy as one specific method of organizing political power. The events studied are
- the abolition of slavery in America,
- the feminist movement,
- the fall of the Soviet Union,
- the end of apartheid in South Africa, and
- Khatami's reform movement in Iran.

These are only a few examples of significant transformations in the modern era. They all occurred within international contexts and were to varying degrees inspired by developments elsewhere in the world, but the dream of change came from within the respective cultures. The fundamental similarity of all these events is that major changes in politics and culture were initiated not by the international community, but by leaders within the old system—leaders who were far from idealists. Gorbachev was a loyal communist, after all. F. W. de Klerk had a long history of defending apartheid. Most abolitionists, including Abraham Lincoln, believed that the white race was superior to the black but fought wholeheartedly for emancipation even so.

There were idealists within the abolitionist as well as the feminist movement, but they were considered too radical for their time to ever rally popular support for their cause. They were external to the mainstream movement. Real transformation was carried out by those who were in principle loyal to the foundations of the old systems but wanted only to reform it.

Once the reform movements were unleashed, the process often spiraled out of hand and more comprehensive transformations resulted, such as the complete collapse of the Soviet state. But the leaders who initiated the changes never intended to rock the foundations of the whole system.

A group of radical Iranian dissidents in exile called for Islam to be abolished as the state religion in Iran, but they too were far outside the current cultural framework in Iran and their demand amounted to little more than background noise. A similar pattern has been evident in contemporary US politics, where President Obama's perceived idealism stirred up the Tea Party movement against him during the 2010 midterm elections. President Obama can only succeed in staying in power if he portrays himself as a centrist within American politics. Ironically, being a centrist, i.e., being a follower of the culture of Washington (however corrupt it may be), is the same as walking away from his promise of change, which brought him to power in the first place.

As will become clear in Part II, the institution of slavery, gender inequality or centralized rule in the Soviet Union were not merely isolated political patterns that could be transformed easily by toppling a figurehead or altering simple aspects of the power structures. They were deeply-rooted cultural phenomena. Changing them required gradual cultural evolution. Slavery was not only a system of extorting labor from the slaves; it thrived on a whole culture of racial prejudice. Discrimination against blacks was not confined to the Southern states. In spite of the abolitionist movement, many Northerners were just as fearful of the emerging free black population as their fellow Southerners.

The American Civil War tardily adopted as one of its goals the abolition of slavery, and it was unquestionably successful in that, but the war was not imposed on Americans by outside forces. It was an internal struggle, the culmination of decades of legislative attempts to achieve a consensus agreeable to all. Neither was the welfare of the black population its chief concern, as shown by the abject misery of the system that was allowed to replace it. In any case, as chapter 3 will show, many Southerners already shared the North's ideas about the institution of slavery and were haunted by guilt, and at the same time most Northerners shared the white supremacist ideology of the South. (Even Great Britain had only ended slavery in the Caribbean a few decades before; and their racial attitudes too remained largely unchanged.)

Gender inequality was not only about men subjugating women; a whole culture of gender prejudice existed in which both men and women sustained the inequalities. Another example is the custom still widespread in some developing countries, where mothers participate alongside fathers to impose forced marriages on their daughters. Both genders play a part in sustaining the culture of oppression. Neither are the authoritarian regimes in the Third World only an expression of one man or the elite class suppressing their populace. There is a culture of violence and chaos from which only a brutal leader can emerge to restore a degree of law and order. Without far-reaching change in attitudes, the respective cultures would sustain the old ways. If a dictator falls, another dictator will rise up to fill the gap quickly, as long as the culture stands.

One may always find a black swan, or an exception to any rule, and this author does not mean to say that no outside pressure can ever bring positive change. But what makes a policy reliable is the overwhelming evidence of past successes. The record from the period under investigation rather tells a poor story about the ability of external players or military operations to effect fundamental and positive transformations in the world, if any.

CHAPTER BREAKDOWN

Chapter 2 examines the inconsistency of the West's democratization projects. It also evaluates the effects of democracy in developing countries. Two opposing views are discussed in detail.

Chapter 3 focuses on the institution of slavery and its collapse. The slave trade in the Western Hemisphere largely went hand in hand with the idea that blacks were inferior to whites. Among those who engaged in the battle to free the slaves in the US were idealists who believed more literally than others that "all men were born free and equal." But was the slave trade ended by these idealists? The battle for emancipation of the slaves needed a leader who would condemn slavery but not radically break from the white supremacist ideology. Abraham Lincoln was the right man for this job. As the chapter will show, he held racially biased views that in today's world would have been totally unacceptable, but they allowed Lincoln to draw sufficient support from a vast majority of white voters who despite believing in the superiority of the white race were in favor of ending the slavery. Thus, Abraham Lincoln was by no means a stranger to the supremacist ideology. He was an "insider" himself, but a progressive insider who wished to abolish the worst consequences of the white supremacist ideology. This chapter reviews the events leading up to the Civil War, the destruction of slavery, and the leadership for change.

Chapter 4 is on the battle for gender equality. The feminist movement has gone through three waves of struggle over the past two centuries. Today, it is clear that the history of feminism represents one of the greatest social transformations of our modern time. However, the fight for social and economic equality did not start until 1960s. Apart from feminists such as Voltairine de Cleyre and Margaret Sanger, the first wave of the Western feminist movement was primarily concerned with a few political rights such as women's suffrage (or vote). The notion that men and women were equal had not yet been fully formed at the time. Throughout the first wave, the idea that gender differences justified unequal treatment of men and women was widespread among members of both sexes in this early period in the history of the movement. Before the feminist movement could gain the leverage to campaign for full gender equality, a much more limited battle had to be won by the "insiders" of the old gender culture first. Though these insiders did not necessarily believe in full equality between men and women, their fight pioneered changes that would fuel a more progressive struggle later. The chapter will critically examine the forces of change within the three different waves of feminist movement.

Chapter 5 deals with the Soviet Union under the Cold War and Gorbachev's revolution. The West's containment policy played a pivotal role in hindering the global expansion of communism after World War II, but the containment policy alone proved insufficient to break down the Soviet state itself. The Soviet Union was strong for at least four decades post World War II, and with its help regional communist regimes still managed to pop up on both sides of the ocean. For the communist state to change, it needed a leader from within the organization. Mikhail Gorbachev was such a leader. He was a dedicated communist and an insider of the culture of Kremlin, who aspired to change the system culturally and politically from within. His stated intention was to preserve communism as the leading ideology, but his work ultimately opened up the pathway for forces that would rid Russia of communism altogether. The chapter describes the astute leadership of Ronald Reagan during the Soviet transformation, but argues that only a leader from within the communist system could ever gain the kind of leverage that Gorbachev had to break down the old system. The chapter will elaborate Gorbachev's legacy, his rise to power, his ideological battle and ambitions, and finally, the events leading up to the fall of the communist state and its dramatic aftermath as its economic system crumbled.

Chapter 6 scrutinizes apartheid in South Africa. Though there must be no doubt that the international sanctions put effective pressure on the apartheid regime, it was not sanctions alone that changed the South African system. It took a leader within the system to finally break through the barriers and bring about the political change in the country. That leader was F. W. de Klerk, a white ex-apartheid leader. As the first black president,

Nelson Mandela became indispensable in the transitional government. His efforts and calm style limited the civil unrest during this delicate period. But even Mandela could not have triggered the change by himself. He was imprisoned at the time de Klerk began engineering the transformation. De Klerk was by no means an idealist and he had for many years defended segregation, but he ultimately ended the system. The chapter discusses why and how the system of apartheid was defended by the white constituency in terms of national security and self-defense. De Klerk's early views in favor of segregation allowed him to survive as a political figure in the apartheid system. Had he acted as an outsider and campaigned for change from the outset of his political career, he might not have won the presidency, and thus he might not have arrived at a position from which he could end apartheid. The chapter also highlights ANC's shrewd maneuvering through the negotiations, which speeded up the fall of apartheid and brought Mandela to power.

Discussions about Iran are organized in Chapters 7 and 8. More space is devoted to Iran because Iran's problem is evolving, both with regard to its internal political aspirations and its external standoff with the US on the nuclear issue. Chapter 7 looks at Iranian nationalism, its democratic objectives, and the origins of the country's distrust of Western powers. It briefly reviews Iran's history from the glories of the Persian Empire up until the 1979 Revolution that brought the Islamic regime to Iran, but the chapter focuses primarily on Iran's first democracy that followed the 1906 Constitutional Revolution and the 1953 CIA-orchestrated coup d'état that deposed the Iranian prime minister and replaced his power with the despotic shah.

The focus of Chapter 8 is on Iran as an Islamic republic. Regime change has been one of the items atop the agenda for US's Iran policy. Various measures ranging from sanctions to supporting political dissidents have been applied to this end. Every time the US stepped up efforts to topple the Islamic Republic, the Islamic Republic gained strength by drawing upon anti-American sentiments in the population. In 1997, Mohammad Khatami won the presidential election. Soon he embarked on a master plan for cultural and political change in Iran. Within a short period of time the political arena became much freer, women gained increased rights, and a wealth of newspapers and books flourished. Iran became a more open society. Although unlike de Klerk and Gorbachev, Khatami did not succeed in completing a lasting change in the country, his case is another example of change initiated from within a system. Khatami was an insider to the system. His vision was to create a more progressive Iran, but he was still an Islamic cleric who aimed at preserving the role of religion in politics. A real change that would have divided religion from politics might have happened later had he succeeded in completing his agenda first.

The chapter reviews Khatami's legacy, what he achieved, how he failed, and why only a leader from within the Islamic Republic has the best chances of initiating change. This raises a question about the West's security while Iran's democracy is in the making. The chapter deals with the Western fear of Iran's current hardliner president, Mahmoud Ahmadinejad. It seeks to explain his policies in an original approach by interpreting his behavior in the light of imminent threat of a US invasion under the Bush Administration. It argues that far from being fearless, as Ahmadinejad has often been delineated in the media globally, his vitriolic language was deeply rooted in an extreme anxiety about the possible US aggression on his country. The chapter raises also the point that while his aggressive rhetoric was unavoidably damaging for Iran's image in the long run, it helped him ward off the invasion. The image of a "mad man" who might retaliate stopped the hawks in Washington short of attacking Iran. Without his theatrical rhetoric the war might have been inevitable and many lives might have been lost. Drawing from lessons learned in Iraq and Afghanistan, an invasion of Iran would have potentially been extremely devastating for the whole region, for the US military, and global security, as it could have vastly inflated anti-Western sentiments and international terrorism. In this regard, the number one enemy of the American people was not Ahmadinejad but the hawkish aspirations of the Bush Administration. By guarding against a highly possible war, the chapter argues, Ahmadinejad became, inadvertently and ironically, the best friend of peace and of American people.

The chapter suggests that the often-cited security threats from Tehran have no deep roots and that under a new policy approach the country can quickly cease to present any major threat to the West and become instead a positive player in the world. So far, President Obama has failed to create a new policy approach for Iran.

Chapter 9 connects the dots, concluding that the Western approach towards the developing countries has often done more harm than good, even if the intentions were to help the region change for the better. The chapter argues that a different vision must be invented for the future relationship between the two worlds. The chapter starts off with a short analysis of the Iraq and Afghanistan Wars, and shows that military operations can hardly serve the West's own interests in the long run.

Finally, Chapter 10 ends the discussion by proposing that, in exact opposition to the mainstream view that wars are an inevitable part of human culture, we are never more than one single generation away from a culture in which war is not recognized as a solution. Up until the nineteenth century it was believed that slavery was an inevitable fact of life. During the period leading up to the US Civil War, many in the Democratic Party argued that focusing on the state of the economy was more important than worrying about the abolitionist movement. Fifty years after Emancipation, slavery was entirely a thing of the past, even though racial prejudice persisted in the country. Women were subordinated up until a few decades ago. In the US, they did not have voting rights until 1919.

These examples give reason to hope that, on the whole, once the culture is changed in a fundamental way and there has been general consensus about that change, it only takes one generation to put it beyond reversal. And if it is difficult to find ways to advance towards a culture of lasting peace, it is increasingly becoming more difficult to find ways to justify wars.

The style of this chapter is speculative, but no book in politics is truly worth the paper it is written on unless it offers at least some ideas about how lasting peace may be achieved. The chapter shows that the hawks are not candid when they sell a plan of war as the "last resort." War is in fact considered as the quickest way to achieve desired objectives—until proven wrong. This chapter proposes how the journey to lasting peace can start.

2. Democracy or Illusion? — Two Opposing Views

The American people have been united under the illusion of advancing democracy in the Third World since World War II. Democracy has been held up as the golden principle behind many US military operations. Is democracy even the right model of governance for the Third World?

For those who consider democracy a moral imperative, detached from all other considerations, the question seems pointless. If democracy is obligatory, it ought to be implemented; and if despotism is evil, it ought to be rooted out at any cost. Bringing democracy into the moral sphere, as opposed to conceptualizing it in terms of its practicality or efficiency in organizing power, it seems *prima facie* that even outside observers will be morally required to intervene on behalf of the oppressed. Now, if I witness that you are trimming a plant as a matter of aesthetics and I disagree that your garden will look prettier that way, I have no right to impose upon you my sense of beauty; but if I witness you chopping off the head of your political opponent to augment your power and I view such acts with moral abhorrence, I seem to have an urgent duty to stop you, and to do so with force, if necessary.

This is the opinion cherished dearly by many people. It is rooted in the idea that moral principles are universal and imperative. The German philosopher Immanuel Kant is credited with the thesis of the universality of moral precepts. For Kant, an action ought to be in conformity with moral imperatives regardless of what outcome they are likely to produce. Kantians oppose utilitarianism, which seeks to maximize utility (or benefits) for the maximum number of people as the basis for all morality.[9]

Western democracy works as a double-edged sword. Democratic principles, understood in a moral sense, are commendable not only in a utilitarian approach, in that "people power" (one definition of democracy) maximizes the fruit of liberty for the maximum number of people, but also it is often accepted as a universal moral imperative as in a Kantian tradition. But it is a valid question whether intervention could make matters worse. If I see a stranger lying on the ground unable to breathe, I have a duty to rush to his aide; but if I am not a physician and my attempt to preserve his life could instead hasten his death, my duty is to refrain from intervening and wait for assistance. In other words, this book does not reject a general duty to intervene in matters of a moral nature anywhere in the world, but it attempts to highlight the complexities of culture and social events in the modern era to show that some interventions cause more harm than good.

The issue has gained renewed urgency with regard to the twenty-first century's rise of fundamentalism in the Middle East and North Africa. Americans see a world where despotism, fundamentalism, and terrorism are on the rise; this has created an acute sense of national insecurity. But is democracy the right solution for combating fundamentalism and if the answer is yes, how far should America go to press for political and cultural change in the world?

One answer is provided by Anuradha Kataria, author of *Democracy on Trial, All Rise!*[10] She puts democracy on trial in a remarkably honest and bold fashion, showing the flaws in Western thinking about pushing ahead democratic reforms in the developing world. Her analyses of democratization projects both in pre-industrial Europe and the developing world are highly edifying, and her book is a must-read for everyone concerned about the direction the world is taking.

Kataria demonstrates that democracy has been damaging to stability and development in the Third World. Congo gained independence from Belgium in 1960, and five years later a coup brought Mobutu Sese Seko to power. Seko was an authoritarian ruler whose personal wealth concerned him more than the wellbeing of his nation. But his strongly anti-communist stance drew Western support and under his reign, Congo remained a relatively peaceful country for 32 years. After the fall of communism, Laurent-Désiré Kabila led a rebellion to overthrow Seko and established the Demo-

cratic Republic of the Congo with a promise to hold free elections and promote democratic rule. A year later a civil war broke out, causing an unprec-
edented level violence. Laurent-Désiré Kabila was assassinated in 2001 and
his son Joseph Kabila assumed the presidential office and began negotiating
with ethnic rebels. Despite attempts to solidify the democratic system, DR
Congo has been plagued with disorder and brutal ethnic infighting. The
International Rescue Committee (IRC) puts the number of people killed
to 45,000 per month. This number exceeds by far even the worst estimates
of deaths in Iraq since 2003 (the worst estimates put the death toll to up
to one million over the seven-year period the country has been under conflict. These figures have been disputed by the US and European officials
who puts the number to less 100,000 deaths.). Over five million people have
died in Congo since 1998. Rape has increased 17-fold, according to Oxfam,
and 56% of the assaults occurred in the victims' homes in the presence of
family members, including children. Rape, mutilation of organs, and arbitrary genocide are used in Congo as weapons of war. Kataria believes that
the problem in Congo is due to lack of a strong centralized leadership and
the inability of democracy to calm down the situation in a conflict-riddled
country. World media is peculiarly quiet about all this.

In June 2009, the entire world's focus was on the allegedly rigged election in Iran and the anti-Ahmadinejad demonstrations which took nineteen
lives, but little mention was made about the soaring violence in Congo—
perhaps because, as Kataria contemplates, it is harder to pinpoint a per-
petrator in a democracy than a dictatorship where one person can be held
accountable.[11]

Similar patterns of chaos caused by the introduction of democracy are
prevalent all over the developing world. Nigeria experimented with democracy a couple of times since its independence in 1960, but it descended into
chaos and ferocious infighting among its predominantly Muslim North,
Christian East, and the mixed West. The military took control and soon
stability resumed. In 1979, Olusegun Obasanjo introduced democracy voluntarily, only to see chaos return to Nigeria with full force. Corruption,
economic mismanagement, and rigged elections in 1983 capsized the fragile democracy barely four years after its inception. A series of coups and
countercoups ensued until democracy was restored once again in 1999, but
the second round of democracy continues to suffer from communal violence. Kidnappings, extortions, and murder have become rampant in recent

decades. There have been allegations that local politicians bribe youth to stir up violence against their opponents in the run-up to elections. Thus a country known for its substantial oil reserves remains poor and underdeveloped. About 64% of Nigerians live below the poverty line.[12]

Kenya is a diverse country with in the neighborhood of 40 different ethnic tribes, yet it remained peaceful for nearly three decades under its totalitarian ruler Jomo Kenyatta. The ethnic groups were integrated fairly in the government and social life, the economy was reasonably well-managed, and foreign investment poured in as a result. Following international and domestic pressure, a multi-party system was ushered in. The result was that each ethnic group created its own party and clashes broke out among them during the election periods. Kataria claims that the problem of Kenya is not tribalism but the democratic system in a country that is not ready for it yet. The proof of her statement is that the same people lived alongside each other and intermarried across tribal lines under Jomo Kenyatta, but now tribal differences are being exploited by factional politics of elections contesters to win the vote.[13]

Examples from other countries in Africa, Latin America, and the Middle East, including the present conflicts in Iraq and Afghanistan, are clear testimony of democracy gone astray. The core message is that democracy does not function well in poverty-stricken countries because politicians can exploit the desperation of the poor and under-educated class to derail fair elections in their own favor. It is more expedient that poor countries focus on becoming richer first before jumping into an open political system, rather than vice versa. It is hard to get one's head around democracy with an empty stomach. Kataria draws from experiences gained from half a century of democratization efforts in the Third World to show that democracy does not guarantee stability and economic prosperity, but that economic development and stability—even when provided through a centralized government—offer the best chances for a democratic future. In other words, democracy is not necessarily a prerequisite for peace and economic wellbeing, as always assumed by the West, but economic growth seems to be a prerequisite for the wellbeing of democracy.

Even here in the United States with a long democratic tradition, the experience from Great Depression and recent economic meltdown since 2008 suggest that law, order, and democracy come under threat at times when people are dissatisfied with their economic standing; extremists on both left and right side of political spectrum gain strength; established political institutions come under attack; immigrants and ethnic minorities are threatened; the political discourse turns increasingly into propaganda, containing little substance and more political symbolism promoted by agitated radicals. People power turns into protest marches and bitter squabbling, and sometimes worse.

Kataria writes in detail about how democracy in India, the country celebrated as the world's largest democracy but also as a country with one of the highest rates of poverty and illiteracy in the region, has effectively hampered development because contesting politicians persistently avoid long-term, but unpopular, interests, such as investing in technology to combat India's ticking water depletion problem, and instead invoke short-term tactics, such as pledging the vast poor electorate cash handouts, in order to get elected. Despite praiseworthy developments in recent decades, democracy bears exactly the guilt for impeding a faster pace of economic progress in that country, according to her.[14]

In modern Europe, democracy was ushered in first after a very long period of cultural evolution and economic empowerment, and even then democracy came only piecemeal with the privileged elite who possessed property to be enfranchised first. Europe went through the Renaissance, Enlightenment, Scientific Revolution, and Industrialization before democracy was even a plausible idea. Up until the seventeenth century the giants of philosophy and social life, such as the English philosopher Thomas Hobbes, argued against democracy, believing that it would produce a weak and dangerous leadership for his country. Gradually, the electoral property requirements were reduced in England as the growing wealth and education level of the nation produced a well-informed middleclass. Property requirements were abandoned a few decades later, but women were excluded from the ballot until the twentieth century. England achieved democracy through a "stepwise evolutionary path"[15] and only after the country had culturally and economically developed to a critical level to absorb the people power peacefully. The French, on the other hand, did a quick shortcut to democracy following the French Revolution in the period 1789-99. The French monarchy was ousted and a national assembly was established. Within three years of the start of the revolution, all males were granted the suffrage. As in France revolution took the place of an English-style evolutionary democracy, violence replaced the peace that the English had enjoyed. The chaos of a premature democracy unleashed the radical elements and in 1793 Jacobins ascended to power and began large scale arrests and executions as a way of preserving the revolution. As a result, the French Revolution is remembered today just as much for its horrific massacres as for its pioneering democratic aspirations. The situation finally calmed down when Napoleon Bonaparte reintroduced a totalitarian rule in 1799 via a military coup. France regained stability and economic development. Under Napoleon, France soared to the heights of international power and became a rival to the British Empire, colonizing vast territories in Africa, before its growing wealth and better educated people translated in a new wave of democracy. What France experienced in the eighteenth century with its sudden democracy and the pursuant totalitarian regime of Napoleon is reminiscent of the direction the developing countries take, when they are pushed by the international community to adopt a fully open political structure abruptly and prematurely. Kataria asks rhetorically why should a sudden and premature implementation of democracy work for the developing countries, when it did not work for Europe and why should the Third World not be given a chance to develop culturally and economically under peaceful centralized governance first like in Europe before democracy is attempted.[16]

Sure enough, the evidence is overwhelming in favor of this thesis. History demonstrates that democracy usually works best, if it is introduced stepwise, initiated by the people and not imposed by the international community, and if an educated middleclass is available to absorb the impact of people power. In the absence of the right conditions, democracy has indeed proven to be counterproductive. In Kataria's words, "[democracy] is not a ready-to-install product but a process. A nation has to undergo evolution socially as well as economically before it is ready to take on the mantle of people power. In our eagerness to have the fruit of liberty, we want to skip all the painstaking stages of its formation and demand that a seed turn into a fruit on command...But in reality when we jump gun like this, we not only fail to solve the existing problems of poverty but to our horror we often let loose bigger catastrophes."[17]

But Kataria's theory has its limitations too. She appears to be implying that the West should wash its hands of the Third World and let the developing countries grow at their own pace and free from international pressure, but in today's world, this is hardly plausible.

Firstly, the world today is integrated in global trade. To achieve economic growth and feed the growing populations in the Third World, the developing countries need to exchange goods with the developed countries and to do so, the developing countries need to take into account the emotional reaction of the Western world against human rights abuses under their watch. Without trade with the West, the developing countries may never gain the economic growth needed to usher in democracy at a later point in time; and without improving their human rights records, the West may not be willing to trade with them. The cost of stability through totalitarian government is arrest, torture, execution, or in other ways repression of thousands of political dissidents. In an age where the people have access to Internet, where dissidents can easily post accounts of atrocities online for everyone to view, it is more likely that the West will continue to protest and stir up dissent further by doing so—or soon or later cut short its trade. For instance, the militia groups in Congo are known to sell vital minerals used in electronic components in order to finance heinous war efforts. Congo is not under centralized government. Nevertheless the example is relevant in this context, as it reveals Western reaction in dealing with a country, where human rights abuses are rampant. The Congo Conflict Minerals Act of 2009 requires companies that are registered with Security and Exchange Commission (SEC) to disclose annually, whether they use minerals from Congo or adjoining countries in their products. If they do, they are obligated to implement due diligence in selecting the source and supply chain for their mineral requirements.[18]

Sanctions initiated by governments or popular boycotts initiated by the people can cripple the foundation for economic growth that is badly needed in the Third World. Examples of international sanctions and trade embargoes against apartheid, Cuba, the former Eastern bloc, Iran, and other countries show that economic isolation does not necessarily change the behavior of repressive governments, but it does encumber their economies in the long run. Iran's economy was crippled in the 1980s due to the Iran–Iraq War and international sanctions. The sanctions were eased in 1990s as relations with the West improved and trade routes began to open up. The country's economy reached an annual growth rate of up to 7% under former President Mohammad Khatami. Iran made substantial domestic reforms before it succeeded in attracting Western goodwill. But economic growth began a downward trend as soon as the incumbent president, Mahmoud Ahmadinejad, was elected to office and relations with the West regressed.

After nearly three decades, Vietnam is emerging as a strong economy on the world scene, but to achieve its growth rate of 7 to 8%, Vietnam has steadily improved its relations with the West. It is clear that global trade routes are increasingly vital for any modern economy to survive. But trade routes are at the same time sensitive to emotional reactions of the trading countries.

For instance, upon learning about child labor, Western consumers are unlikely to simply hope that patience will resolve the issue. People will demand reforms, and if no progress is forthcoming, people may boycott their products. Especially, Americans are increasingly at risk of opting for isolationism as strategy. Having fought two recent wars in the Middle East with disappointing results, Americans may decide in the future simply not to engage in substantial trade with regimes that they do not like.

China is a country with a strongly centralized government and strong economic ties to the West. The relationship between China and the West has been tense and the Chinese leadership has constantly sought to balance between defending its system of governance on one hand, and addressing Western concerns and internal outcry by gradually granting greater openness on the other hand (though at a slow pace). Meanwhile, the West's dependence on low-cost Chinese goods has grown beyond the point at which the West can levy sanctions against the Chinese without hurting itself. Other and smaller developing countries are not in this position and can easily be pushed aside by the West. To lift the Third World out of poverty, Western technology, expertise, and markets are needed, and to access all this, the developing countries have no choice but to address Western concerns regarding issues of human rights, freedom of expression, and democracy—one way or another.

Secondly, lessons from the War on Terror show that if the Westerners are made to believe that democracy is not the right solution for the Third World, this conviction may likely be followed by a new brand of dangerous stereotyping that could be just as damaging in the long run for the developing countries as premature democracy would be. Many American troops were deployed to Iraq and Afghanistan believing that they would help free those nations from repression. Some of them came back convinced that democracy would not work in the Middle East, while at the same time they had developed a degree of distaste for the Middle Eastern culture.[19] Democracy's failure in that region seems to have caused increased prejudice and intolerance. The expectation that the West should sit back patiently and let the developing countries grow piecemeal may not work once the propagandists have emphasized their negative qualities.

The political landscape looked different 300 years ago. Public conscience had not developed to the level of today's standards; the Internet and mass media had not yet seen the day's light; and nations were more isolated. Britain trammeled on human rights in India and elsewhere, but could still trade with other markets. As a result, they traded, developed a powerful middle class, and became democratic later.

The same roadmap cannot work for the developing countries in modern era. The world is now polarized, with a democratic West on one side and centralized governments or nonfunctioning democracies on the other side. Tensions between the two blocs could create an impasse. The developing countries need to be integrated into world trade on an equal footing in order to combat poverty. Kataria does not offer any answer as to how the Third World can buy the West's goodwill without becoming democratic.

Thirdly, Kataria has convincingly shown that the current situation in the Third World does not warrant immediate democratization, but for how long shall the developing countries be dictated by central governments? Her answer is, until the poor are lifted out of poverty and a reasonably well-off and well-educated middle class is created to absorb people power constructively. But how do we know that the leaders in power will voluntarily step aside and usher in democracy when that critical middle class is created? If there is no pressure, if there is no one pressing for democracy at all times, and if totalitarian leaders shall simply be allowed to crack down on dissidents in the name of stability, what guarantee is there to expect that the system will eventually loosen up? What would make a dictator give up his or her power, if the dissent is nicely suppressed and the West is sitting on the fence waiting and being understanding? What mechanisms would bring change, if there is no internal friction, no internal leadership for change, and no external pressure on dictators?

The question is particularly important in the case of solo dictators. The former Iraqi president Saddam Hussein was a strong totalitarian ruler. Under his first few decades, Iraqi economy grew. All Iraqis gained access to free education and healthcare and women were empowered and encouraged to participate in public affairs. Economic and social development did not, however, translate into more freedom. Instead, Saddam was elected as eternal leader by "100% of voters" through a theatrical pseudo-election.

China, on the other hand, has responded to internal and external pressure. It has been opening up to some extent, although the pace of change has been a slow marathon run. China is led by its elite. Internal friction among its leadership ensures a degree of pressure. Iran too is led by a group of clerics. Internal strife between the hardliners and reformists has created a platform for change. The country saw dramatic liberalizations post the death of Ayatollah Khomeini, culminating in Khatami's reform movement. But in the absence of critical pressure or a concrete long-term plan for democracy, no change is guaranteed in any of these countries.

The people of Europe did not have a role model 300 years ago. The rule of kings, queens, and dictators were considered the normal way of life and many Europeans accepted it until ideas about democracy were born. In today's world, the people of the developing countries look into how power is organized in the West and demand the same freedom. Strong factions all across the developing world keep the anti-government opposition and internal tensions smoldering, making centralized governments less stable and more oppressive. It is right that democracy must be implemented in the Third World through a stepwise evolutionary path and that in the interim a totalitarian rule may be necessitated as a "transient model"[20] in order to maintain calm and to build the economy in the short term. But if the dictators do not give up power voluntarily when the time is ready, a popular uprising will become the only option and Kataria's fear of chaos will become the reality anyway. The upheavals in Tunisia and Egypt in January 2011 are examples to this effect. The call for a transient period which can help the developing countries to alleviate poverty first and progress towards democracy gradually and peacefully requires that dictators have a plan for future democracy. It is unlikely that many dictators would have such plans in the absence of pressure.

The Iranian Islamic Revolution of 1979 offers again an interesting example that contrasts the central tenet of Kataria's thesis. Iran under the shah became the foremost regional power militarily, economically, and culturally. The average Iranian's disposable income 30 years ago was about double of what it is today. Women gained a higher social standing. The education level soared and many students were sent abroad to pursue higher education in Europe and the United States. But the shah did not give in to popular demands for democracy despite the growing wealth and education. He continued his rule and the more people protested, the more he oppressed them. The West was more than understanding—it actively backed the shah in every way. What happened next were the revolution, chaos, and disorder, which finally brought Khomeini to power. Contrary to the above thesis, here it was not poverty that led to chaos and agitation. It was the growing wealth of the middleclass that unleashed the people's aspiration for a better future, which was materialized in its opposite: Khomeini's Islamic Republic. Iran still had a sizeable poor segment in the villages, but the revolution was led by rich cities, not poor areas. Many Iranians claimed after the revolution that "people rose up against the shah because their bellies were full. If you are hungry, you think about bread, not revolution." This is quite the opposite of the point illustrated above. One example does not refute a thesis, but it shows that the picture is far more complex.

Fourthly, totalitarianism does not guarantee long-term peace and prosperity either, even if we were to embrace peace obtained in such manner. Authoritarian central governments in Egypt, Saudi Arabia, and other countries in the Middle East have proven effective in restoring law and order in the short term. In the petroleum rich parts of the region, oil money has built impressive cities with big towers. But inhumane treatment of the dissent radicalized many intellectuals that today account for Islamic extremism. Al Zawahiri—who has been named as one of the masterminds of Al Qaeda—was radicalized after he was incarcerated in Egypt following Sadat's assassination, where he was allegedly brutally abused.

Fifthly, as pointed out in the previous discussion, the West has not always supported democratic movements, but sometimes the opposite. Dictators such as the shah of Iran and Augusto Pinochet in Chile were supported precisely in the interest of stability, but it did not work. *Democracy on Trial* does not address this question at all.

Kataria recognizes that democracy should be the ultimate goal, but by overemphasizing the need for centralized governance in a transient phase without highlighting how internal dynamics and leadership within the developing world could eventually create enough pressure to mobilize a democratic movement, she risks oversimplifying the situation and only raises more questions.

The pressure must come from within a system to be effective. International pressure could sometimes play a part in encouraging change in developing countries, but never substitute the internal mobilization and leadership. It must be acknowledged that because of the cultural distance between the two worlds a degree of tension will always persist. This tension can translate into constructive pressure for change, if international actors respect the primacy of internal dynamics for social transformations, or destructive violence that results in chaos, if actors rely on military firepower.

WINNING THE ARGUMENT OR WINNING THE WAR

On the other end of the ideological spectrum, the author of *The End of Faith: Religion, Terror, and the Future of Reason*, Sam Harris, argues in favor of US intervention backed with the full measure of its military firepower, including torture if needs be, to root out threats to the Western civilization. His is another candid and must-read book, but one that must be taken with a grain of salt. Writing in the immediate aftermath of 9/11, he is more concerned about stamping out terrorism than about implementing democracy in the Third World; and while he is critical of all religions (and dogmatic ideologies), his attention is focused primarily on Islam. Yet his analyses are relevant in this context because they imply the legitimacy, necessity, as well as practicality of Western (for him, in particular America's) application of force to impose change around the world.

Writing extensively about "the problem with Islam," Harris concludes that the danger the West is facing is not confined to the Islamic extremism. As he contends, "[w]e will see that the greatest problem confronting civilization is not merely religious extremism: rather, it is the larger set of cultural and intellectual accommodations we have made to faith itself. Religious moderates are, in large part, responsible for the religious conflict in our world, because their beliefs provide the context in which scriptural literalism and religious violence can never be adequately opposed."[21]

The above statement targets all religions. But focusing on Islam, for the sake of the argument, Harris claims that no reading of the Koran can be good enough because Islam, like any other religion, by its nature is a dogma (or word of God), and clashes between the West and Islam will persist "as long as it is acceptable for a person to believe that he knows how God wants everyone on earth to live."[22]

Even though Muslim moderates are tolerant and respect the beliefs of others, the problem with religion is not solved, according to Harris, because, as he writes, "...religious moderates are themselves the bearers of a terrible dogma: they imagine that the path to peace will be paved once each of us has learned to respect the unjustified beliefs [beliefs that are rooted in religion and not in hard evidence or scientific data] of others. I hope to show that the very ideal of religious tolerance—born of the notion that every human being should be free to believe whatever he wants about God—is one of the principle forces driving us toward the [man's inhumanity to man]."[23]

With these statements Harris makes a form of extremism of his own, but so far not one that is as overly dramatic as the types of extremisms that lead people to crash planes into buildings or to blow up trains and buses. What makes his thesis more problematic is what he says next: "...the West must either *win the argument or win the war* [against Islam]. All else will be bondage" (italics added).[24]

If the demand of either winning the argument or the war is made in a different context and its target is extremists and terrorists, most people, including the overwhelming majority of Muslims, will in principle approve of it. There would, of course, be a discussion as to whether winning either the argument or the war is realistically even possible given the experiences from the War on Terror, but this is beside the point. The point here is that most people would in principle agree that terrorism must somehow end. But reading Harris's demand in light of his other assertions about religious extremists and moderates alike, the issue becomes alarming. To take the first part of his demand first, what does it mean to win the argument against the terrorists? If it means to convince them to lay down their weapons, change their ways, and adopt a more moderate and tolerant interpretation of Islam, then the problem is still not resolved, shall we believe Harris. For Harris, religious moderation is still a problem. So the only other option for winning the argument in the way Harris likes to see is to convince all Muslims, moderates and extremists alike, to abandon their religion, but is it not naïve to believe that over one billion Muslims in the world would simply follow Harris's advice and abandon their religion any time soon? As long as religious moderation is not permitted, there is no way the *argument* can be won in the real world—at least not for quite some time, if not ever.

What does winning the war mean, to Harris's taste? Certainly, killing merely the terrorists is not enough because as long as the moderates are left alone, Harris will be troubled by the possibility of "man's inhumanity to man," as he states that religious moderation will always provide the context in which scriptural literalism and religious violence can never be adequately opposed. In Harris's world there would be no Muslims, and since it is naïve to believe that any war can force over one billion Muslims to abandon their religion, only one option remains available to win Harris's war. Harris himself does not spell it out, but it follows from his logic inadvertently: a holocaust of Muslims like the world has never seen thus far; a holocaust that will dwarf any atrocities the Islamic terrorists have done to the West or to other Muslims in the entire history of Islam; a holocaust that would make Hitler look like a mild man; a pogrom in the name of ending "man's inhumanity to man."

To put it differently, the combination of holding religious moderation guilty of providing the context for terrorism and the zero-tolerance against anything believed to accommodate terrorism is what makes Harris more extreme than the extremists, whom he tries to fight.

Without a doubt, Harris does not mean this. Harris has earned a reputation as an intellectual, though a radical one, but not an exterminator. It is important to remember that *The End of Faith* was in part a reaction to 9/11, which clearly attests to Harris's respect for human life and his strong aversion for murdering over 3,000 innocent people. Holocaust does not fit within this worldview. As much as Harris's words will lead to a worldwide holocaust of Muslims if implemented literally, given a proposal he offers right before his demand to win the argument or win the war, it is clear that he does not want the destruction of the whole Muslim world. He proposes: "Given the constraints of Muslim orthodoxy...I think it is clear that Islam must find some way to revise itself..."[25]

Here he is offering co-existence provided Islam revises itself. Apparently, in his zeal to save the world from the evils of religions, he has confused himself by on one hand categorically rejecting all religions and religious moderations—refusing to *tolerate* the faith itself—and on the other hand, still be willing to go in bed with his worst enemy provided it revises itself.

Former British Prime Minister Tony Blair expressed in one respect the very opposite of Harris's idea, but in another respect a modified version of the same concept that the problem with international terrorism is not confined to Muslim extremists only. In a recent interview broadcast by Charlie Rose on PBS, Blair complained about the general notion upheld by many moderate Muslims that the West is at war with Islam as the underlying factor encouraging international terrorism against the West. He called on moderate Muslims to declare this notion "nonsense." In the last chapter I will discuss that Blair himself bears much of the burden for unintentionally promoting this idea by employing rhetoric that inflated what should have been a surgical military operation to take out a limited terrorist cell into a major civilizational crusade to defend the "Western way of life," by which the signals sent to the Muslim world were that Islam itself was the enemy. Much of the language of the War on Terror resembled Samuel Huntington's thesis, which defined Islam as the rising power against the Western civilization.[26] Whether or not Islam with its present orthodox interpretation of Koran is a serious threat to the West is an open question. But as long as the war was defined in such broad terms as in defending the Western values, it became difficult for Bush/Blair coalition to communicate clearly in the pandemonium of the war that the enemy was not really Islam itself.

Harris, nevertheless, does entertain the idea that Islam itself is the enemy. He puts it quite blatantly that, "[w]estern leaders who insist that our conflict is not with Islam are mistaken...Our enemy is nothing other than [Islam and all other religions].[27] On the account of his categorical opposition to all forms of faith and his advocacy of violence and torture, Harris has often been rejected out of hand by his adversaries. Opponents label him extremist and do not want to deal with him. This is not fair. Harris is an original thinker, who displays eloquent reasoning and oratory skills. He has made a significant contribution to the post 9/11 discourse on faith in general, and Islam in particular. He fares surely to the extremes, but his ideas are never so dangerous because they are based not on dogmas but logic and reasoning—and arguments can be met with arguments.

The underlying attitude that makes Harris an extremist is not that he dislikes faith, but his uncompromising stance that if something is bad, whatever it may be, then it must be eliminated at any cost and by any means. In this regard, Harris is a perfectionist. Harris complains that religious intolerance impedes social progress and he creates stricter intolerance of his own in response. In other words, his rejection of faith is not unjustified. It is only his intolerance of it that is illegitimate. It is legitimate to reject a religion (or any ideas), but to tolerate that others may appreciate it. Reaction against Islam is not unexpected given many conflicts over the past twenty years, from the *fatwa* (Islamic decree) on Rushdie's head for the publication of *The*

Satanic Verse to the sectional infighting from Africa to the Balkans, which have gone under the name of this religion. But rigid intolerance renders otherwise legitimate criticism ineffective or worse, counterproductive. To borrow from his own phraseology, Harris's "intellectual accommodations" to an intolerant outlook about faith, makes it harder for him to "adequately oppose" religious intolerance without running into contradictions.

Even if we allow that Muslim moderates too are responsible for the religious conflict in the world, because their beliefs provide the context in which scriptural literalism and religious violence can never be adequately opposed, as Harris complains, a war against all Muslims cannot be justified. Every atrocity in the world could be said to have its roots in cultural and intellectual accommodations that made it possible. At some point the Nazi had the majority backing in Germany. A long history of European feuds against the Jews coupled with the imperialist culture of vying for power enabled Hitler to execute his vicious ambitions. Whole cultures in America provided the context in which slavery or segregation of blacks occurred. Whole cultures embraced or tacitly permitted the skirmishes that led to near extinction of aboriginal Indians in early American history. Yet, no one calls for all Germans or Americans to perish on account of it. The excesses of a culture do not warrant the elimination of the whole people.

Harris's rejection of cultural relativism and his platonic view of political leadership are testimonies of his perfectionism.[28] Plato believed that only the learned should be elected to political office. The English philosopher John Stuart Mill, writing over two millennia later, argued that the merit of democracy was not about finding the right solutions but rather about empowering the people. Even if an omniscient God knew what was best for the people, the people were still better off making their own mistakes than being pacified by following the word of God, Mill asserted.

Democracy, understood as such, is not an ideal of a perfect society—as it is often assumed; it is only a minimum requirement for how power should be organized in the society. Democracy on its own is not the best a society can be; it is only the least a society must have to have a fair division of power. If democracy is an ideal, it is the ideal of a minimum requirement for arranging power, not an ideal of social perfection: it is the ideal foundation on which a castle is built; not the castle itself. Democracy requires tolerating adversary views. Tolerance is a concept in moral philosophy which admits of morally objectionable practices even though they are considered bad, but as long as they are not too bad (by accepted social standards) to be prohibited. Democracy is therefore open to imperfections by its nature. The problem with countries like Iran is that it does not offer any space for deviations, imperfections, or any behavior deemed anomalous by the establishment. Iran wants to be the perfect society judged by the standards of the establishment, and so the Iranian culture remains stagnant. Western democracies are full of deviations from the mainstream standards, oddness, and contradictions, which materialize in a dynamic and progressive culture in the end. Tolerance is the heart of democracy and the engine for social progress in the Western civilization. Harris wants to go to war to defend the Western civilization, but offers little tolerance for anything that deviates from his ideals. Without tolerance and respect for civil liberties, there would be little left of Western civilization worthy of defending.

Kataria too misinterprets democracy as an ideal of a perfect society, but in her view it is an ideal that does not work in the present situation of the Third World. She compares democracy with antiquity's ideals of the perfect circular orbits of the sun and stars, which the ancient scientists defended strenuously despite observations to the contrary.[29] The analogy is interesting but not accurate. Scientific observations sometimes force us to change our perspectives; other times the knowledge learned helps us manipulate the nature. In the case of orbits, whatever views we may entertain about circular motions, the Earth and stars continue their paths independently. But by changing our views about democracy, we actually always change the prospects for our society, for human development, and for our future in fundamental ways—whether in good ways or bad ways. Her point that democracy—whether as a concept describing the ideal society or as a minimum requirement for organizing power—cannot and shall not be implemented prematurely is well-taken, but her active support for totalitarianism, without an indication that some form of pressure must inevitably exist to root out despotism in the end, is disputed.

Harris and Kataria are two authors at the opposite ends of the ideological spectrum, while they both exhibit considerable insight in making their cases. But both authors misinterpret democracy as an ideal of the perfect society; both are peculiarly tolerant but in their own respects—one tolerating war and torture for the sake of defending the West and the other tolerating the evil of totalitarian rule for the sake of stability in the Third World; both intolerant in other respects—one categorically rejecting all religions and the other categorically rejecting all calls for democratizing the Third World—and they finally arrive at two very different conclusions. As expected, one calls on the West to either win the argument or win the war and the other calls on the West to wash its hands of the Third World.

INEVITABLE PRESSURE POINTS

There will inevitably be pressure points between the developed and the developing worlds, as long as the two worlds follow incompatible ideologies, and as long as these pressure points exist, the relationship between the two worlds will continue to be at odds.

Ideological rivalry is by no means a phenomenon for modern era, and there is no reason to believe that the rivalry will end anytime soon. Christian missionaries have in all ages since the birth of the religion attempted to spread the message of Jesus. The Muslim conquest stretched all the way to Spain. The ancient Persians, the Romans, Ottomans, and the colonial Europeans all tried to impose their notion of civilization on others. The communists yearned for exporting the ideology. So did even Iran's Khomeini. The passion to push everyone else over to one's own ideological base has remained strong through all ages. There is no guarantee that history will repeat itself, but there is no reason to believe that it will not, either. The failed wars in Iraq and Afghanistan are clear setbacks for the United States. These experiences coupled with the current financial crisis may change the US foreign policy in some way, but it is unlikely to stop America's old approach towards the Third World altogether as long as the US remains powerful. After the Vietnam War many forecast that US foreign policy would radically change, but it didn't. Before Americans had a chance to come to terms with the legacy of the Vietnam War, the US military started new adventures in Latin America, though in smaller scale. The same pattern repeated itself right after the Iraq invasion, when failure to find Saddam's smoking gun did not discourage the Bush Administration to look for WMD in Iran. With the US military bogged down in Iraq and Afghanistan, the Bush Administration and his successor, the Obama Administration, launched verbal attacks on China for its currency policy and North Korea for its nuclear arsenal. America has learned that its world dominance will go down, as soon as it drops the ball—so it will try to keep the ball rolling as long as it can. The White House today uses just as many of the old ploys as the Roman,

Ottoman, or European empires did. To expect, as Kataria does, that the two worlds can completely ignore the ideological friction between them in an increasingly globalized reality is utopianism. To expect, as Harris does, that the Western world can completely win the argument or win the war against the Third World is another fantasy. Our best bet and the only feasible way to ease these pressure points is to acknowledge the interests of both sides and at the same time to incessantly remind us that no nation can impose its way on other nations in the long run no matter how powerful one may be.

PART II

FOUR HISTORICAL TRANSFORMATIONS

3. The Battle for Emancipation

The modern outlook on human worth, dignity, autonomy, and equality makes it impossible to fully grasp how the evil of slavery could evolve to such large scale in the history of mankind. As Steven Mintz has pointed out, "[e]ven those who think that they know something about this nation's past tend to misunderstand slavery's cruelties and its central role in the nation's politics and economic development."[30]

To assert that the American antislavery movement was a splendid event that forever ended the trading and enslaving of human beings is to state the obvious. But to put things in perspective, abolishing slavery was in one sense even more important than the American Revolution. The American Revolution is regarded as the single most important incident in American history, but in fact this country could have perfectly well remained a part of the British Empire. There is nothing morally repugnant about that. But the case of slavery is different. The institution of slavery could have continued had no one fought for abolishing it, but by today's moral standards, we can never accept it as a moral possibility.

It is not a surprise, therefore, that the history books in schools have cast the abolitionists as righteous men and women. Early in the nineteenth century heroic men and women, mostly from the northern states and most of them religious, stood up and demanded an end to exploitation of human beings. These individuals bore a conviction that slavery was a sin. But as will become clear in the discussion below, the circumstances that ended the institution of slavery were much more complex than the story of these righteous men and women.

ABOLITIONISM GAINS MOMENTUM

Abolitionism, defined as a movement to extirpate slavery, was not an alien concept brought to existence instantaneously by some form of superior moralists. It evolved gradually, but it intensified in the nineteenth century. The first debates about the legitimacy of slavery can be traced back to antiquity. But during the ancient and early European history Persians, Greek, Romans, and people of any race or color frequently ended up slaves.[31]

In the second half of the second millennium a racist form of slavery evolved, using a narrative in which non-"white" skin was evidence of inferiority and justified enslavement. This version of slavery put blacks at a permanent disadvantage by birth. The race argument freed slave traders from any pangs of guilt. Hundreds of European merchant ships began transporting enslaved Africans to Europe and America. But for many whites, slavery always seemed inconsistent with moral ideals. Precisely for this reason slaveholders and proslavery intellectuals often resorted to the most innovative ideas to excuse the practice. It was held that slavery was an economic necessity (an argument famously articulated by Aristotle). The person who is most remembered for the Declaration of Independence, Thomas Jefferson, embraced briskly argument of economic necessity, pointing out the role that slaves had played in building the great Greek and Roman civilizations. He believed America's greatness was equally dependent on the benefits of the institution of slavery. Thomas Jefferson defended the inferiority theory in his *Notes on the State of Virginia*, suggesting that blacks had different blood color.[32] Southern slaveholders postulated that slaves were better off enslaved in the West, where life's basic necessities were granted by their masters, than free in Africa. Considering slaves as mere property, proslavery advocates objected that the abolition of slavery would infringe their (the slaveholders') Constitutional right to private property. Some slaveholders attempted to escape moral responsibility by contending that they only bought their slaves from a third party and that their slaves would have remained enslaved by another buyer anyway even if they had not made the purchase. Even some ostensibly antislavery ministers supported the institution to appease the slaveholders. Missionaries from the Church of England worried that the message of emancipation would render slaveholders resentful and unwilling to allow their slaves learn about Christianity. To spread the Christian teachings among the slaves, these missionaries were willing to ignore the brutality and immorality of this institution.[33]

The more the slaveholders were challenged by the antislavery activists, the more they sought to invent economic, religious, moral, or pseudoscientific justifications for holding slaves. As Paul Finkelman has demonstrated, all these arguments were ultimately tied to race.[34] To excuse the exploitation the slaveholders regarded the slaves of lesser value racially.

The abolitionist sentiment continued to threaten the institution of slavery. A wave of antislavery movement spread through the northern states around the eighteenth century. The first calls for emancipation of slaves were modest, most demanding the implementation of a gradual path to abolition. This phase went under the name *gradualism*, which assumed that better moral education and piecemeal reforms in society would slowly but inevitably end slavery in America. These abolitionists were optimistic about the American sense of morality. They believed that once the moral conscience is awakened, most slaveholders would freely choose to manumit their slaves. Many prominent politicians and missionaries both in the North and South subscribed to this view. Gradualism remained prevalent throughout the movement, but in 1830s, a new school of thought began to infuse the abolitionist campaign. This new doctrine was coined *immediatism*. Contrary to popular misconceptions, immediatism was not about credulously demanding the instantaneous freeing of all slaves. The immediatists were acutely aware of the kind of human and social tragedy that could follow, if thousands of slaves were freed at once but no provisions had been made to house them or to absorb them in the job market. They were also aware of the political and cultural obstacles to immediate emancipation of slaves, and acknowledged the need for gradual emancipation. Their idea was anchored in the realization that human nature was inclined to delay progress; and that only a call for immediate abolition had a chance of delivering gradual manumission. Immediatism was, in other words, a mental attitude that put the urgency into the antislavery cause. A century of moderate campaigning for abolishing slavery had not only proven ineffective in producing any noteworthy results, but the intimidated slaveholders had stepped up their grip on power in the South to ensure status quo with regard to the slavery question. For immediatists the choice was apparent. If they wanted to see full abolition of slavery at some point in the future, they needed to make it urgent; they needed to demand it now.[35]

But urgency made compromise impossible, intensifying southerners' resentment and need for self-defense. As Dillon noted: "By their remorseless agitation [the immediatists] sharpened sectional antagonisms; by their insistence upon viewing all issues in terms of principle, they transmuted sectional controversies into titanic moral struggles, thus rendering compromise unlikely if not impossible. Southerners, reacting to their verbal attacks, defended slavery and "Southern Rights" more stubbornly."[36]

Multiple factors accounted for the evolution of immediatism, the most notable one being religious revivalism during the first half of the nineteenth century. Distinguished ministers, such as Charles G. Finny of New York and Lyman Beecher of New England, deployed a new evangelical teaching about benevolence and brotherhood. They called on Christians to accept immediate and personal responsibility for the evil of slavery. This brand of evangelicalism saw emancipation the immediate right of the slaves and the immediate obligation of all free Christians. It provided a new vision, a new language, and a new set of tactics for the abolitionist movement; one which put urgency at the center of the movement. The historian Gerald Sorin has pointed out that immediatism was not a church movement and that the immediatist clergy was generally unable to convert their churches to their cause.[37] But the majority of abolitionists—about two-thirds according to Gilbert H. Barnes[38]—were ministers and pastors even though this does not imply that the majority of religious people were abolitionists. Other religious sects also stepped up their antislavery efforts. Quakers rejected the notion that the color of skin of African-Americans was God's punishment for ancient sins. They insisted that the benevolent God loved all man and that no sin would warrant perpetual divine retribution. The Quakers offered some of the loudest voices against slavery in antebellum America.[39]

William L. Garrison was one of the leading figures of the antislavery movement, who rapidly rose up to the forefront of the immediatist struggle. As a young activist, he flirted for a short while with the American Colonization Society. The society advocated deportation of freed slaves to Africa, as a way of avoiding interracial conflicts in American mainland. Garrison quickly realized that this racial prejudice against African-Americans had been the very cause behind the institution of slavery, and came to advocate that abolition was possible only if all prejudice against African-Americans

3. The Battle for Emancipation

were rejected immediately and all free slaves integrated in the American society as equals to whites. Garrison apologized publicly for his engagement
with the American Colonization Society and joined the immediatism cause.
He worked as the editor of the successful magazine, *The Liberator*, which for
over three decades fervently advocated immediate abolition of slavery until
he concluded his mission accomplished and closed down the magazine in
1865, after the end of the Civil War.[40] The theologian Theodore D. Weld,
the silk merchant, Lewis Tappan, the businessman Gerrit Smith, and the
lawyer, Henry B. Stanton, were among other leading abolitionists, who in
one way or another agitated for reforms.[41]

The changing economic environment is seen by historians as another
major factor for the rise of immediatism. Industrialization made the northern states less dependent on slave power for their economic growth, while
the cotton farms of the south relied heavily on slave labor. This diverging
economic development created conflicting interests between North and
South with regard to the slavery question. Additionally, as the southern
cotton farming grew more prosperous, southern states became increasingly
independent from New England. Southerners gradually developed social
codes and political institutions along their own cultural lines. The North's
declining influence alarmed the New England clergy and politicians, whom
in order to reassert their authority pressed southern leaders to abolish slavery. To this extent, abolitionism was about political control, not morality.[42]

African-American activism played an important role in the movement.
African-Americans complained that the institution of slavery contradicted
the democratic values upon which this country was built. They vigorously
opposed the American Colonization Society, claiming that the colonization
scheme was a charade designed to exclude resourceful freedmen from the
American society, so to make it easier to continue the shackles of slavery.
Mounting fear of a coordinated African-American revolt led the slaveholder
states to toughen "black codes," which severely restricted African-American mobility, curtailed their ability to congregate in public places, use public facilities, or seek education. A plot for a rebel, masterminded by the former slave Denmark Vesey, was uncovered in Charleston, South Carolina, in
1822, which led to Vesey's arrest and execution. The repressive black codes
and the danger of a bloody African-American uprising made both black and
white abolitionists to seek immediate emancipation.[43]

The fugitive slaves also played a crucial role in the antislavery movement. The proslavery propaganda portrayed the slave states as benevolent paternalistic states, in where slaves were delightful for being cared for by their masters. According to this picture, slaves were inferior beings whose lives and wellbeing could be threatened outside the stability and the benevolence of the institution of slavery. The fugitive slaves challenged this view. They exposed the miseries of slavery, the whippings, the chains, and despair the slaves had to endure in the hands of their masters. Many of fugitives published poignant accounts of their escapes. These publications circulated widely in the North and were read with great appetite by blacks and whites alike. For many northerners these writings were the only way they could gain insight into the realities of the world of slavery.[44]

Finally, the role the foreign impulses played in bringing about stronger abolition advocacy must not be overlooked. The emancipation of one million slaves in the British West Indies in 1831 set a powerful example for those who aspired to abolish slavery in America. Americans thought of themselves as the champions of freedom. If Britain could emancipate one million slaves, why should Americans not do the same? British Baptists, Methodists, and Presbyterians toured the US in mid nineteenth century to disseminate religious arguments against the practice of slavery. The British immediatism did no exert a direct influence on American abolitionists, but it inspired them and acted as a model for progressive American leaders and activists.[45]

THE HYPOCRISY OF NORTH AND THE DECEPTION OF SOUTH

The abolitionist movement owed its existence to the inhumane treatment and exploitation of slaves in the South, but at the same time the movement suffered remarkable racial prejudice within its own ranks. While expressing an acute abhorrence for the sins of slavery, many white abolitionists, who otherwise would have put their heads on the line for the cause, still believed in the supremacy of the white race and rejected the idea of black integration into white society. The ex-slaves, "freedmen," in the North lived in segregated areas and under appalling conditions. They lacked jobs, amenities, and decent education. Established social norms prevented them from integrating in the white society. Most whites believed that the black race was inapt for prerogatives afforded to the white race. Racial inequalities in the North discredited calls for abolition in the eyes of southern slaveholders, who often referred to the dreadful treatment of northern blacks as a mark of hypocrisy in Free states.

Many abolitionists feared that interracial interaction would eventually lead to race wars. Leon F. Litwack reports the mood among the abolitionists in the following: "Since racial mixing flouted the prevailing social code and might easily lead to mob action, antislavery advocates faced a real dilemma. If an abolitionist fought for equal rights, some argued, it did not necessarily follow that he must also consort with Negroes socially."[46]

Others were concerned about racial amalgamation, worrying that it could lead to interracial love and marriages that could potentially spoil the white race. In 1833, a group of about fifty abolitionists from ten states founded the American Anti-Slavery Society, headquartered in Philadelphia. The organization adopted a Declaration of Sentiments, aiming at bringing about "the destruction of error by the potency of truth—the overthrow of prejudice by the power of love—and the abolition of slavery by the spirit of repentance."[47] Yet, such was the extent of racism among abolitionists themselves that many of them advocated the exclusion of free black activists from the organization. As a liberal abolitionist Charles Follen claimed that excluding black activists from the organization would comply with the prejudices that underpinned the institution of slavery, asking "how can we have the effrontery to expect the white slaveholder of the South to live on terms of civil equality with his colored slave, if we, the white abolitionists of the North, will not admit colored freemen as members of our Anti-Slavery Societies?"[48]

The question fell on deaf ears. Even some liberal abolitionists, who in principle agreed with Follen, argued that mixing with blacks might jeopardize the "effectiveness" of the antislavery cause. Lewis Tappan proposed inviting a black minister to speak at a meeting, insisting that "we must act out our principles," but he was warned that the time for mixing with blacks had not come yet. At another meeting an activist threatened to resign if blacks were to join the organization.[49]

After a long and heated debate the antislavery society in Philadelphia voted in favor of permitting black membership in 1837 by a margin of two votes.[50] Under this racist climate Tappan admitted that he had once dined with black members of the executive committee of the American Anti-Slavery Society.[51] His admission was a sign of great courage considering the racial atmosphere of the time, but also a reminder of the scope of racism at the height of antislavery movement. Female abolitionists seemed more inclined to racial intermingling, but neither could women escape racial prejudice altogether. The Female Anti-Slavery Society in Fall River, Massachusetts, embraced black membership despite strong opposition, while their sister society in New York denied black women the right of membership. The Anti-Slavery Convention of American Women approved in 1838 a resolution by Sarah M. Grimké urging abolitionists to associate and interact with them both in public and private as they did with white fellow citizens. A few weeks later, two Philadelphia abolitionists asked prominent blacks to renounce publicly any desire to mingle with whites in order to avoid "destruction and bloodshed."[52]

Despite widespread prejudice among whites, black abolitionists soon constituted a substantial proportion of the Anti-Slavery Society in New England. Black leaders, such as, Lewis Clarke, William W. Brown, Henry Bibb, and Frederick Douglass worked tirelessly to advance the cause for freedom. Blacks' input in the movement was represented at all levels, from participating in the sales of abolitionist materials to representation at the board level in white anti-slavery societies. The blacks formed their own anti-slavery societies too.

The American Colonization Society sought to expatriate legions of freed slaves to Liberia. Many whites and a few blacks thought of this plan as favorable to newly freed slaves. If they were not tolerated in white communities, if they could not find a job, housing, and a decent life style in America as freedmen, they would be better off, they argued, to be shipped to Liberia, where they could start a new life far away from vicious slaveholders. The black businessman Paul Cuffe assisted successfully thirty-eight free blacks to resettle in Sierra Leone in 1815, but the majority of black leaders believed that expatriation would be nothing more than a death trap for millions of freed slaves.[53] Black abolitionists worked hard to put to rest the colonization question.

About four million slaves and freedmen lived in America at the time. It is hard to imagine the scale of human tragedy had over four million freed slaves been transported from America to a land they knew nothing about, and asked to begin a new civilization with little or no resources. The black abolitionists convinced many of their white peers that colonization was unacceptable and that the only legitimate roadmap for abolitionism was to combat prejudice and integrate manumitted slaves into the wider society as equals to the white man. For them, nothing short of brotherly love and racial justice would be consistent with the God's will for mankind.

In spite of their prejudices the abolitionists remained true to their sense of moral responsibility to purify the nation from the sins of slavery. They saw their cause as instrumental to God's plan for a perfect world. Strenuous efforts to crack down on prejudice did begin gradually to pay a dividend. Garrison and his followers had realized that better education would increase job prospects for black laborers and lift them out of poverty. When the blacks began to handle skilled labor, make a decent living, and have the opportunity to demonstrate their tenacity and acumen, racial prejudice would fade slowly from public mind, Garrisonian abolitionists hoped.

Attempts to establish a technical college for blacks in New Haven, Connecticut, failed in the face of local resentment, but by 1845 black children won the right to attend public schools alongside their white co-students in Massachusetts, Salem, and a few other cities. Success stories in these communities triggered slowly but surely a chain reaction in northern states. These states were gradually stripped of the laws of segregation. In some states blacks gained virtual legal equality, yet the prejudice and discrimination persisted stubbornly and continues to haunt the modern day's America.

This history exhibits an important lesson: the abolitionist struggle was never a clear-cut and internally consistent movement. It mobilized legions of people to the cause; some who wholeheartedly and completely submitted to the ideals of racial equality; but many more who despite fighting for the cause, held ideas inconsistent with the underlying abolitionist ideology. The ideology was not born over night. It evolved through decades of bitter internal conflicts. The abolitionists were guilty of much of the same prejudices, class attitudes, hypocrisy, and factionalism within their own ranks, as they blamed southern states for. Yet as Litwack rightly points out: "The fact that abolitionists did not allow these weaknesses to interfere materially with their struggle for civil rights is a tribute to their sincerity...Although frequently hesitant and uncertain in their own social relations with Negroes, abolitionists nevertheless attempted to demonstrate to a hostile public that environmental factors, rather than any peculiar racial traits, largely accounted for the degradation of the...Negro."[54]

POLITICAL ENGAGEMENT

The abolitionists endured numerous attacks on their persons or property by angry proslavery vigilantes. Their houses were vandalized; their meeting halls burned in New York and Philadelphia; Theodore D. Weld was subjected to physical assault; in 1837, the abolitionist editor, Elijah Lovejoy, who had sought refuge in Illinois to escape persecution in his slave state of Missouri, was shot to death by an anti-abolitionist mob. Garrison estimated about three hundred attacks on the abolitionists between 1830 and 1850. The abolitionists refrained from seeking retribution.[55] The basic tenet of abolitionism was nonviolence and peaceful transformation. They believed in moral awakening, as opposed to armed conflict, as a pathway to eliminating the institution of slavery. Apart from a few radical abolitionists, such as John Brown who organized a guerrilla attack on Harper's Ferry[56], the brunt of abolitionists believed that any form of coercion was immoral. They sought to avert violence as much as at all possible. Moral awakening involved passionate championship of core Christian values. This work required convincing slaveholders to free their slaves and to end the practice out of free will, but many abolitionists realized soon that moral persuasion was not enough. In order to make meaningful progress, they thought, they needed to couple moral enlightening campaigns with political engagement.

Political participation took the form of using the ballot box strategically to elect to political office candidates most likely to advance the abolitionist cause. Other abolitionists decided to start up a separate political party and run for elections. The idea of a specific abolitionist political party caused a schism in 1840 between Garrisonians, who worried that direct political involvement could potentially require a compromise of principle with the proslavery camp, and other abolitionists who saw political action as the only viable way for furthering their mission. Those who distanced themselves from the Garrisonians, founded an independent, radical political party called *The Liberty Party*.[57] One dilemma for the Liberal Party was whether to narrow its focus on the single issue of promoting the abolition of slaves, or to adopt a broader political agenda, dealing with national issues other than the slavery question. The party members settled eventually for the single issue platform, with a division of the party breaking off to found the short-lived Liberty League Party on a broader platform. Another dilemma was to decide how radically to pursue abolitionism. Prevalent racial prejudice amongst the electorate compelled the party to distance itself increasingly from the principle of racial equality. In an effort to moderate the party's image in order to broaden its support base, members of the Liberty Party nominated as their presidential candidate a modest abolitionist: John P. Hale. Hale opposed both the abolition of slavery in Washington, D.C. and a ban on interstate slave trade. The opponent of black suffrage, Thomas Morris, was elected as the vice-presidential candidate.[58]

Other abolitionists joined the ranks of the Free Soil Party. The Free Soil Party was a far more liberal political organization, seeking only to limit the spread of slavery, but not necessarily abolish it. It also categorically opposed any attempt to promote equal rights for black people. By embracing the racism that was common at the time, the Free Soil Party succeeded in attracting many of the half-hearted Liberty members. Yet, it was not until antislavery sentiments permeated through the hearts of Republicans that the political machinery could be put to effective use.[59]

THE BIRTH OF THE REPUBLICAN PARTY AND THE AMERICAN CIVIL WAR

Nearly three decades of organized antislavery activism produced no victory. The few success stories in assisting fugitive slaves to gain freedom were countered by a new Fugitive Slave Act in 1850s. In 1854, the federal government returned the fugitive slave, Anthony Burns, to slavery. Public opposition to Burns' return was so volatile that the government employed naval vessels, Marines, and artillery to enforce the court's ruling. Barricades were erected outside the courthouse to prevent attacks.[60] The proslavery forces both in the North and the South fought harder to preserve their position, triggering suspicions that a major southern conspiracy was in the making to crush the abolitionist movement. When the Supreme Court ruled in 1857 that blacks were not citizens and that the prohibition of slavery in the North was unconstitutional, several abolitionists changed their moderate or nonviolent positions to believing that coercive methods were the only way to deal with proslavery power. The Supreme Court's ruling was a response to a litigation launched by Dred Scott. Scott was a slave who had been taken to free territories of Minnesota and the free state of Illinois. He petitioned the Supreme Court to grant him freedom on the basis of his stay in free territories. The Supreme Court rejected Scott's appeal on the grounds of non-citizenship, but also went on to declare the Missouri

Compromise, which barred slavery from spreading out north of the 36°30′ parallel line, unconstitutional. The ruling opened up potential expansion of slavery throughout the United States. The Supreme Court based its verdict on the Fifth Amendment to the Constitution, which bans confiscation of private property without proper legal action. The Court interpreted slaves as chattel.[61]

Such grave setbacks for the abolitionists and the accumulation of public resentment on both sides of the conflict prepared the ground for the Civil War. A year before the Supreme Court's decision in the Dred Scott case a group of political agitators in the North, who called themselves "Friends of Freedom," formed the Republican Party. The Republicans were deeply concerned with the moral hazards of the institution of slavery, but like most other white Americans they viewed the blacks as inferior and had no program for dealing with a large mass of freed slaves once slavery was abolished. However, as a young and vibrant party, the Republicans grew rapidly, drawing membership from former Whigs and dissatisfied Democrats and Liberty members. They became soon a serious counterweight to the proslavery Democratic Party. In a sweeping election in 1860, only four years after their inception, the Republican Party candidate, Abraham Lincoln, won the presidency. The brunt of Republican support came from the North. Fearing disunity among their southern supporters, the Democratic Party had steadfastly held a proslavery position throughout the election campaign, alienating the northern voters while the magnitude of Democratic electorate in the South proved insufficient to sweep them to power.[62] With Republicans firmly in power the fate of the Union was in jeopardy. Although Lincoln himself worked hard to reassure the South that his office would never strive to abolish slavery at the expense of the Union, sectional pride and fear for the North's power propelled southern states to secede from the union to form the Confederate States of America (or popularly known as the Confederacy), of which Jefferson Davis became the president.

The split of the Union heightened the animosity between the North and South. On April 1861, the Confederate army attacked the Union troops at Fort Sumter. Lincoln had been terrified by the prospect of war. He had worked to near exhaustion to prevent the conflict from escalating, but after the Fort Sumter attack, he saw no option but to reciprocate. The war that followed was devastating, but it marked the end of slavery in America. Lincoln himself insisted that the Civil War was a war to save the Union, not to abolish slavery. His aides even strove to reassure southerners that Lincoln had no design to abolish slavery. Congress enacted a constitutional amendment to guarantee slavery in the South. But the abolitionists were adamant that the war effort would be a great waste of opportunity, if it only returned the southern states to the Union but did not emancipate the slaves. As the Civil War raged on, abolitionists became increasingly worried about ending the war without ending slavery. If that became the case, they feared, slavery would become even more robust and could soon spread through northern states too. To prevent this outcome the abolitionists abandoned their nonviolence ideology and instead began a meticulous campaign to convince Lincoln making the abolition of slavery the objective of the war. The Confederate army deployed thousands of slaves in its war efforts against the Union forces. The abolitionists argued that emancipation would substantially weaken the southern army by depriving it from the opportunity of deploying slave soldiers. They urged Lincoln to manumit all slaves by a presidential decree. Even though the abolitionists did not consider slaves as property but as human beings, they argued that emancipation of slaves by presidential decree could be justified on the grounds of confiscating private property during war. The Constitution granted the President the power to impound property in war times. In January 1863, Lincoln issued a limited emancipation proclamation to free all slaves in war areas. A year later 400,000 people endorsed a signature campaign in favor of an abolition amendment to the Constitution. Finally, on January 31, 1865, only a couple of months after Lincoln's reelection for a second term, the Thirteen Amendment was passed in the House with some Democrats voting for the bill or abstaining. The amendment abolished slavery throughout the United States, and the abolitionists got to have the last laughter.

Throughout the war the Union had maintained a superior position, being technologically more advanced and financially stronger. The Union could also draw from a large pool of freedmen and fugitive slaves from the South, who joined the Union army, as well as a number of foreign residents in the US—particularly Irish and German immigrants. The South's only hope was to involve the British or French in the war against the Union. The South was a major exporter of cotton to the European textile industry. In 1861, the South embargoed the cotton export to force Britain intervene, but the plot (often dubbed as cotton king or cotton diplomacy) failed as Europe had a surplus of cotton in that year. As added salt to injury, Europe was short of corn and the North's corn export to Europe increased.

THE LESSON FROM THE ABOLITIONIST MOVEMENT

The abolition of slavery was without a doubt a monumental accomplishment. Success brings confidence, enthusiasm, and a desire to keep pushing forward. The abolitionists had fought and won a battle against injustice. The success of abolishing slavery would become part of a lasting American identity. It would reinvigorate Americans' morale and combat spirit. During and after World War II, this identity emboldened those who maintained that American power should be used to eradicate the Earth of all injustice. They entertained the view that if Americans could free millions of slaves; if they could engage in a bitter civil war and opt for peaceful coexistence and brotherly relations only a few years later; if North and South could join forces to rebuilt this country anew right after a devastating civil war; if they could then carry on defeating the Nazis, beating the gender inequalities, and working to improve the race relations; if despite all past injustices, this country could reemerge strong and proud of its achievements; and if nothing could ever stop the American quest for building a better future, why should America not use its "God-given" power and valor to cleanse the earth from all sin? This has become the dream of those Americans who believe that cleansing the earth from all sin is not only an American prerogative, but it is an American duty. Deposing authoritarian rulers from positions of power and installing democracies around the world is an obligation, they maintain, that follows the American might. A strong moral value underpins this attitude. To yearn changing the world for the better is morally righteous and commendable. Unfortunately, however, in our zeal to change the world we often overlook the complexity of social change and the requirement for popular willpower among the people that we seek to change. Ignoring this fact alters the nature of well-intended efforts to bring about democracy into some hypocritical imposition of alien values to a people who never asked for them.

The problem with this school of thought for the example in this chapter is that it fails to recognize the critical role of internal factors both in the Union and the Confederacy that contributed to the success of the Civil War in eradicating slavery. The abolition of slavery was a home-made transformation, not an international imposition, and that must be the lesson for how successful transformations generally occur. The Union forces were not an external power with an alien ideology or culture to the same degree as the US forces would be in foreign regions, such as in countries in the Middle East, Africa, or Latin America. Although the South strenuously defended the institution of slavery, historians Charles Sellers and William Freehling have demonstrated that the Southerners in the antebellum America cherished the same liberal and revolutionary values about freedom and the equality of all men, as those living in the Union.[63] As the author Gerald Sorin stated, "...for five decades after the Declaration of Independence, Southerners were openly apologetic about slavery. But the huge economic investment in it and the fear of a huge free black population always came between their *awareness of the evil of slavery* and the act of emancipation. Thus these Southerners clung stubbornly to the institution while continuing to feel acute guilt or at least significant tension [italics added]."[64]

The abolitionist ideology was not foreign to the southerners. Sorin points out, for example, the resolution by Virginia Revolutionary Convention in 1774 declaring that the abolition of slavery was "the greatest object of desire," or the resolution by the Georgia County Committee in 1775, acknowledging the "unnatural practice of slavery," which they endeavored to eliminate from the state.[65] But as Sorin has correctly pointed out, southerners suppressed their libertarian ideals in favor of the economic and social benefits of slavery. They began increasingly to stress the rights of states (to hold slaves) instead of the natural rights of man. Despite all odds between the North and South, the Union and the Confederacy shared a common history, a common background, and much of the same culture and ideas. The Union succeeded in ending the system of slavery because mechanism for change were already present both in the South and the North, as opposed to regions of the world where the internal leadership, internal will, or internal mobilization do not converge with the wishes and objectives of the United States. Without favorable internal mechanisms, no coercive measure will succeed in bringing about a lasting change; a change embraced by its people. American idealism to end repression and bring about positive change in the world is perfectly admirable, if and only if the local populace joins the cause overwhelmingly. If there is no internal will, the US's efforts will run the risk of creating authoritarian ways of its own.

There existed an apparent ideological divide between the Union and Confederacy. Yet, contrary to the US's foreign engagement, where there exists a cultural chasm between the US army and the locals with whom the army is engaged, cultural and historical proximity in antebellum America enabled both parties to the Civil War to end the dispute in unity. If the southerners were culturally close to the northerners in that deep in their hearts they knew that slavery was wrong, as implied above, the northerners were also culturally close to their southern brothers in that they endorsed the same racial prejudices and the same fear for a black population on American soil. The abolitionists who considered all men as equal and worked to cleanse the nation of all racial prejudice constituted only a small minority of the populace. Mostly ministers, they did not even manage to pull support from their churches or congregations. Rather than developing a strong antislavery vision, most northerners had developed a form of "anti-southernism." What concerned most of the Union citizens more than the slavery itself was the adverse effect of the conflict on civil liberties for themselves, not for the slaves. Before the war broke out southern interest groups lobbied Congress for legislations to crack down on antislavery opposition. The southerners were particularly nervous for widespread slave uprising as a result of abolitionist agitation. To prevent a rebellion they saw it necessary to curtail the abolitionists' freedom of speech. Already in 1835 President Andrew Jackson addressed Congress condemning the dissemination of "inflammatory" abolitionist mails through the southern states and called for a law to "prohibit, under severe penalties, the circulation" of such literature.[66]

Some proslavery extremists interpreted such statements from the President and other prominent officials as a license to step up assaults on abolitionists across the country. Mailmen in the South took the law in their own hands and stopped delivering antislavery literature. Those who sympathized with the abolitionist cause in the South remained silent or fled to North. Popular concern for civil liberties reached to a head, when in 1830s Southerners forced a bill through Congress prohibiting Congressional meddling with slavery. In a symbolic act of defiance large number of Northerners rushed to sign an antislavery petition to Congress.[67] The "gag" rule in Congress—as it became known—provoked ferocious opposition from senior politicians and at the grassroots level, but many Northerners hoped to evade a black uprising at any cost. Their loud protests aimed at preserving the American values for the white population rather than targeting the evils of slavery. Many Northerners who were not abolitionist activists but condemned slavery, did so mostly because they thought the dispute with the South was harmful to American civil liberties and the Union power. The slavery issue was of secondary import to most Northerners other than a core group of idealistic abolitionists.

Lincoln's role during the Civil War was instrumental in bringing an end to slavery. Yet other factors had already made the institution of slavery unsustainable. With Britain banning the importation of slavery, the slave market was drying up, forcing the South to abandon the practice anyway. As soon as Lincoln was elected president, he was determined to resolve the slavery conundrum one way or another, even though he did not define the Civil War as a war for emancipation of slaves. In a private farewell to his law partner, Herndon, he said: "I am decided; my course is fixed; my path is blazed. The Union and the Constitution shall be preserved and the laws enforced at every and at all hazards. I expect the people to sustain me. They have never yet forsaken any true man."[68]

Lincoln often spoke in religious terms. Phrases such as "Divine Providence," "God," "the Providence of God," "that God who has never forsaken this people," "the Divine Power, without whose aid we can do nothing," "that Supreme Being who has never forsaken this favored land," "the Maker of the Universe," "the Almighty," and "Almighty God" frequently appeared in his speeches.[69] He would sometimes speak as an uncompromising leader: "Away—off—begone! If the nation wants to back down, let it—not I." He told a Missouri Republican that he "would sooner go out into [his] back yard and hang [himself]."[70] Yet Lincoln was no abolitionist. He was solemnly and primarily concerned about the status of the Union. He believed that the partial abolition of slavery had jeopardized the unity of the country. Despite occasional uncompromising rhetoric, he considered to reconcile with the Confederacy, if it could help save the Union. As he said in 1862: "My paramount objective in this struggle is to save the Union, and is not either to save or to destroy slavery. If I could save the Union without freeing any slave I would do it, and if I could save it by freeing all the slaves I would do it; and if I could save it by freeing some and leaving others alone I would also do that."[71]

Lincoln also felt a responsibility for his party. The Republican Party was young, inexperienced with party politics, and fragile. It had no real foothold in the American politics other than in the slavery question. The party members came from an amalgam of interests and backgrounds. The slavery issue was the uniting force that held them together. Otherwise they could have trickled down to factionalism and perhaps separation. Lincoln was determined to maintain the unity of his party, and to do so he constantly had to weigh and balance his actions.[72] He would not simply adopt a radical antislavery position that could further aggravate the southerners, but he would not discard the slavery question either in order to appease his party men. Furthermore, as a private person, and as a lawyer, Lincoln was a constitutionalist. Though he was not actively abolitionist, he believed that the Constitution afforded all men freedom. He was quite willing to sacrifice principles closest to his heart to save the Union, but on a personal level he was morally certain that slavery was wrong. Yet he contended that blacks were inferior to the white man. As he asserted: "I will say then that I am not, nor ever have been in favor of bringing about in anyway the social and political equality of the white and black races—that I am not nor ever have been in favor of making voters or jurors of negroes, nor of qualifying them to hold office, nor to intermarry with white people; and I will say in addition to this that there is a physical difference between the white and black races which I believe will forever forbid the two races living together on terms of social and political equality. And inasmuch as they cannot so live, while they do remain together there must be the position of superior and inferior, and I as much as any other man am in favor of having the superior position assigned to the white race. I say upon this occasion I do not perceive that because the white man is to have the superior position the negro should be denied everything."[73]

Lincoln could only be successful if he could dissociate himself from the abolitionists' ideas about black equality. At some point he even flirted with the idea of colonizing freed slaves, as a way of reconciling with his anti-black constituency. Some other Republicans followed in the same footstep. For instance, in Oregon the Republicans used racism to their advantage by arguing in favor of a ban on slavery to keep Oregon for "white race" only.[74]

The Emancipation did not mark the end of African-American suffering; it marked only the beginning of the end. After the institution of slavery was eliminated, the population of freed blacks increased many fold, and with the growing black population the black code and black phobia intensified. Blacks were excluded from many social goods, such as employment, schooling, medical care, and decent housing. In the south a violent and highly black phobic organization was formed, known as Ku Klux Klan, which committed horrendous acts of aggression including many murders against African-Americans.[75]

Just as Iraq and Afghanistan are slow to transform themselves into democracies even after their dictators have fallen, it took a century for the Civil Rights Movement and the death of Dr. Martin Luther King Jr. before African-Americans won equal rights even on paper, and another half a century before America could see its first black president. Racial prejudice persists in this generation; a generation baffled by why it is taking so much time for Iraq and Afghanistan to become democratic states!

The abolitionist movement had a long history. This chapter has by no means touched all aspects of this movement. Similarly, the American Civil War was an eventful epoch in the history of this country. We barely touched a few headlines, leaving out other defining moments of this war. Our aim has been to show the complexity of cultural workings behind social transformations, and the stories outlined here will suffice as examples to underline this aim.

4. THE ROAD TO GENDER EQUALITY

The One Thousand and One Nights is a classic fictional story from the Middle East which portrays a woman's battle against a fictional Persian king, Shahri`r, who kills his adulterous wife. In vengeance, he decides to marry a virgin each day, take with her to bed, and order her execution the following morning before marrying his next victim. In his anger, King Shahri`r stereotypes women as a group by labeling them unfaithful and turning them into sex objects. Scheherazade became the last virgin to be married to the king: as a witty storyteller she managed to defer death for one thousand and one nights. She told a new tale every night and dragged it on skillfully till King Shahri`r fell asleep before the story concluded. The curious king had to postpone her execution in the morning to hear the end of the story. In one respect, Scheherazade lived as a slave because she had to bargain for her life. But she took control over her fate by being proactive, until King Shahri`r decided eventually to spare her life.

The One Thousand and One Nights provides an interesting context for this chapter because it is a classic tale of one protagonist who reduces the other protagonist to one dimension (in this case, sex). But the female character gives him more valuable than that, something that turns out to be irresistible.

At some point during the nineteenth century women began demanding more rights—gradually, they began demanding equal rights—and stopped placing their sole focus on pleasing their men, as a way of bargaining for their rights. But why? What happened? How did the transformation of gender relations occur, and who did it? What can be learned from the story of the feminist movement?

What Triggered the Feminist Uprising?

The patriarchal society was not a phenomenon specific to the nineteenth or twentieth centuries. For thousands of years men monopolized a superior social role in most places in the world, although a few examples of matriarchal power are still known. Women held leading positions in some African and South American tribes. They could, for example, marry more than one husband while the husbands were prohibited from marrying more than but one wife. The examples of the ancient Egyptian female Pharaohs, Merytneith and Nimaethap, or the biblical Jewish woman Deborah, are testimonies of matriarchal power in the Near East. But for the most part, patriarchy has been the rule since ancient times. The Buddhists, Jews, Christians, and Muslims characterized men as the lords and their wives as servants.[76] If patriarchy prevailed for thousands of years, why exactly did the nineteenth and twentieth centuries become the era for women's uprising, and why did it occur first in Europe and America?

The feminist expert and writer Estelle Freedman believes that the answer lies in the diminishing status of women during the industrialization period in the West. As she points out, women in the hunter–gatherer society and even in feudal Medieval Europe had a degree of authority and control over their homes. Men and women shared the responsibility for bringing food to the table. According to her reading of history, industrialization distorted the traditional household, reducing the importance of women in some ways. Industrialization led to the growth of specialized markets and specialized labor. The birth of specialized labor tended to create separate spheres for men and women. Increasingly, jobs outside the confines of the home were reserved for men, and all the daily duties inside the home were assigned to women. The new gender roles were soon sanctioned by a whole array of scientific explanations and legislation. Charles Darwin's evolutionary theory of sexual selection suggested that natural reproductive strategies produced stronger and more pugnacious and innovative males than females. Darwin's theory justified and intensified sharp gender divisions.

As Freedman writes: "[w]hen factories replaced home-based, artisanal production, the gap between men's paid and women's unpaid labor widened. Women became more economically dependent on men, enjoying less leverage within marriage and fewer opportunities outside it. Equally important, capitalism encouraged political theories of individual rights and a social contract between the people and their rulers. This new definition of citizenship drew sharp exclusionary lines. In place of older, divinely ordained hierarchies, the concept of 'natural' rights distinguished between rational white men, who could be independent citizens, and the irrational, dependent, or less human categories of women, servants, and nonwhite races, who could not."[77]

Industrialization required a much higher level of technical insight than ever required before. The dazzling technical advances by the white man led them to believe that the white male had superior intellectual capacity and therefore had a right to maintain a superior social position over women as well as other groups of human beings. Feminists such as the British Mary Wollstonecraft would argue later that with proper education women could be just as intelligent as any man.

According to Freedman, it was the gender roles in this period—which reduced women to being mere accessories to men—that fueled the women's uprising in the nineteenth and twentieth centuries. After the Industrial Revolution enlightened women who saw their social status diminishing and their human rights being nullified in urban industrialized Europe and North America began to challenge the patriarchy.

Marxist women joined the revolutionary camps to claim equality and better working conditions for women in the labor market. Wealthy women used the opportunities created by the capitalist system itself to change women's social status from within the system. As Freedman points out: "...both industrial capitalism and democratic revolutions disadvantaged women in relation to men. But they also provided critical new resources that allowed women to question gender inequality. Within the middle class, education exposed more women to new ideas about citizenship. When families accumulated wealth under capitalism, some women who gained new leisure used it to write or organize. Even the ideology of separate spheres provided a resource for women who rejected older views of female inferiority and claimed that their maternal calling required education and citizenship... [W]herever capitalist economic relations took hold,...middle-class women sought education and property rights...often combining claims [in early feminist politics] of women's equality to men with an insistence that gender difference carried its own entitlements."[78]

The Western women were also suppressed sexually more than women in many countries. There is evidence that, while the practice of female circumcision in parts of Africa and Asia is an example to the contrary, many African, Asian, and Latino women enjoyed in general a better familial and sexual status than the Western women during the Victorian and the early industrial era. In Chile adulterous women were tolerated in the same way as men. Moral considerations aside, this demonstrates that the Chileans recognized female sexual passion in the same way as that of men. Islamic Sharia law granted women the right to sexual gratification. Impotent men were by Sharia law obliged to compensate their wives financially. Muslim women could seek divorce on the grounds of their husbands' impotence. The Victorian West viewed the ideal woman as a nonsexual being and the sexuality as a tool for reproduction, whereas Islam acknowledged women's rights to sexual gratification within marriage.

For these reasons women in the West had more to be "liberated" from than women elsewhere. Intensified suppression provided a rapt audience for feminists such as Emma Goldman, Voltairine de Cleyre, and others whose voices echoed loud across the Western world. At the same time, Western women had access to better resources for their fight. Once the movement was ablaze, they could deploy those resources to go further than women in the Third World.

First Wave: The Battle for Suffrage

The women's liberation movement, or feminism, has produced a colossal body of literature, but few authors truly recognize the significance of this movement beyond the manner in which it has altered the domestic and social role of women over the past two or three centuries. The failure to realize the full import of the movement is because authors have sharply conflicting views as to the scope of the concept of feminism, both with regard to whom and to what aspects of the women issue the concepts shall include. They also fail to recognize that if the feminist movement shall be regarded as a moral crusade rather than a self-centered factional struggle for gender equality, the principles laid down by feminism must apply to any egalitarian movement.

Feminism has been a contentious term. Some women advocacy groups use it as a generic tag to denote the women's movement in general; others dispute the label, viewing it as signifying only a subcategory of the movement, such as the radical feminism which deviates from the main stream women's movement by entertaining a militant agenda.

The term "feminism" appeared first in France in 1880s and entered the English-speaking world around the turn of the century, but until the 1980s it remained a derogatory term, from which most progressive reformers sought to distance themselves.[79] Throughout the nineteenth century the woman issue had three main objectives: suffrage, the rights to education, and the rights to own property. A group of women discovered their power to mobilize and enforce change through the abolitionist movement.[80]

Emboldened by their successful campaign in the nineteenth century to emancipate the slaves, women rallied to advance their rights. This period of activism was coined simply "the woman movement." The woman movement activists believed that there existed a common ground between women from all backgrounds, which rested on a unique female identity that was created through shared experiences as being subjugated by the patriarchal society. It was thought that this common identity would be able to sustain divergences in the movement and not be submerged by them.[81] The woman movement linked the social authority of women to the role of motherhood. The right to education was sought based on the argument that women played a decisive role in the early years of a child's development. As mothers, they insisted, women needed to be educated. Property rights were sought as a pathway to political representation. The English constitution reserved political representation not to individuals, but to property ownership. Only men with property had a voting right and the interests of women were represented through their husbands. Women's identity was therefore inseparable from their identity as housewives. Suffragists argued that women constituted a separate social category with distinct values and wishes. They needed the voting right to represent their interests, women activists argued. Some activists asserted that the values held high by women would benefit both men and women; hence women's political representation was a social imperative for the society at large. Fearing that the claim for full voting rights for all women would be too radical a demand for their time, many suffragists compromised with the established family laws and supported only bills that excluded married women from the voting right. This group of suffragists saw the partial voting right as a stepping stone towards a universal right to vote at some point in the future, and they justified their temporary compromise by averring that they would be able to represent the best interests of their married sisters in the meantime. The battle for suffrage is coined "the first wave of feminism."

The first wave of feminism distanced itself from calls for total gender equality.[82] They ridiculed such calls either because they believed that there were essential gender differences that justified unequal treatment of men and women or because they feared that a radical feminist agenda in early days of the movement could potentially harm the cause. The first step needed to be taken first, and that step was to win the right to vote. Suffrage was considered the medium, through which women could promote more comprehensive reforms in the future.

Second Wave: Demanding Equality

A new wave of activism, popularly known as "the second wave of feminism," emerged in the 1960s and demanded equality with men at home, workplace, and in politics, but neither this group of activists readily embraced the term feminism. These activists considered themselves as liberators of women from the bondage of the patriarchal society; hence their battle went under the banner "women's liberation movement." Several factors led to the outburst and success of the movement. The 1960s and 1970s saw a surge in the number of women who were willing to roll up their sleeves and carry the torch for freedom. In 1963, Betty Friedan published *The Feminine Mystique*, which questioned the degenerating role of women as housewives and called for liberation. In the years that followed thousands of women joined the liberation movement. By the end of the decade and beginning of 1970, The National Organization for Women (NOW) was founded, claiming half a million members from both sexes. The organization's openness to sympathetic male membership was the reason why it was named The National Organization *for* Women rather than *of* Women.[83]

The 1960s and 1970s was also a period of impressive feminist writings. The writings of John Stuart Mill, Jeremy Bentham, Marquis de Condorcet, and Mary Wollstonecraft, and Karl Marx (especially in Europe) were revitalized, as well as, a whole host of new feminist writers appeared in this period. Authors such as, Kate Millett, Gloria Steinem, Susan Brownmiller, and Juliet Michell are but a few names of feminist writers who resorted to the power of pens to defeat the patriarchy. Their writings drew the attention of national media, which in turn created a vibrant climate for change.[84]

The liberation movement identified spheres in gender relations where women were subjugated by men. The spheres did not only relate to commonly practiced prejudices that impeded women's progress at workplace or in politics, but also highlighted issues such as, rape, sexual harassment, marriage and divorce, abortion and pregnancy. What the activists called sexual harassment many men simply considered innocent flirtation. The activists assumed two strategies in their battle against sexual harassment and rape. They lobbied Congress to enact laws protective of women, and they implemented measures to educate women as to when to say no and educate men as to what women consider legitimate flirtation. One contentious but in the end successful move was the campaign for reclassifying rape as a crime of assault. The feminists also scored victories in their campaigns for rights associated with divorce, birth control, and abortion.[85]

The second-wave feminist issues provoked strong controversy throughout the Western world. The male-dominated media adopted the sarcastic term "libbers" to refer to the liberation activists. Antifeminist propaganda in media and Congress fueled the animosity on both sides and helped unleash radical forces within feminist circles, who adopted a confrontational language and in some instances militant actions. Some of these feminists called for women to stop all sexual relations with men. They claimed that because sexuality was a male construct, any heterosexual relationship was so designed to enslave women. All sex with men was therefore a case of rape, they insisted.[86] For many radical feminists the only solution to gender inequalities in family and society was to deny men any form of sexual contact.

Judging with the benefit of hindsight, it is hard to dispute that it is not the radical feminists but the moderate women who ultimately must be credited with bringing forward equality between men and women. The radicals were too divisive to be able to substantially promote the liberation movement. They did not want to have anything to do with men. They exhibited such bitter anger that they alienated both men and women. It was the moderate women who succeeded in breaking down traditional barriers to male society and penetrating male-dominated jobs. They proved their acumen and determination. They lobbied men in Congress, joined forces with men to promote equality, and bid for high level jobs despite unfair conditions. Women like Shirley Chisholm and Martha Griffiths succeeded in reaching to the top social stratum. In an environment where men still held a dominating position, an overly hostile attitude would secure neither the interests of the individual woman who vied for power nor the cause as a whole.

But the role of radicals must not be completely discounted either. It was the radical feminists that effectively campaigned against rape and sexual assault. To shake up the system some women needed to go a distance. The radicals helped open up new opportunities, which the moderates used to promote women's social standing. The demand for the same pay for the same work could not be materialized unless women held the same jobs as men in the first place, and women cannot work side by side with men unless they are willing to work together cooperatively and to entertain good relationships with their male colleagues. But to arrive at the point at which women could share those jobs with their male colleagues, a fierce battle for equality needed to be won. This battle would inevitably produce both radicalism and moderate voices. Both groups of radicals and moderates played a role in the women's liberation movement. The synergy between the radical feminists' campaigns and the moderate women's efforts created "the power to change," which finally broke down the patriarchal chains in the West, though arguably only the moderates could build new and sustainable gender relations over time.

THIRD WAVE: FEMINISM COMING OF AGE

Throughout the second wave of activism, the moderate women feared that affiliation with the radicals could harm the women's cause. Because of the stigma attached to the radical agenda the moderates refused to call themselves feminists. The term feminism took hold in the West as an acceptable tag for women liberation activism first in 1980s and 1990s with the advent of the "third wave" of women's liberation movement. In this period a whole host of specialized labels were used in conjunction with the term feminist such as, black feminists, Latino or Asian feminists, radical feminists, socialist feminists, lesbian feminists, and so on. As Rosalind Delmar writes in the beginning of 1980s, "[t]he fragmentation of contemporary feminism bears ample witness to the impossibility of constructing modern feminism as a simple unity in the present or of arriving at a shared feminist definition of feminism. Such differing explanations, such a variety of emphases in practical campaigns, such widely varying interpretations of their results have emerged, that it now makes more sense to speak of a plurality of feminisms than of one."[87]

The prevailing view after 1980s was that if feminism was concerned with questions affecting women, then anyone who shared this concern, (for some) including men, was a feminist. Some defined feminists as those entertaining an *active* role in women's liberation movement, leaving out sympathizers of both sexes who did not directly participate in the struggle.[88] By this definition, if taken plainly, a man such as, John Stuart Mill, could be named one of the world's first feminists, as he vigorously advocated women's rights in the British Parliament already in mid nineteenth century. Feminism refers, according to this definition, to activism, not the gender of the activist. In other words, the essential component of the power to change is activism, not gender. But men descended gradually to a secondary role in the movement, as women increasingly took charge of their own battle for equality; hence women gained the power to change on their own terms.

Delmar contends that: "As recently as 1972, Simone de Beauvoir could refer to feminists as 'those women or even men who fight to change the position of women, in liaison with and yet outside the class struggle, without totally subordinating that change to a change in society.' Now, in the mid-eighties, it is practically impossible to speak of 'male feminism.' Feminism is increasingly understood by feminists as a way of thinking created by, for, and on behalf of women, as 'gender-specific'."[89]

While feminists continued to demand equal treatment for women, the egalitarian ideal was abandoned "by developing much more than previously the concept of inescapable differences between the sexes."[90] Ideas about inescapable differences between the genders created a paradox for the ideology behind the struggle for equality. If there are inescapable differences between men and women, how can they be treated equally in every manner of social life? No one has perhaps worded the paradoxical variations of feminism better than Nancy F. Cott. As she writes: "Feminism is nothing if not paradoxical. It aims for individual freedoms by mobilizing sex solidarity. It acknowledges diversity among women while positing that women recognize their unity. It requires gender consciousness for its basis, yet calls for the elimination of prescribed gender roles. These paradoxes of feminism are rooted in women's actual situation, being the same (in a species sense) as men; being different, with respect to reproductive biology and gender construction, from men."[91]

In order to resolve this puzzle, feminists needed to move away from a culture of demanding equality on the basis of natural rights to the idea that biological distinctions by gender does not justify privileged treatment of one gender from the other. What does this mean exactly and how did this ideological/cultural transition occur?

The Essence of the Feminist Movement and American Wars

The concept of natural rights is closely related to the concept of human rights, which holds that all human beings possess certain rights by the power of nature. These are not rights created by the society or the law. They are intrinsic rights that follow all humans regardless of their social standing; rights the breach of which cannot be justified under any circumstances. As members of human species, the argument goes, women have the same natural rights as those of men,[92] that is, the right to autonomy and to be respected as equal and intelligent beings. This idea rests on the principle of equality, or justice for sameness, that is, same beings deserve same rights and same opportunities. This position has been vigorously defended by organizations, such as The National Woman's Party. But as mentioned above, feminists also argued for having the same rights as men based on their differences with men. They reasoned that firstly, the values women represent—values of care and peace—would benefit all of mankind, and secondly, as a distinct group women needed to have a level playing field with men to promote their own distinct interests. This seemed like a clever tactic to reconcile the argument from sameness with the argument from difference to resolve the aforementioned paradox in the movement, but what really was interesting was the manner in which arguments for natural rights eventually evolved to the notion that biological distinctions does not justify privileged treatment of one group over another.

The evolution of this new ideological platform was rarely explicitly articulated. It related rather to cultural maturity. A cultural transformation eventually replaced the paradoxical sameness difference position at the root of the feminist movement. Once women won voting rights, entered the male-dominated labor market and proved themselves as capable employees, or excelled in academic or political circles, a shift in attitudes followed. Women's performance proved that they could participate in and contribute to the economy in a wide range of roles, just as they had in earlier eras.

As the shackles of suppression broke down, natural rights arguments were no longer needed to maintain gender equality. Gender equality (to the extent it is practiced) became a permanent feature of the new culture without requiring any ideological backup. In fact, when the suffragettes were about to compromise in order to win the voting rights for unmarried women at the expense of married ones, the British feminist Christabel Pankhurst reasoned that winning voting rights for some women would automatically void gender as a basis for excluding women from suffrage. For her, it did not matter which women were franchised first.[93] What was more important was to defeat the principle of exclusion. The power of this argument is that once a notion has been broadly established that specific biological differences do not justify discrimination, the concept of natural rights need no longer be invoked to maintain it. Natural rights are useful tools in a movement until a pattern is firmly instituted. This pattern takes the form of a cultural evolution, which starts off from an ideological platform, but ends needless of any ideology that backs it up unless its foundation is being threatened.

The idea that biological distinctions between different genders do not justify discrimination is a negative argument in the sense that it negates the principles that allow one group to suppress another. In other words, it is a defensive argument, as opposed to a positive argument of demanding the same rights. To win the battle for equality women needed a more forceful argument. Demanding the same rights was the winning strategy on the battlefield. But for at least two reasons the defensive, negative, argument is more sustainable than the argument rested on natural rights. Firstly, the argument from natural rights requires a philosophical justification. The person who demands natural rights must justify the concept of natural rights, that is, she must show why certain rights are natural rights and why should certain groups enjoy those rights. The burden of proof is on the person who demands natural rights. But the notion that gender differences do not amount to a reason to discriminate against one group reverses the burden of proof. In this case, it is not the person who avers this statement, but the one who wants to oppose it—i.e. the person who wishes to maintain that biological distinctions between men and women do indeed justify privileged treatment of men (or women)—that needs to justify his position.

The second reason why the defensive argument is more sustainable is that this argument smoothes out the paradox in feminist ideology by simply asserting that regardless of whether biological distinctions make men and women different in any respect, those potential differences do not warrant discrimination.

Once women achieved a more equal footing in the society, once men became habituated to seeing women in powerful positions, and once the society as a whole realized that differences in gender did not distinguish women from men in a way that would justify discriminating them, there was no turning back.

This cultural evolution provides a more solid foundation for equality than any argument from sameness or difference can do. Mill's stepdaughter, Helen Taylor, makes this point precisely in her address to the skeptics of the theory of natural rights. She supports female suffrage as a birthright of women, but says that to consider "a *birthright* as not of *natural* but of *legal* origin is in conformity with modern habits of thought in regard to civilized men, the natives of civilized societies; but exactly as it is opposed to any a priori theories of the rights of man, it is also opposed to any attempt to give or withhold privileges for merely *natural* reasons, such as differences of sex."[94]

The significance of this insight for the discussion about US military intervention in the Middle East is that the notion of individual rights and democracy with its full meaning and implications was never established in Iraq or Afghanistan. Hence, the Iraqi and Afghani people did not embrace the Western democratization project and lack of local endorsement compelled the West to invoke the language of human rights to render a positive argument for imposing change through force. But by doing so, the West violated the rights of those same humans whose rights the West purported to protect.

The Universality of Feminist Values and the War in Afghanistan

The feminist revolution was based on values—i.e., universal moral principles—that not only dealt with the case of women, but also with the worth and status of human beings in general. The universality of the principle of equality was already established during the abolitionist movement. The idea that biological descriptions, such as sex, race, or color of skin, do not constitute a right to discriminate applies to both gender and race. Additionally, the universality of the principle of equality is in the West upheld as a principle that applies across borders. For this reason the battle for equality is, at its core, inseparable from a larger struggle for equality for all suppressed groups in all societies. This understanding has far-reaching implications. It means that no equality movement is complete unless justice is achieved for all mankind, including people in the Third World.

This notion of universal female values is invoked to justify the US military intervention in Afghanistan. It is held that we have a duty to maintain a presence in that country to safeguard the interests of the Afghani women, not to mention the interests of all other Afghani groups. But the question we have to ask is will the battle for justice succeed exclusively on terms laid down by a military force without internal mobilization and leadership? What would have Americans done had the feminist ideology been forced upon them at gunpoint by a foreign force?

As will be mentioned below, the US military intervention has not produced a success story for women in Afghanistan or Iraq.

The Lesson from the Feminist Movement

The history of the feminist movement represents one of the most fascinating transformations in modern time. It is fascinating because it became a synchronized movement across the globe. Even though the West has progressed far beyond other parts of the world, the movement drew support from feminists from both Near and Far East. But perhaps it is most fascinating because after a prolonged period of subjugation, stretching hundreds of years, it took only a few decades for women to emerge as strong as they are today. The battle for gender equality has by no means come to an end. Women still earn 20 percent less than men on average. Prejudice and discrimination continues in the job market and elsewhere to this day, but what has been accomplished so far is no small achievement. Women have penetrated most of the traditionally male dominated jobs. A dozen countries as far east as, Pakistan, India, and Australia to as far west as Brazil have already seen female presidents. This would have been unthinkable only half a century ago. Although queens and female pharaohs have ruled in parts of the world for millennia, they were not democratically elected. For a democracy to elect female presidents, the gender attitudes in the population needed to be changed. The examples from Pakistan, India, and elsewhere are thrilling tales of female achievements, despite the fact that men are still favored above women in almost all of these countries. The feminist movement did not only improve the familial and social standing of women, but it also radically altered our perspective on sexuality, on what it means to be a human, on how humans shall behave and treat one another, and on how power relations between individuals and groups shall be organized.

This book explores the power to change in major transformations in recent history. As laid out in chapter one, the book seeks to demonstrate that change, even if inspired and encouraged by outside sources, often requires internal mobilization and leadership to materialize. The history of feminist movement is a clear example of this thesis. Anyone reading this history cannot help but be amazed by the complexity of ideas and controversies that the movement has produced over time. For feminists to win the argument, for them to win the battle for equality, and for a male audience to finally submit to the feminist demand for change, the feminists needed to go through a complex and painful process. They needed to bring awareness to the plights of women, to engage in debates, write books, assemble in demonstrations, lobby Congress, and do all that they did to arrive at the point where we stand today. Many sacrifices were made throughout this process. Male feminists such as Bentham and Mill supplied crucial arguments in favor of change, but the movement would not have reached anywhere without women's leadership. Women needed to change their own attitudes before changing the attitudes of men. They were themselves part of the culture, which suppressed them. For generations women had embraced patriarchy tacitly, rearing their sons and daughters to conform to traditional gender roles. Once they changed their own attitudes, they needed to mobilize and take the fight to their men and the wider society. Wives fought from within the family; woman advocacy groups fought from within societies; and lesbians fought from within the movement itself. Internal mobilization and leadership was essential to the success of the movement. The feminist accomplishments were not the makings of an external force, but the results of a meticulous internal struggle.

Having made outstanding improvements in gender relations in the West, it is easy for us to believe that we can help other nations to break down their traditional gender roles. But this move must come from within those nations. The plights of the Afghani women; news of young girls deprived from the opportunity for education; honor killings in Pakistan; female circumcision in Africa; heartbreaking images of suppressed mothers and daughters circulate in the media and arouse the emotions of morally conscious Americans. We see it justifiable to use the iron fist against a suppressive ideology that dominate in those regions, but is it really possible to free a people without first that people develop on their own terms a cultural basis that embraces the freedom? Is it possible to liberate a nation, when the oppressor is not a single person, but an ideology or a culture? Is it possible to introduce sustainable change through military measures? Many Americans, who are otherwise opposed to military operations, support the operation in Afghanistan because it helps many Afghani girls gain the right to go to school. This is undoubtedly a positive achievement. But if we advanced the role of Afghani women through military operation, the effect of the Iraq War on Iraqi women was to diminish their social status. Women, who participated in all manner of social life alongside men under Saddam's regime, were now forced into the role of housewives. To the extent that the welfare of Iraqi women is used as an argument for American military engagement in the country, the US forces have failed. If improving the social and familial status of women can justify violence, the net gain for the US military, when both wars are taken into account, is a zero-sum game—not to mention that there is no guarantee that the Afghani women can retain their newly-won rights after the coalition forces are withdrawn from the war zone.

In stark contrast to this, women in Iran have gained far better access to education over the last two decades. The Iranian leadership has prioritized education, which again shows how success can be achieved when there is mobilization and willpower from within a culture. Iran witnessed a cultural revolution through 1980s and 1990s. The ministry of education in Iran receives about 20% of the government budget and employs about 41% of the country's civil servants. As a result, national literacy rate rose from 50% in 1970 to about 85% in 2000, and women literacy rate increased from 35% in 1970 to about 80% in 2000. The literacy rate grew for both genders, while the gap between literacy rate for men and women narrowed from 15% in 1970s to only about 5% in 2000.[95] The figure for female participation in higher education is even more promising. About 51% of university intakes in 2000-2001 were female. Iranian women have over the last one or two decades competed with men more or less evenly in higher education and their participation in the workplace is also growing, although at a slower pace. This is an incredible success story based on determination from within the Iranian society alone. Interestingly, positive events in the Third World rarely hit news headlines in the West.

The lesson from the feminist movement must be that sustainable change, whether with regards to the status of women or anything else, must take root in a popular movement that starts from within the system. It must go through a process that mobilizes the support of a large segment of the population. Change is a process, not a ready-to-install solution that can be brought down on a people from above. Considering the complexity and richness involved in social transformations, it is hard to understand how the iron fist can succeed in altering cultures.

5. GORBACHEV AND THE END OF THE COLD WAR

The Soviet Union was a union of socialist republics which dominated the Eastern bloc and rivaled the power of the United States of America. It was formed under Vladimir Lenin in 1922 following five years of revolution and civil war, when the Socialist Federative Soviet Republics of Russia, Ukraine, Belarus, and the Transcaucasian Republics (which included Georgia, Armenia, and Azerbaijan) signed the Treaty of Creation of the USSR and designated Moscow as the capital. The abbreviation USSR stands for The Union of Soviet Socialist Republics.

During World War II, the German–Soviet Nonaggression Pact enabled the Soviet Union to occupy the Baltic states. These states were then permanently added to the Soviet Union until it collapsed in 1991. With the inclusion of the Baltic region, the Soviet Union encompassed as much as one-sixth of earth's land area. The Soviet Union had a strong centralized government based on a single-party system and a planned economy. The Communist Party (in this chapter we call it the Party) was the only legal political party in the country. Voting was organized through Party Congresses, which elected the Central Committee. The Central Committee in turn appointed the highest political offices, the Politburo and its General Secretary (who acted as the head of state of the Soviet Union).

The Party was based on a Marxist–Leninist platform that intended to create, but never fully succeeded, economic equality by controlling the means of production and reducing exploitation of simple workers to the benefit of the elites. The system was code-named the dictatorship of the proletariat. In a nutshell, the idea was that the free market economy inevitably leads to capital accumulation among a small privileged group with resources at the expense of the masses. To counter this outcome, the Party took full ownership of all economic activities on behalf of the proletariats (wage earners). Economic planning and distribution of resources were centralized under the state oversight.

The system failed ultimately and the ideology proved little more than Utopia because barriers to accrue private capital and the guarantee for equal pay irrespective of performance eliminated incentives for individual initiative-taking and entrepreneurship, and lowered productivity. Instead of raising the standard of living for the masses, meager productivity lowered the economic prospects.

The system experienced a crisis in the 1980s and collapsed under Mikhail Gorbachev's leadership. The analysis below will review some of the possible causes for this collapse. But in the meantime, it is important to point out that the Soviet economy actually grew substantially for several decades under its planned economy. Starting off with radical reforms under Lenin and the collectivization project under Lenin's successor, Joseph Stalin, the industrial sector gained strength, the Soviet military was modernized and considerably expanded, and agriculture was made more efficient though at the cost of forcefully relocating millions of peasants to collective farms, many of whom perished of disease and hunger in the process. While the productivity rate was lower in the Soviet Union compared to the Western countries, the per capita income grew at an average annual rate slightly above the global average until the end of 1980s. The growing Soviet economy and military expenditure married with an ideology that opposed the Western capitalism intensified the rivalry between the country and the US and led to what came to be known as the Cold War.

The Cold War was a period of jealous rivalry after World War II between the US and the Soviet Union to dominate the world. It divided the world into two spheres of influence, the West bloc and the East bloc and countries, which refused to align with one of the two superpowers, were subjected to pressure, including sanctions, military assaults, espionage, coup, proxy war, or propaganda war from one side or another. The doctrines of domino-effect or liberating the oppressed people were invoked by the superpowers to justify the measures taken to realign noncompliant states under their wings. The domino-effect was a doctrine utilized by the United States to justify its efforts to block the Soviet Union at every turn, hinged on the idea that a communist takeover in any country could potentially encourage other countries to follow suit, possibly even triggering a worldwide communist revolution. The communist revolution was the medium through which the Soviet Union was perceived to be attempting to promote communism internationally. The Marxist tradition maintained that the class conflict between the haves and have-nots would eventually spark a full-blown upheaval that would end in workers taking control of production (or in Leninist tradition, would end in a centralized socialist state).

For over four decades, the Cold War either directly defined or at least indirectly provided the context for every international relation.

The Effect of the Cold War

The competition between the US and the Soviet Union offered postwar Western Europe breathing room from internal rivalry. The old rivals, France, Germany, and England, needed to ally with the US to provide benefits to their populations in order to dent any appeal that the communist model might have held. To foster peace in Europe, a scheme of economic cooperation was invented. Shortly after World War II, Germany was included in the international framework for economic activity, and in 1958 Belgium, France, Italy, Luxembourg, the Netherlands, and West Germany founded the European Economic Community (EEC)—which became the predecessor to the European Union.

The costs of the Cold War were enormous. The conflict led to the fastest and largest arms race ever. It divided the world sharply. The Berlin Wall became the most tangible symbol of this global divide, but the real upshot of this partitioning was its damning effect on international trade and on the exchange of culture and technology between the East and West for over four decades. The growth of Islamic terrorism was also one of the adverse and unforeseen consequences of the Cold War.

Islamism was born in the nineteenth century as a reaction to the British and French colonialism. Jamal ad-Din al-Afghani (1839–97), Hasan al-Banna (1906–49), and Sayyid Qutb (1906–66) were pan-Islamists and political activists, who believed that only a revival of politicized Islam could stop colonialism and the European influence in the Muslim world.[96] The creation of Islamism had initially no reference to the Cold War, but it was the policies during this period that eventually led to an expansion of violent Islamism as an adversarial international force.

The CIA-orchestrated coup in Iran in 1953 that overthrew the democratically-elected government of Mossadegh was one such policy. The coup was sold in Washington at least partially as a measure to contain Soviet influence in Iran, though Chapter 7 argues that there was no real evidence that Iran would fall in the hands of the communists. The coup, followed by President Johnson's unconditional support for the oppressive regime of the shah, exasperated the Iranian people and the Iranian clerics masterfully played on the memories of the coup to foment hostility and to justify violent attacks against the West.

In Afghanistan the competition between the two superpowers resulted in a decade-long proxy war. In the 1980s, Washington supported the Islamist fighters, Mujahideen, financially and militarily following the Soviet invasion of country, only to see the Islamists turning against the US itself after the Soviet withdrawal.

There were many other incidents that contributed to the Cold War rivalry between the two superpowers. The 1948 communist takeover of Czechoslovakia and the Soviet invasion of the country twenty years later; the Korean War in the beginning of 1950s; the 1956 Hungarian uprising; the Vietnam War in the 1960s and 70s; the Bays of Pigs Invasion of Cuba in 1961; the Cuban missile crisis of 1962; and other incidents became all part of the game of rivalry between those who wanted to plan the economy and those who believed in the free market.

In the aftermath of the Cold War, many differing views and interpretations have been proposed about the nature and impacts of the transformations that ended the Cold War. Gorbachev often used the language of freedom and economic liberalization. For many Western commentators he became the champion of democracy and human rights. The end of the Cold War reduced the possibility of a nuclear war. That alone was a major achievement. Others have pointed out that the collapse of the Soviet Union left a power vacuum that proved detrimental for the country. Many ordinary Russians turned their back to Gorbachev, as his reforms rather reduced their standard of living and increased the hardship. Some international observers saw the fall of the Soviet Union as a major victory for the US. Without strong rivalry, these observers saw the US as the sole superpower with unlimited might and opportunity to influence the world. Others yet have argued that American influence benefited from the game of power between the two superpowers. The fear of communism was a uniting force among the Western countries. The US utilized the perceived threat of communism to enforce its agenda, this group argued. The collapse of the Soviet power eliminated this dynamic, hence weakened the US's position in the world, according to this opinion. There are signs that several countries are gradually moving away from the American power bloc. The European Union, for instance, began talks about creating a form of military cooperation alongside, but separate from, NATO—right before 9/11. More recently, France and the UK have been engaged in talks about bilateral defense cooperation. Not to mention that Bush's Iraq War polarized the world, leaving the US isolated during 2003.

By the time the Cold War ended the Eastern bloc was bankrupt. The planned economy was dismantled quickly, before a viable free market economy had been built. The Soviet state was thrown into such dire financial condition that it even struggled to fulfill its rental obligations for its embassies around the world. In Oslo the Norwegian government had to bail out the Russian Embassy. With great humiliation Gorbachev toured the world asking for money to help salvage his country from economic ruin. But the Reagan Administration failed to provide Gorbachev anything more than a nominal aid package, which proved insufficient to help the Soviet economy stay on its feet.

WHAT CAUSED THE FALL OF THE SOVIET UNION?

Experts disagree broadly about the causes of the collapse of the Soviet Union, but most commentators agree that some combination of the factors below created a hostile environment that eventually helped bring down the Soviet might.

Firstly, as mentioned above, the Cold War era led to an unsustainable arms race. The Soviet defense industry absorbed much of the country's resources at the expense of the civil society. For over four decades the Soviet leadership succeeded in matching the US's defense build-up, even surpassing the US in the area of space technology. But with a Conservative administration in charge of the White House in 1980s, a massive arms race was initiated by Reagan, forcing the Soviet Union to up its defense investment as well. Defense spending nearly doubled in the US from 1980 to 1989, from $134 billion to $253 billion annually—or about 7% of the GDP in 1989. The respective figures for the Soviet Union were increased from 22% to about 27% of the Soviet GDP. Nearly a third of the Soviet's national wealth was squandered on weapon build-up.[97]

Secondly, Saudi Arabia increased its oil production substantially in mid 1980s, which led to a dramatic fall in the price of petroleum. This proved detrimental for the Soviet economy, as it was heavily dependent on its oil income.

Thirdly, the Soviet economy suffered from an acute productivity deficit compared to Western economies, which made the planned economy unsustainable; even so, the Soviet economy was still growing somewhat faster than the world average up until the eve of its collapse. This fact coupled with a chronic culture of corruption that had permeated through all levels of the society took a toll on the Soviet system. Furthermore, lack of transparency disillusioned the Soviet populace. As a result, the Soviet apparatus gradually lost its popular support base.

Fourthly, the Reagan Administration maintained a hostile posture towards the Soviet leadership until Gorbachev initiated a process of change. It has been speculated that Reagan played an active role in forcing the dismantling of the Soviet system, both through hostile policies before Gorbachev and through collaborating with Gorbachev to aggressively speed up its fall. Ronald Hilton points out, for example, that Reagan's controversial defense initiative, codenamed SDI, was unrealistic and extravagant. He implies that the initiative was primarily designed to push the Soviet leadership to increase their military budget, which then could drive the Soviet economy to the verge of bankruptcy.[98] There have also been speculations that Reagan lobbied the Saudis to increase their production of petroleum in 1980s in order to effect a drop in the price of oil.[99] However, the US economy was dependent on Middle Eastern oil and Reagan had an incentive to press for cheaper oil anyway. And to the extent Reagan collaborated with Gorbachev after mid 1980s, it was clear that it was Gorbachev, not Reagan, which was the main player. Nonetheless, Reagan's decision to dramatically increase defense spending and his refusal to extend meaningful financial aid to the Soviet leader in 1990, helped push the communist regime off the edge.

Fifthly, a decade long Soviet occupation of Afghanistan from 1979 drained the Soviet system of resources. Here, the Reagan Administration worked actively against the Soviet Union by supporting the Mujahideen's resistance movement against Soviet army.

In the end, an amalgam of all these factors created a difficult breathing room for the Soviet system, but there were also indications already during Gorbachev's early days as a leading bureaucrat of the Department of Agriculture that the young leader aspired to open up his country's political and economic structures. Gorbachev's vision for a better Soviet Union when he became the General Secretary of the Party might have played just as much of a role in unleashing the forces of change as the economic and political factors.

THE DYNAMICS OF SOVIET CHANGE

Lenin's death in 1924 cleared the way for the young Joseph Stalin to assume power in Moscow. Stalin's vision was to resurrect the country's economy, which had been devastated by World War I, the Revolution, and the civil war, and he used extreme violence to achieve his goal. Shortly after taking power, he launched a central economic plan for rapid industrialization and economic collectivization through forced labor. The industrialization effort was a dramatic success early on, transportation and railways expanded across the country, and the need for labor virtually wiped out unemployment. The number of hospitals and schools rose markedly. In a few decades universal literacy was achieved, and in particular the position of women in the society improved dramatically within this period. However, these successes came at an incredible cost. Forced labor radically diminished the standard of living for a vast number of workers, who often had to work up to eighteen hours a day seven days a week. The collectivization process forced many peasants to leave their villages to work on farms hundreds of miles away from their families or to move to urban areas and work in factories. Those who refused to leave were threatened, killed, or prosecuted for anti-revolutionary crimes. Failed farming reforms led to a severe food shortage. In particular Ukraine was hit hard by famine. Millions of Ukrainians lost their lives due to hunger. In the 1930s Stalin ordered an intense process of internal cleansing within the ranks of the Communist Party, which became known as the Great Purge.

Stalin tightened the grip further after World War II as he was faced with threats from the West. The Cold War was born. Despite his declared goal of building "socialism in one country" and his denunciation of Trotsky's ideas of "world revolution," Stalin's efforts to consolidate his power beyond the Russian borders after the war alarmed Western policymakers.

The Stalin era effectively laid down the long-term direction of the country for the remaining part of the Cold War. After Stalin the Soviet leadership turned conservative. Efforts to reform the system were sporadic and not very successful. The former head of the secret security agency and a close aide of Stalin, Lavrentiy Beria, did release several political prisoners and allowed some freedom of expression. However, he had earned a reputation as the executor of Stalin's terror state while heading the secret agency, and his opponents in the communist leadership moved fast to remove him from power only months after Stalin's death. Nikita Khrushchev picked up the thread where Beria left it. In a speech to a closed session of the Twentieth Party Congress in 1956, he denounced the crimes committed on Stalin's watch and advocated an easing of the relations with the West, claiming that capitalism would eventually decay from within. Khrushchev's speech gave him a boost of support from the more liberal communist leaders and the political dissidents who had suffered under Stalin, but it weakened the Soviet Union's authority and prestige among communists in other parts of the world. After his speech millions of prisoners were pardoned. Censorship was relaxed and the Soviet relationship with the West improved. Meanwhile, the hardliners within the Communist Party resisted Khrushchev in order to preserve the status quo.

There were, however, impulses and pressures coming from abroad during this period. The economic success of the West quickly tore down the Soviet Union's stature on the world scene. As a result, a growing attraction to the Western economic model spread across the East bloc. The decisive blow came from China's successful market orientation: if China could do it, why should the other communist countries not do it?

This put the Soviet state on the defensive with regard to its economic structure. Then the 1979 Islamic Revolution in Iran alarmed the Soviet leadership. With a large Muslim population, the Communist Party feared a similar uprising in its own backyard. This fear was reinforced in 1980s by their failure to ensure stability in Afghanistan. Despite their state-of-the-art military technology, the Afghan puppet government lost the war to the

Islamist fighters. At the same time the Soviet leaders were feeling the heat from US presidents. President Ronald Reagan famously dubbed the communist regime "the Evil Empire" and refused to collaborate with Moscow. All of these events spurred those liberal segments of the Soviet leadership who craved for change, but played into the hands of the conservatives who feared the Western threat. Around mid 1980s a process of transformation began, which ultimately led to the collapse of the Soviet system. That process was initiated by Mikhail Gorbachev. Gorbachev was a loyal communist leader who knew the system in and out but had a new vision for the future.

GORBACHEV'S ASCENT TO POWER

Gorbachev started his career at Moscow State University, where he studied law. After graduation he moved back to Stavropol, a rural province in southeast Russia where he was born, and began a modest career as a provincial Communist Party bureaucrat. Only one year into his job he was named first secretary of his town. Two years later he was promoted to the head of the department of propaganda, a key position within the communist bureaucracy. After another two years he became the first secretary of the whole province of Stavropol Krai. With this post under his belt he positioned himself for a big job in the Soviet state. Stavropol Krai was the province to where many of the Soviet Union's top leaders went for vacation. For Gorbachev this meant plenty of opportunities to meet with and impress the top communist leaders.

Gorbachev soon got a job with the Agricultural Department of Stavropol, where he became responsible for coordinating crop production for a number of farms. It was in this period that he began to develop ideas about political transparency. He experimented with what later became known as his policy of *glasnost* (the policy of openness and transparency in government and politics). His policies increased crop production and boosted Gorbachev's image as an able young leader. The central party newspaper *Pravda* featured a front page article hailing him for his expertise and leadership and urged other provinces to follow his example.

In November 1982 the long-serving leader, Leonid Brezhnev, died and the head of KGB, Yuri Andropov, took over the Soviet leadership. As the head of KGB, Andropov had earned a reputation for his cruel tactics to silence the opposition. He had wasted no time in sending the dissident writers and intellectuals to show trials and having them jailed or executed. Some dissidents ended up in psychiatric hospitals, and others were exiled or forced to emigrate. But in the few months that he took over the Soviet leadership after Brezhnev, Andropov appointed young and bright politicians and servicemen to key posts. As the chairman of KGB, Andropov had witnessed the state of the Soviet economy first hand. The information was kept highly secret, but Andropov knew well that the standard of living had deteriorated steadily during the Brezhnev era. The economy was stagnant; unemployment was high; corruption was exorbitant; people were destitute, and increasingly turned to alcohol as their only consolation from everyday life's hardship. In some families, children as young as fifteen years of age had already developed alcohol-related problems. The health costs related to drinking and stress were immense, and the government seemed unable to deal with the problem. The Soviet republic ranked fiftieth place in the world for infant mortality, and thirty-second for overall life expectancy. Half the schools did not have central heating, running water, or a sewage system. A quarter of the students attended school in split shifts. More than half of the students suffered from ill health due to lack of proper ventilation or other poor conditions in the classrooms. The system had failed to provide basic necessities. Many Soviet households had no telephone line. Transportation, roads, and new constructions were inadequate, especially in villages.

Andropov was determined to reform the system and chose young and dynamic Party members as his aides to carry out his reform plans. Gorbachev's responsibilities were extended by Andropov. Gorbachev's hard work and loyalty paid off. On his deathbed only a few months later, Andropov put Gorbachev in charge of the Party secretariat. Gorbachev was now practically the head of the Soviet Union, though not in name yet.

He now had to make one last move on his precipitous path to the top. The Party member and diplomat, Konstantin Chernenko, was by a core and mighty group of Party officials considered a better fit for the position of general secretariat after Andropov's death. Gorbachev acknowledged the power of this core group and decided to put his support behind Chernenko. Chernenko won the top post in February 1984, and the reconciliation with the Chernenko supporters earned Gorbachev goodwill. Chernenko was an old and ailing man, who served parts of his thirteen month tenure as the General Secretary from his hospital bed. When Chernenko died, Gorbachev was ready for the big job, and the big job became his at last. As the next

candidate in line, a long and loyal serving Communist Party member, a successful bureaucrat of the Ministry of Agriculture, and a likeable comrade he
became the natural choice for the post of General Secretary of the Party—a
post he held from 1985 to the collapse of the communist system in 1991.

TOWARDS MORE OPENNESS

Five weeks into his new position, Gorbachev summoned his Party officials to a special Central Committee meeting in order to launch his new
policy program. Gorbachev presented an extensive reform program. The es-
sence of his plans was captured in the two phrases *glasnost* and *perestroika*.
Glasnost was the policy of transparency and openness, including freedom
of expression. The media became freer to express views of the opposition,
and political prisoners were awarded amnesty. Perestroika was Gorbachev's economic and political restructuring plan. He advocated more efficient
scientific and technical solutions to increase labor productivity and output.
He believed that real participation in and ownership of economic activities
would encourage the large mass of laborers to work better and harder. He
advocated that the workers should be given the power to hold the executive
branch accountable and to monitor government performance. Gorbachev
saw democratization as consistent with the core Leninist–Marxist ideology, which encouraged worker self-government. In his Central Committee
meeting, he told his comrades that Lenin had taught communists to base
everything they do on the interests of the working people, to scrutinize life
deeply, to evaluate social phenomena realistically and from class positions,
and to engage in a constant, creative search for the best ways to implement
the ideals of communism. He urged them to reexamine their deeds and plans
against Lenin and his "great ideas", and to live and work in accordance with
Lenin's behests.[100]

Throughout the reform process, Gorbachev played the game of a double
agent. He would seek the support of the opposition against the conservative
forces, and he would seek the support of the hardliners to limit the opposition for the benefit of a balanced approach.

Real domestic reforms had to wait another three or four years before
materializing. Gorbachev needed to consolidate his power as the General
Secretary before major changes could take place. But internationally, Gorbachev scored quick points early in 1985, when in April that year he an-

nounced a unilateral suspension of the deployment of SS-20 intermediate-range missiles in Europe. The missiles had upset the balance of power in Europe, and had led NATO to respond the move with deploying Pershing II and cruise missiles. In September the same year, Gorbachev proposed a mutual halving of the American and Soviet nuclear arsenals. He then embarked on a reconciliation tour to Paris and Geneva. These policies quickly improved his country's international relations, helped alleviate the conservatives' fear for the West within the Party, and enhanced Gorbachev's position at home and abroad.

Yet, by late 1987 the reform process seemed largely to have failed. The economy remained weak. Corruption was still rampant. Gorbachev's first reform project was to combat alcoholism by raising the prices on beer, vodka, and wine. Excessive drinking habits had caused acute health and social problems. But the anti-drinking campaign forced much of the alcohol industry underground. Doctors began reporting cases of alcohol poisoning, as drinkers consumed cheap industrial alcohol. The state budget suffered tens of billions of rubles in lost revenue from sales of alcohol. Not surprisingly, the then First Secretary of Moscow City Committee and a notoriously heavy drinker, Boris Yeltsin, became one of the staunchest critics of Gorbachev's new alcohol policy.

In December 1986, Gorbachev personally invited the physicist and human rights campaigner, Andrei Sakharov, to move back to Moscow after six years of internal exile. Sakharov had been exiled for his political views, and human rights campaigners pressed hard for his release. Following his return to Moscow, Sakharov was hailed as a national hero. Glasnost had noticeably opened up the press media. New publications blossomed; some openly critical of the old system. The publication of Bukharin's testament signified the effect of glasnost. Bukharin was a political oppositionist who had been executed by Stalin decades earlier. In anticipation of his arrest, Bukharin had written a letter to the future generations of communist leaders, where he condemned Stalin's crimes and talked of his innocence. Bukharin's widow, Anna Larina, had memorized the content of the letter, as she did not want to keep the hard copy out of fear for getting into trouble with the secret police. Glasnost made it possible to publish it in *Moscow News* in 1987. But even glasnost seemed to be diminishing in 1987. Capitalizing on Gorbachev's failures, the conservative elements were trying to consolidate their power and push back the reform plans. Several publications became subjected to the old ways of censorship again. The newspaper *Ogonyok* was prevented from publishing a criticism of the police in Uzbekistan. Hardliners' confrontational approach in this period concerned Gorbachev's security officers. He was advised to stay in his cottage outside Moscow.

Gorbachev remained, however, determined to press forward with his reforms. What would become characteristic of his leadership over the years were his tenacious and tireless efforts to make change happen despite stiff obstacles. Occasionally, he experienced a setback that jeopardized the reform process. The setbacks often triggered crises, and the crises spark new life into the reform process that allowed new breakthroughs to come to fruition. In February 1988, he announced that he would withdraw Soviet forces from Afghanistan within ten months. Again, the announcement boosted his image in the West, but concerned hardliners who worried that the withdrawal could weaken the Soviet Union's international standing. Later in the same month, an ethnic clash broke out between the Armenians and Muslim Azerbaijanis, leaving several dead and injured. Thousands of terrified Armenians and Muslims left their homes and moved to other areas in search of safety. The army was ordered in to take control of the situation. Glasnost came once again under threat, as the details of the Armenian-Azerbaijani conflict were heavily censored in the Russian media.

The conservative Party members used the newly won press freedom against Gorbachev himself. In an article entitled "I Cannot Deny My Principles" published in *Sovietskaya Rossiya* in March 1988, a chemistry lecturer at the Leningrad Technological Institute, Nina Andreyeva, strongly criticized glasnost and defended Stalinism. The article made an impact among the conservatives, but Gorbachev's tolerance of criticism against him, which was unusual for Soviet leaders before him, put the leader on moral high ground and strengthened his message of openness and honesty among his followers.

THE COLLAPSE OF THE SOVIET UNION

The dismantling of the Soviet system led to a breakdown of the Soviet Union, both internally and externally. The speed in which this happened was spectacular. In December 1988, Gorbachev made another move toward détente. He announced that the Soviet Union would unilaterally reduce its armed forces by 500,000 troops in two years. Fifty thousand Soviet troops and five thousand tanks would be withdrawn from Eastern Europe. The announcement meant a much needed cut in the Soviet military budget. But it was also a powerful signal to the East European bloc and the countries within the Union that the Soviet Union was losing ground.

The highlight of a series of events that marked the end of the Soviet Union was the fall of the Berlin Wall on November 9. 1989. The incident was monumental. It came as the culmination of nearly five years of struggle for reform. One by one the Eastern European countries abandoned the Soviet Union's camp.

The end of the Cold War opened up the pathway for political and economic cooperation between the East and West. As events were unfolding, fear ran high as to how the Soviet Union might respond. The answer became clear soon. Gorbachev had seemingly made the decision to stay out of the troubled waters and let the occasion run its natural course. Observers speculated whether or not Gorbachev actively encouraged the dismantling of the Soviet Union. A short while before the collapse of the Wall, Gorbachev was asked if it might one day come down—to which he had answered, "Nothing is eternal in this world." Gorbachev talked openly about democratization to his East European counterparts. He had just come back from a tour to China, where his speech about the need for democracy was believed to have sparked the street riots that led to the Tiananmen Square massacre. Whatever role Gorbachev played in this, November 9 saw a sea of East Germans taking to the street where the Wall had divided the East from West. With the help of axes, shovels, bare fists, kicking, or whatever tools in their disposal, the rebels broke open the Wall resolutely and ran through the streets of West Germany, while conservative Soviet leaders watched the demise of Soviet power with horror. Gorbachev did nothing to stop it. In his book, *Perestroika: New Thinking for the Country and the World*, published in 1987, Gorbachev had stated: "the time is ripe for abandoning views on foreign policy which are influenced by an imperial standpoint. Neither the Soviet Union nor the United States is able to force its will on others. It is possible to suppress, compel, bribe, break, or blast, but only for a certain period. From the point of view of long-term, big-time politics, no one will be able to subordinate others."[101]

Around August 1989, the political situation in the Baltic republics began to challenge the unity of the Soviet republics. Growing nationalism in Estonia, Latvia, and Lithuania sought to break loose from the Soviet Union and establish sovereign states. Around the same time, turmoil erupted in Georgia and Uzbekistan and troops were sent in to restore order. Around four years of glasnost had allowed the nationalist voices in these states to grow. Old ethnic animosity and frustrations from the Stalin period were revitalized. Many Lithuanians still vividly remembered how their country had been forcibly seized by Stalin. On Stalin's order, tens of thousands of Lithuanians had been slaughtered and many were expelled to Siberia and elsewhere.

Gorbachev became increasingly anxious about the internal situation of his country. He rejected calls for independence, pleaded with the states to show restraint, and blamed the media for playing up the conflict. To tighten the grip on the Union, Gorbachev sought and was granted by the Congress of People's Deputies increased presidential power, including the power to order military action. This drew criticism both domestically and internationally. Gorbachev's staunch ally and the country's Foreign Minister, Eduard Shevardnadze—who became later the president of Georgia—resigned in protest in December 1990, warning that "reformers have gone and hidden in the bushes. Dictatorship is coming."[102] Shevardnadze's move seriously undermined Gorbachev's authority and reputation.

In the meantime, the Sajūdis, a Lithuanian non-communist independence movement, declared on March 11, 1990, independence from the Soviet Union. The Soviet Union reacted by imposing economic sanctions on Lithuania. As Lithuanians remained defiant, the Soviet troops attacked the Vilnius TV Tower killing at least 13 civilians on January 13, 1991. In the same month, Soviet troops moved into Baku to suppress the Azerbaijani insurgency. Gorbachev had in 1990 been awarded the Nobel Peace Prize for his leading role in ending the hostilities between the East and West blocs. The military actions in Lithuania drew massive international outrage and calls for revoking the Nobel Prize. Gorbachev responded that any attempts by Lithuania to secede from the Union would jeopardize the whole reform program. He seemed, however, to have run out of luck. He was now being bombarded with conflicts from every corner. He fought hard to keep the Union intact, but to no avail. The West's support for the Lithuanian cause encouraged the Latvians to rise up. In a clash with the security forces there four people were killed. Gorbachev took a more conciliatory tone this time, allowing secession from the Union through a proper legal process. He hurriedly drafted a new union treaty based on voluntary membership in a democratized Soviet Union. A referendum was held in March 1991 to determine the formation of the new Soviet Union. But on August 19, before the treaty was signed into law, hard-line Party officials within the armed forces executed a coup, putting Gorbachev under house arrest for three days.

During those three days Yeltsin tirelessly led massive demonstrations against the coup. He often spoke to demonstrators from the top of his car. Owing to his defiance Gorbachev was freed and restored to power, but in the meantime, Yeltsin's reputation had surpassed that of Gorbachev as the heroic national leader. Yeltsin had been elected as the first President of the newly formed Russian Federation on June 12. Leading the opposition to the coup was his first serious challenge in his new role, and he proved himself a strong and courageous leader. He was now using his popularity to press ahead for a speedier transition to market economy, even if this meant to dissolve the Union. In the end Yeltsin got what he wanted.

Within a few weeks Belarus, Moldova, Kyrgyzstan, Estonia, Latvia, Lithuania, Ukraine, Georgia, Armenia, Uzbekistan, Turkmenistan, Kazakhstan, Tajikistan, and Azerbaijan became independent states. The nationalistic aspirations of the Baltic and Central Asian republics, and the August coup had gravely weakened Gorbachev's power. The master of democratization had lost his grip; the imperial power of the Union and its internal structure had collapsed; the communist hardliners had been defeated; and now it was time for the Party itself to rumple under the weight of speedy transformations. A series of events over the next few months quickly led to the collapse of the Communist Party, the closure of the Congress of People's Deputy, and the ascent of Yeltsin to the forefront of politics in the country. Gorbachev resigned on December 25, 1991, and a day after the Soviet Union was formally dissolved.

Later, Gorbachev offered a different account for the Vilnius TV Tower massacre. In his memoir, he writes that in an attempt to prevent bloodshed he summoned the key officials the day before the massacre to discuss the Lithuanian crisis. They agreed on sending representatives to Lithuania to negotiate a possible solution, but before the delegation arrived the local branches of the armed forces and KGB acted on their own initiative to attack the Vilnius TV Tower. This demonstrates that Gorbachev had lost control over the situation during this most sensitive period of the Soviet Union's transformation.

THE LESSON OF THE SOVIET TRANSFORMATIONS

When the Cold War ended, McDonald's opened up its first restaurant in Moscow. The day it opened its door to customers hungry for novelty in 1990, tens, if not hundreds, of Russians queued up in a line stretching far outside the restaurant for an American-style burger. The incident was widely echoed in the media across the world. Just as the Berlin Wall became emblematic of the iron curtain, the queue outside McDonald's became the most visible symbol for the Western media of the Russian people's desire for change. But their hope was soon shattered, as the economy grew worse.

Gorbachev's popularity was rapidly diminishing towards the end of his tenure. The sudden collapse of the Soviet system left the country in shambles. By the time Gorbachev gave away power to his successor, the Russian economy was completely ruined. The economy was stagnant under the communist regime, but the rapid transformations in Gorbachev's last year in office destroyed the economic infrastructure before an alternative system was built first. Gorbachev lost control of the reform process ,and with the economy in free fall the country was hit with severe food shortages and hunger. There was an acute lack of sugar, meat, potatoes, and other basic necessities. Grocery store shelves were bare, while Gorbachev carried on talking about civic participation in society, individual ownership of economic output and the ordinary people's right to hold the Party accountable for its conducts. People had embraced this program because they believed that it would help improve the economy, but it failed. The health of the Soviet economy did not improve; it worsened. Unemployment did not shrink; it grew. And the people's outlook for the future did not become more optimistic; they became more pessimistic. For this reason, while Gorbachev was by and large hailed internationally for his leadership in ending the Cold War and freeing the East bloc from Soviet dominance, domestically his approval rating crumpled. This was evident in 1996, when he ran for the presidential office for a last time. He only received half a percent of the votes—a humiliating defeat for one of the most innovative leaders in the country's history.

The story of the collapse of the Soviet Union offers an interesting example of our desire to change the world faster than the world can absorb change, and before an internal infrastructure is built to replace the old order without producing chaos and destruction. It shows our limitations for forcing democracy prematurely. As discussed earlier, the extent of Reagan's role in demolishing the Soviet Union is disputed. But as we pointed out, there are good reasons to maintain that Reagan's policies at least speeded up the process that brought the Soviet system down.[103] Reagan might not have played the dominant factor, but he was a part of the synergy that rendered the critical force behind the destruction of the Soviet Union.

If Reagan played his cards to replace the "Evil Empire"[104] with an open and democratic Russia, the result became a tragedy for the Russian economy and the Russian people. Of course, it eliminated America's main rival, and from purely an American perspective this was a positive outcome. But the threat of the Soviet Union to America's national interests and the question of whether that threat was of such nature under Gorbachev that it would warrant the immediate destruction of the Soviet structure before the country had made an alternative economic infrastructure are not the point of discussion here. The point here is that Washington always purports to be interested in liberating the oppressed nations and building democracies around the world. Taking this stated goal on its face value, to the extent Reagan was involved in the event his accomplishment was in the negative.

The fact that the Cold War ended was a significant achievement. Ending the Cold War has been said to make the world safer from possible nuclear warfare and destruction. The fact that the former Soviet republics gained their sovereignty was, too, a positive outcome, when considered in isolation. These states sought independence, and massive Western pressure and media focus helped them achieve what they wanted. But the speed and manner in which it happened left a power vacuum that ended in factional infighting, ethnic cleansing, and bloody civil wars in Albania, the former Yugoslavia, and elsewhere. Kyrgyzstan, Tajikistan, and Uzbekistan have become basins for terrorist groups, which might potentially threaten world security just as much as the US–Soviet rivalry ever did.

We have to ask the question again: Is it possible to liberate a nation when the oppressor is not a single person, but an ideology or a culture? It appears that the United States has formidable power to demolish other powers across the globe, but not to rebuild those nations, or even to clear the rubble. It is always easier to destroy than to rebuild.

The power to rebuild a nation must come from within that nation. If the oppressor in a nation was a single dictator, then America might have had a chance to demolish the dictator's power and let that nation rebuild itself.

But as it turns out, there is never a case of a single oppressor dominating a whole nation. One individual, one isolated system, or one political institution can never rule over a whole nation unless there is a culture that enables that individual, system, or institution to exert power over everyone else.

In any case, the key figure in the process that brought down the Soviet Union was the Soviet leader himself. Gorbachev had never intended or anticipated his "revolution" to go as far as it did, but the transformation process spiraled out of hand and slipped further than he would have permitted, if he could stay in control. Gorbachev intended to remove the barriers to the Soviet Union's progress, but he wanted also to preserve socialism, which seeks to allocate resources equitably, and the unity of the Soviet republics. His crusaded against the communist hardliners who had monopolized power, but he did not intend to terminate the Communist Party as whole. When the system was shaken and people were granted the rights to free political engagement, they adopted a variety of competing ideologies, some of which were strongly anti-communist. The immediate impact of this was the elimination of government power and an economy in free fall before an alternative infrastructure was put in place.

In 1990, the Communist Party was finally feeling the heat of glasnost. The weakening of the Communist Party's hold on power had given rise to scores of political parties, associations, clubs, labor organizations, religious groups, popular movements and assemblies, and other interest groups in every republic of the Soviet Union. An article was published in February that year in *Nedyelya*, a weekly magazine detailing about 350 such organizations. The Communist Party found itself in a tense competitive environment, and desperately needed to safeguard itself against the rivals. Some of the liberal Party members came up with the innovative idea of changing the Party's name and ideological platform in order to maintain a competitive edge, but Gorbachev opposed the idea calling it, "a serious blow to the Party's ideological foundation, [which] would disappoint many Party members and non-Party people who support the Communist Party as a party of lofty ideals."[105]

All along, Gorbachev refused to see the perils that he had helped create in the new Russia. In an interview for Time magazine in May 1990, Gorbachev explained that: "To be a communist, as I see it, means not to be afraid of what is new, to reject obedience to any dogma, to think independently, to submit one's thoughts and plans of action to the test of morality and, through political action, to help working people realize their hopes and aspirations and live up to their abilities. I believe that to be a communist today means first of all to be consistently democratic and to put universal human values above everything else."

Gorbachev never faltered in his vision about a special place for the Communist Party in the Soviet politics. When the Communist Party was no longer viable in the new Russia, he was incapable of engineering different political machinery that could take control of the disintegrating economy and power structure. He advocated political pluralism that opened up constructive debate and opposition, but hoped that the Party would stand. When the Party fell, he lost foothold.

In July 1989, the Siberian coal miners went on a strike to protest about their harsh working conditions, low pay, and food and housing shortages. The strike was a serious blow to the Communist Party, whose effort had failed to produce better living standard for the Siberian workers. Gorbachev took the side of the coal miners, but he was also clearly concerned about the health of his own Party. He summoned senior officials to reinvigorate a new life into the Party. He said, "The most important thing now is to extricate the Party from what I would call a state of siege and to impart dynamism to it."[106]

Throughout the reform process, Gorbachev was fighting the battle on two fronts. He fought hard to restructure the economic and political system of the country, but he also fought hard to protect the Communist Party. He was a reformer that aimed at changing both the country and his Party, but at the same time preserving both the Union and the Party. He failed on both fronts.

The history of the Soviet transformations exhibits how only an internal leader like Gorbachev could mobilize his nation and unleash the forces of change, and how even a change-maker like him would fail, if he did not sufficiently understand the cultural and social dynamics of change and power.

6. The Fall of Apartheid

The term apartheid means "apartness" or partition. It refers to the attempted formal partitioning of the ethnic and racial groups in South Africa into separate geographical areas called "homelands," each with its own distinct administrative units and independent economic foundation. This system was initiated in 1948 by the predecessors of the early Dutch settlers in Cape Peninsula. The idea was to amputate the British colonial power as well as the influence of blacks in South Africa by partitioning the country, but the system was never completed. Black resistance, changing demographics, economic dynamics, and international pressure forced white South Africans to dismantle apartheid after more than four decades of failed attempts to partition the country. The founders of apartheid phrased the concept in rosy pictures. Partitioning was believed to offer people of different race and ethnicity the opportunity to coexist in peace and prosperity, but in truth it turned out to be an efficient repressive machine. Apartheid confiscated land from black people and foreign workers, deported them from "white areas," and effectively suppressed the non-white section of the population. By the end of 1980s, apartheid had turned into a brutal police state. According to an opinion poll taken in 2000-2001, a sizable majority of white South Africans still believed that the basic idea of apartheid was good,[107] but most of them acknowledged that the system had in reality led to unjust distribution of wealth and power.

This chapter discusses the period before apartheid, the ideology and practice of apartheid, the black resistance, why apartheid could never be completed, and finally the mechanisms for change and the birth of the democratic rule in South Africa.

THE BIRTH OF SOUTH AFRICA

For thousands of years South Africa remained an isolated tract of land filled with wilderness and outside the purview of the European invaders. In 1487, the Portuguese captain, Bartholomeu Dias, set sail on a mission to find a direct trading route to the Indies. As his voyage ventured around the Cape of Good Hope in the southwestern part of what is called South Africa today, his ships anchored briefly in Mossel Bay in a storm and the weary sailors forced the expedition back to Lisbon. Ten years later another Portuguese expedition spearheaded by Captain Vasco da Gama rounded the Cape of Good Hope, sailed through the Indian Ocean to Calicut in India and sailed back, losing two of his four ships during the mission. With a direct route to India the Portuguese government commissioned annual fleet round the Cape of Good Hope to the Indian Ocean and the Portuguese trade with Asia boosted as a result. However, due to strong currents around the Cape peninsula and fear of the region's tribal inhabitants, the Portuguese rarely entered any territory in South Africa. Instead, they preferred to sail to trading posts along the east coast of Africa, where they frequently stopped to replenish water and food supplies and to trade in arms and other European goods with the locals for their slaves, dried skins, ivory, pepper, and gold.[108]

White settlement in South Africa had to wait until the seventeenth century, when the Dutch East India Company decided to build a base there to support the company's fleets en route to Batavia in Java. The company was losing half of its sailors on the sea owing to diseases and malnutrition caused by unbearably long voyages. In 1652, Jan van Riebeeck was sent to Table Bay to build a fort that would provide a hospital, a vegetable garden, and other amenities to the company's sailors. Initially, the company did not intend to establish a colony in South Africa, but five years after van Riebeeck and his men arrived at Table Bay the company freed nine of its servants and allowed them to establish private farms in the newly occupied land. These men were to produce food that the company could purchase for its sailors at a cheaper rate than what it would cost the company to assign staff and slaves under its payroll to produce the food. With time more servants were freed and allowed to settle in Cape peninsula and beyond. Gradually, the French, Belgians, and Germans arrived and settled in South Africa, but under exclusive Dutch governorship. From 1658, the settlers began to import slaves from other parts of Africa to work the farms. Some of the slaves were later manumitted, adding to the population of free burghers of the newly formed colony. By the end of the eighteenth century the colonial population had risen to some 14,000 men, women and children.

As white settlers grew in numbers, they became more and more aggressive in claiming native lands. The *Afrikaners*—white settlers from Dutch origin—forced the local African tribes to withdraw from their fertile land and fresh water sources or to remain on their land provided they worked as servants of the white farmers.[109]

When Van Riebeeck invaded what became South Africa, he had found only a scattered population of African tribes. In 1713, smallpox was brought to the colony by a Dutch ship, which devastated the Khoikhoi—a native tribe—who had no previous experience with the disease and so no immunity against it.[110] They eventually capitulated and let the white settlers take full control of their land. Soon they practically served the Afrikaners as their slaves. On the other hand, the colony had gained a degree of autonomy from the European powers, though formal authority was in name under exclusive Dutch governorship and the Council of Policy. The Council of Policy was formally organized under the Council of Seventeen in Amsterdam and the governor-general in Batavia.[111]

Within a few decades the colony became a highly stratified society, yet with a primitive culture, rudimentary infrastructure, and booming corruption. It offered little opportunity for education. The slaves were deprived from the right to marry, acquire property, or enter legal contracts, while a small group of affluent white businessmen and farmers with political connections controlled most of the colony's resources. During the eighteenth century only one out of every six hundred slaves was freed. Free slaves were required to speak fluent Dutch and be baptized. In addition, to make manumission harder a law was passed to require every freed slave to have a guarantor who could sponsor him or her, in the event he or she became destitute.[112]

During the early period the colony had a marked surplus of male settlers. This was because sailing was exclusively a job for men. Many of these men had decided to settle in the newly found territory, contributing to a male-dominated gender distribution in the colony. A male surplus meant that many men had sexual relations with their slaves or tribal women. As result, a substantial number of multiracial children were born. They were named "coloreds" and under apartheid ranked as a separate group of South Africans whom were discriminated against.[113]

Early British Interest in South Africa

The British became interested in South Africa first after considerable diamond, gold and other mineral reserves were discovered around 1870. Until 1870, South Africa provided little of value to the British. Without British interference, the Afrikaner settlement remained rural for the most part. It consisted mainly of unsophisticated farmers, called *Boers*. For the British the term Boers came to gain a derogatory overtone.[114] Compared to the United States, which by 1870 had gained a population of 32 million people of European origins, about 53,000 miles of railroad, and a vibrant political infrastructure, South Africa had grown to no more than a quarter of million white people and a meager 70 miles of railroad.[115] The Boers supplied wine, wool, ivory, and animal skins to the British merchants.[116] The value of this trade was insignificant for Britain, but to prevent the Cape Peninsula from falling into Napoleon's hand, the British colonized the territory in 1795. The British merchant vessels to and from Asia needed also a stopping post and the Cape seemed like a good place to stop for refreshments.[117]

The British colony was initially intended as a provisional post. Though Britain assumed formal control over the colony, they intended to preserve the status quo as much as possible. Until the formation of a full-fledged British imperialism in South Africa at the end of the nineteenth century, little effort was made to change the Afrikaners' way of life. The only serious British challenge to the Afrikaner culture in this period was the emancipation of the slaves and campaigns to improve the lot of the Khoikhoi tribe. The British Parliament enacted a law freeing all slaves in the British Empire, including the Cape. Ironically, the law granted damages to slave owners for their loss of "property," but no compensation was offered to the slaves for their long and hard suffering at the hands of their masters. Around the same period, the British missionaries and the Anti-Slavery Society in Great Britain campaigned for an end to abusive treatment of the Khoikhoi laborers, who worked Afrikaner farms under near-slavery conditions. The House of Commons in Britain issued directives to enforce fair treatment of tribal people in South Africa. These directives included fair compensation for work done by tribal workers, regulations for limiting the number of hours tribal laborers could be forced to work by their employers, and limitations on retribution. The employers were, for instance, required to keep a journal entry for inspection whenever they punished their workers.[118] These changes were not always easy to enforce. The Afrikaners did not hesitate to resist the new laws and regulations, and the colonial governors often turned a blind eye when the laws were broken.[119]

In what came to be known the Great Trek, thousands of disgruntled Afrikaners migrated north to avoid British hegemony. Between 1836 and 1854 Afrikaans men, women, and children traveled in caravans, fought with African tribes and confiscated their land north of Orange River, where they established an Afrikaner government named Zuid-Afrikaanse Republic (South African Republic)—commonly known as ZAR.[120]

After the discovery of vast gold and diamond deposits in South Africa, the nature of Britain's role altered radically.[121] To tap into these resources Britain needed firstly to expand their presence further north where gold and diamond had been found, and secondly to build up a robust mining industry to extract this South African treasure. Soon the British entered the Transvaal area and towns such as Kimberley and Johannesburg became basins for the quest for gold and diamond. The British advance led to two bloody Anglo-Afrikaner wars—known as Boer Wars. The first war was a brief Afrikaner-initiated assault on the colonial British forces in Transvaal Republic in 1881, leaving 280 British soldiers dead and the British commissioner conceded. The second Boer War was fought between 1899 and 1902, when the powerful British forces brought the Afrikaner army to its knees and spread British hegemony across ZAR, creating the Union of South Africa based upon mining industry and racial capitalism.[122]

Sowing the Seeds for Apartheid

The task of creating a strong mining industry in South Africa went to the shrewd British politician and administrator, Lord Alfred Milner. It was Milner who commanded the Boer War to colonize ZAR. He believed that the British people were superior and had a natural right to rule the world.[123]

Milner was an uncompromising believer in racial capitalism, which restricted wealth creation and free flow of capital firstly to the British race, and secondly to the white race. Shortly after arriving in South Africa he embarked on an ambitious master plan to rapidly modernize and anglicize the country. As he phrased his vision: "On the political side I attach the greatest importance of all to the increase of the British population...If, ten years hence, there are three men of British race to two of Dutch, the country will be safe and prosperous. If there are three Dutch to two of British, we shall have perpetual difficulty."[124]

By the end of the nineteenth century South Africa supplied about a third of the world's gold output.[125] The mining industry required a large pool of cheap labor consisting of both skilled and unskilled laborers. Milner's plan was to create an abundant working class by urbanizing as many Afrikaners as possible to supply the skilled labor force needed to work the mines under British management, as well as importing Chinese, Indian, and black laborers from other parts of Africa to work as unskilled workers in the mines.

The influx of black and foreign laborers, called *uitlanders*, to the cities drove the wages down for mineworkers. The destruction of the farming and pastoral society, coupled with the low wages in the cities, created an impoverished Afrikaner class. The Afrikaner community was exasperated by Milner's policies. On one hand the Afrikaners resisted the changes in their rural communities and on the other hand, they were increasingly alarmed by the prospect of becoming "swamped" by the blacks in the cities.[126] Afrikaners constituted less than a fifth of the total South African population. As a small white minority group, they feared that the arrival of great numbers of black laborers would gradually lead to a black dominated South Africa economically and politically. They also worried that competition from cheap non-white workforce would push down the wages further. Milner, on the other hand, was in favor of offering the black and colored South Africans, who met strict educational and property requirements, a limited measure of political participation. Yet he was cautious not to allow the black community any prospect of achieving political power or privileges exceeding those of the white race. Milner left little doubt as to where to place the white race in his social hierarchy. As he stated: "Our welfare depends on increasing the quantity of our white population, but not at the expense of its quality. We do not want a white proletariat in this country. The position of the whites among the vastly more numerous black population requires that even their lowest ranks should be able to maintain a standard of living far above that of the poorest section of the population of a purely white country...However you look at the matter, you always come back to the same root principle—the urgency of that development which alone can make this a white man's country in the only sense in which S. Africa can become one, and that is, not a country full of poor whites, but one in which a largely increased white population can live in decency and comfort. That development requires capital; we have got the capital, but it also requires a large amount of rough labour. And that labour cannot, to any great extent, be white, if only because, pending development and the subsequent reduction in the cost of living, white labour is much too dear."[127]

The Afrikaner community was at the time of Milner a pastoral and farming society. Years of isolation from the European continents had preserved their way life. From Milner's point of view the Afrikaners were a backward and primitive people who needed to be educated and developed according to the English ideals. His view that a major cultural shake-up among Afrikaners was necessary in order to build a strong and prosperous capitalistic economy in South Africa clearly appears from his statement that, "[a] social change is also necessary, viz. the introduction of fresh blood, of a body of enterprising European settlers, especially on the land, to reinforce the Boer population, who have been too few, and far too easy-going, to do even the remotest justice to the vast natural capabilities of the soil, on which, for the most part, they have done little more than squat."[128]

It was Milner's policies of modernizing and anglicizing South Africa and building a capitalist state by opening up the boarders for black immigrant laborers that alienated Afrikaners and laid the foundation for the twentieth century's rise of apartheid. For Milner the Boer War was only the first step for transforming South Africa into a prosperous country, where Afrikaners and Anglos would be integrated into a homogenized white community under the umbrella of British ideals. English was going to become the official language. Afrikaner children were forced to learn English. Dutch was going to be used to teach English only and English to be used for everything else. For Milner, the English culture was a necessary condition for economic growth and prosperity. Instead of embracing the English ideals, the Afrikaner community became unified around the idea of protecting their cultural heritage. As a community of sharecroppers and pastoral farmers, modernity and industrialization were not atop the Afrikaners' agenda. Afrikaners were ill prepared for industrialization and there was no internal leadership for change in the Afrikaner community. Milner's tireless efforts to modernize Afrikaners provoked instead Christian nationalism among Afrikaners. Christian nationalism was based on the notion that all cultures were equally valuable and had a right to exist because God had created them. The Afrikaners emphasized *eiesoortigheid* (own-ness), which claimed that every people should be proud of their "own-ness" and that they had a duty to fight for the preservation of their language and cultural heritage.[129]

The Afrikaners were alarmed by the potential for a black majoritarian rule, that is, a system in which a majority consisted of black South Africans would gain full control over all of South Africa. Gradually, the Afrikaners adopted the view that the best way to preserve their culture and their political power was to separate each ethnic and racial group in distinct geographical areas with strict territorial boundary, within which each ethic group could thrive according to its own cultural heritage. With this idea the apartheid was in the making.

APARTHEID AS AN IDEOLOGY

Apartheid was born, firstly, as a rejection of British imperialism. Milner's industrialization in South Africa required an integrated economic model where black and white laborers could come together to develop the economy. Contrary to economic integration of people of all colors and races, socially South Africa had developed a stratified and segregated society. Milner believed that the society as a whole would benefit from better education of both white and black South Africans. He also advocated a limited number of black and colored South Africans to be enfranchised. But he intentionally pursued a social policy that would marginalize the black South Africans. His administration established segregated reserves for black laborers and enforced a passport system for allowing them into white areas to conduct business. The Afrikaners objected to this policy and advocated a total partitioning; though they enforced a similar passport ordinance themselves to control the flow of black workers under apartheid.

The Afrikaner community complained that capitalism had created a stratified society, putting the white Anglo South Africans on the top of the social strata followed by Afrikaners, then colored and Indian immigrant workers, and at last the black South Africans. According to Afrikaners this model had led to economic integration but social segregation of ethnically and racially diverse groups. They named this phenomenon horizontal segregation, where Anglos, Afrikaners, blacks and colored laborers were integrated on the job, but lived in segregation otherwise. Afrikaners complained that horizontal segregation coupled with labor productivity and efficiency was destroying the cultural values of distinct ethnic and racial groups. For them, apartheid was intended to correct this problem by turning a horizontally segregated society into vertical partitioning of each racial group. Such a partitioning would, it was asserted, allow upward mobility within each racial group in conformity with its own cultural norms and values.[130]

Secondly, Afrikaners intended apartheid as a policy of protecting the interests of the minority groups in general, and the interests of their own community against a possible majority rule by black people in particular. Afrikaners constituted a minority group vastly outnumbered by black and colored South Africans. The mining industry's thirst for cheap African labor diminished rapidly the comparative size of the Afrikaner minority to slightly over 10 percent of the overall population in South Africa. Alarmed by this reality, but also because of their underlying racist attitude, Afrikaner leaders saw no other option than partitioning the country into clearly defined areas, where Afrikaners could live in peace and harmony and isolated from both Anglos, colored, and blacks. These areas were called homelands. In other words, according to the supporters of the apartheid system, the partitioning would keep separate groups that were best left separate in order to avoid racial conflict and to give each group a fair chance of flourishing on its terms.

Some early champions of apartheid viewed the application of cheap black labor in the mining industry as human exploitation. As Christian nationalists, some early apartheid supporters argued that once the threat of black South African domination is eliminated through apartheid, Afrikaners even had a moral and religious duty to assist their black neighbor free themselves from the chain of the British imperialism and help them grow and become prosperous within the boundaries of their designated homelands.[131]

The Christian nationalists rejected racial capitalism on the grounds that it exploited powerless workers. They rejected fascism as unchristian—and they rejected communism because it promoted atheism.[132]

They advocated apartheid as the only way peace and prosperity could be restored among conflicting racial groups. Apartheid would prevent, as they thought, all manner of genocides as were often commonplace in societies that harbored racial tension. As author and anti-apartheid activist, P. Eric Louw, has pointed out, "apartheid was the construction of a minority group [i.e. Afrikaners] deeply fearful about being subjugated (politically and economically) by another group, and/or being culturally swamped by black Africans."[133]

Apartheid would, as it was argued, end the abusive practices of British imperialism and save the black community from moral decay and urban degradation by destroying the slums and returning the black people back to their homelands to thrive on their own terms. Afrikaners believed that apartheid offered black South Africans an opportunity to be in charge of their own destiny. In this idea they found justification for creating separate homelands for non-white racial groups. On the other hand, they justified a white-only area for themselves by pointing out that only the Khoikhoi was a native tribe in South Africa, and that Afrikaners had just as much right to having a country of their own as any other African group who had immigrated to South Africa.[134]

IMPLEMENTING APARTHEID

Although the root cause of apartheid can be traced back to the Milner era, its implementation occurred no earlier than four decades later. Until World War II the Afrikaner community was unorganized and too weak to aspire of its own although they outnumbered the Anglos. The Afrikaner political infrastructure was still rudimentary. Their power to change South Africa was crippled by a lack of internal leadership and internal will in their community. Milner's ambition was to form an Anglo majority among white South Africans by encouraging immigration from Britain, America, Australia, and Canada. He never achieved this. By the time Milner left South Africa in 1906, the Afrikaners constituted about 60 percent of the white population, and they remain the majority of the white South African to date. Owing to their greater electorate they succeeded in securing prime ministership for three Afrikaners, Louis Botha, Jan Smuts, and J.B. Hertzog, but none of these men fundamentally changed the system. Botha and Smuts decided that the imperial power was too strong to be challenged. Instead they worked within the system to improve the social and material standing of the Afrikaner community—often at the expense of black workers. By time of Great Depression in 1929, nearly a third of Afrikaners lived below or close to the poverty line. Smuts and Hertzog's policy was to enhance the living standard of Afrikaners by raising the price of white labor. They did this by reducing competition in the labor market through imposing restrictions on black immigrant workers as well as on highly paid British mining experts. Stiff competition had forced down wages. Yet white South Africans earned on average about eight times more than their black counterparts.[135] In 1907, Afrikaners constituted about 17.5 percent of the mineworkers. By 1936, their proportion had risen to about 75 percent, although during World War II the proportion of black labor force rose again. Demand by the Allied forces for South African minerals used in the weapon industry boosted the country's economy and increased the need for more African workers. Immigration laws were relaxed and income gap between the whites and blacks narrowed to a degree. Some African workers were promoted to semi-skilled jobs.[136] After the end of World War II the income gap between Afrikaners and Anglos diminished considerably, while the gap between white workers and black or colored workers began widening again. In mid twentieth century white workers earned up to 15 times more than the black workers and 5 times more than the coloreds.[137]

For apartheid to be implemented the Afrikaners needed a catalyst and a class of politically minded intellectuals who would break away from the British capitalist tradition and take charge of South Africa's leadership. The catalyst was unleashed in the beginning and after World War II. In 1924, Hertzog had won the prime ministerial post after Smuts. Hertzog never departed radically from the British tradition, as stated above, but he used his position for fifteen years to promote Afrikaner nationalism. When the war broke out in 1939, Hertzog advocated neutrality, while Smuts argued that as a part of the British Empire South Africa should join Britain in the fight against the Nazi Germany. As Hertzog lost the parliamentary vote on this issue, he dissolved his government and asked governor general, Sir Patrick Duncan, to call an election. Hertzog was convinced that he would win a reelection. Duncan was a former member of Milner's team. As a pro-British subject, he did not call an election and instead named Smuts as prime minister. Smuts declared war on Germany immediately after taking over, but his action fueled the anger of nationalist Afrikaners who argued that the democratic will of Afrikaners had been violated. When the war ended a period of decolonization ensued and nationalist Afrikaners argued that the time was ripe to reassert the Afrikaner supremacy and sovereignty from the colonial power.[138]

Ironically, the British themselves had created the class of intellectual Afrikaners, who would eventually rebel against Anglicization of South Africa. Urbanization impoverished many Afrikaners, but it also led a group of young Afrikaners to take up higher education in the cities. This class of highly educated Afrikaners provided the intellectual resources that Afrikaner community needed to mobilize against the British brand of capitalism. On the other hand, the poverty that had followed the uneducated class of Afrikaners because of urbanization provided the fuel for an uprising. Thus urbanization combined with Milner's idea that education was beneficial for an anglicized community were exactly the ingredients for Afrikaners' revolt against the imperial design—education making the engine for the uprising and the poverty supplying the fuel. As a result, Afrikaners' resolve to resist the British hegemony took shape and their power to change South Africa on their own terms gained momentum.

Many intellectuals such as, S.J. du Toit, Hendrik Verwoerd, Geoffrey Cronje, and D.F. Malan, were at the forefront of the class of educated Afrikaners who advocated racial partitioning of South Africa. Du Toit was a rural *predikant* (a Dutch Reformed minister), who formulated the concept of a distinct Afrikaner community based on a unique culture, language, and destiny.[139] Verwoerd was a professor of social work, who became a prime minister of South Africa (1958-66) under apartheid.[140] Verwoerd was concerned about the social and cultural impact of a growing black population on the Afrikaner community. For him apartheid represented the only solution for improving the living standard of Afrikaners and preserving the Afrikaner culture and traditions. Cronje went even further, stating that faced with the rising black population, Afrikaners had no option but to restrain progress among the black people. He acknowledged that this was immoral, but claimed that as long as white and black South Africans shared the same areas the only way forward to preserve white autonomy was to suppress the black population.[141]

Malan, the head of the National Party (NP) who became the prime minister of South Africa in 1948, organized a brotherhood revolt against the Anglo capitalism. Many anti-imperialism radicals campaigned under the slogan "[To] take back our country" from the English, but few advocated a return to Afrikaner pastoralism. These intellectuals were urbanized Afrikaners who had lost touch with their pastoral and faming origins. Instead of campaigning for a return to the old days, they championed a radical plan for continued modernization of Afrikaner community while reasserting their pride and identity through partitioning the racial groups and recapturing Afrikaner autonomy from the Anglos. As prime minister, Malan was primarily concerned with purging British imperialism from South Africa rather than with dealing with the perceived threat from the black population. The task of separating blacks from whites became prominent only after the Anglo power had diminished and Afrikaners regained self-esteem to pursue their aspiration of creating a purely white country for themselves.[142]

Malan was successful in uniting Afrikaners and Anglos against the British imperialism. The United Party (UP), which was traditionally supported by the Anglos, never recovered after its defeat in 1948. Many Anglos supported the nationalists' policy of apartheid—a system of partitioning blacks and colored from whites. The UP adopted desperate tactics to win back its support base, but to no avail. In a bid to outdo the NP in racism, some UP leaders rejected the purchase of more land to be dedicated to black homelands. The UP's liberal members left the party in protest and established the Progressive Party. The UP remained weak and dissolved in 1977, while the NP grew stronger steadily. During its golden years in mid to late twentieth century the NP consistently attracted around 40 percent of the Anglo electorate, and of course, a vast majority of Afrikaners.

The NP's struggle to improve the lot of Afrikaners flattened the income gap between the Afrikaners and the Anglos piecemeal. The income gap narrowed for the average Afrikaner from 47 percent that of an English-speaking white South African in 1946 to 71 percent in 1976. By the time apartheid was dismantled, Afrikaners and Anglos enjoyed almost equal shares of the national income.[143] Considering from this vantage point, apartheid was a successful program in uniting the white segment of South Africa: both Afrikaners and to a large extent the British. But the story was quite different for blacks, Asians, and coloreds. As with anything in the world, theory always deviates from real life. If apartheid was not in theory intended as a plot to subjugate the black, Asian, and colored people, in practice it became just that. Rather than freeing the black and colored community from suppression and giving them an opportunity to develop, apartheid dislocated the black and colored population, suppressed them, deprived them from wealth and fortune, and added to desolation and violence in the homelands.

While white South Africa grew as affluent as the middle and upper classes in the West, people in black and colored homelands lived for the most part in poverty. Public amenities such as schools, hospitals, and public transportation were insufficient. Electricity, running water, sewage systems, and telephone lines were scares. Women often had to walk miles every day for a supply of fresh water. Houses were in poor conditions and often over-crowded. The homelands were steaming with unemployment, disease, and lack of proper education for children.[144]

Estimates from the Ford Foundation and the World Bank demonstrated that 40 percent of South Africans—almost exclusively blacks—received only 6 percent of the national income, whereas the top 10 percent of the white population controlled 58 percent of the country's wealth.[145] The black and colored homelands suffered from inadequate healthcare. The government did not keep detailed medical records from black and colored areas, but infant mortality in black and colored homelands was estimated to be about 7 to 8 times of that in white areas (about 15 per 1000 infants in white areas). The average life expectancy was estimated to about 51.2 years for black males and 58.9 for black females. The figures for white areas were 64.5 for males and 72.3 for females in 1960s and 1970s. In 1979, 45,000 cases of tuberculosis were reported, 78.5 percent of them blacks, 20 percent colored and Indians, and only 1.5 percent whites. Many blacks suffered from pneumonia, gastroenteritis, and other illness common in many third-world countries. Despite the fact that the white population constituted only less than 20 percent of the total population in South Africa, in 1980, only 52 black students, 62 Indians, and 18 colored students graduated from the country's medical schools, while over 650 graduates were whites.[146]

One interesting feature of apartheid was that contrary to some other places in the world where racism was practiced outside a legal framework and politicians simply ignored or even tacitly embraced the practice, Afrikaners were legal perfectionists who were determined to build apartheid on a strictly legal foundation. The Population Registration Act (1950) became one of apartheid's first major moves towards building a legal framework for racially categorizing South Africans. Soon, "Whites Only" notices were mounted in every public place, including libraries, buses, taxis, trains, waiting rooms, hospitals, ambulances, public bathrooms, churches, parks, sport facilities, cinemas, schools, hotels, and restaurants. No legislation had been designed specifically for segregating sport facilities, but white authorities used the Group Areas Act to deny people of color access to sport facilities that were reserved for whites or to become a member of a white-only athletic team. Interracial attendance in churches designed for whites was tolerated only after the Anglican archbishop of Cape Town, Geoffrey Clayton, signed a letter that denounced banning black and colored people to attend church services in white areas.[147]

The Prohibition of Mixed Marriages Act (1949) and the Immorality Act (1950) made interracial marriage and sexual relations illegal. It led to the breaking up of multiracial families. In 1953, the court attempted to roll back racial partitioning. It ruled that segregation could be permitted legally only if public facilities were equal for all racial groups. Parliament moved quickly to pass the Reservation of Separate Amenities Act that legalized inequalities in provision of public facilities such as waiting rooms at railroad stations.[148]

Next, the NP moved to eliminate black and colored representation in Parliament. It abolished the Native Representative Council, and restructured the black and colored reserves into eight (later ten) homelands, which were supposed to operate as independent African "nations" that could develop along their own separate lines. In 1951, an act to remove black and colored voters from the common electoral rolls was passed by simple majority. The Appellate Division—South Africa's highest division of its supreme court—ruled that a two-thirds majority was required for this law, and that the law was therefore unconstitutional. Since the NP lacked two-thirds majority in Parliament in 1950s, the NP tried to get round the Constitution by enacting another law—again, by simple majority—to authorize Parliament to review and annul decisions of the Appellate Division. The Appellate Division ruled that this law too was unconstitutional, as it would allow Parliament to act as if it were the High Court. The NP responded by legislating two more laws in 1955, one increasing nominated members of the upper house (Senate) of the Parliament to create a two-thirds majority in a joint sitting, and the other raising the number of appellate judges from five to eleven, which added more NP friendly judges to the Appellate Division. By packing the Senate in 1956, a two-thirds majority finally validated the 1951 act and shortly thereafter signed into law. With this law, the black and colored people lost their voting rights.[149]

Apartheid hampered radically the freedom of the business sector also. White investors were prohibited from investing directly in the homelands. Stringent regulations restricted the number of black workers in white areas.

Factories in need of black and colored workforce relocated to borderlines, where black South Africans could be granted passes to cross the borders on a daily basis to work in white areas. This regulation enabled the white areas of South Africa to benefit from cheap unskilled labor force without granting black and colored workers access to any benefits in white areas other than the low-paying jobs. Black and colored jobseekers were granted short resident permits in white areas to find a job. Those who could not find a job within the time limit or those who lost their jobs were forced to leave. Areas within the newly created white South Africa, where black and colored owned lands or farms from the time before apartheid, were declared "black spots." The government cleared the black spots by confiscating the lands and deporting the owners to their ethnic homelands. The policy led to rising unemployment in African homelands. A study found later that an estimated 3,548,900 people were removed forcefully from towns, farms, and other strategic and developmental areas in white South Africa.[150] Many of these people had been born and bred in areas declared by apartheid as white areas. They had never been to the homelands they were now supposed to belong to. They were transported with violence, their belongings dumped in these new areas, and they were told to make their livings in places they knew nothing of. As the Department of Bantu[151] Administration stated in 1967: "It is accepted Government policy that the Bantu are only temporarily resident in the [white] areas of the Republic for as long as they offer their labour there. As soon as they become, for one reason or another, no longer fit for work or superfluous in the labour market, they are expected to return to their country of origin or the territory of the national unit where they fit ethnically if they were not born and bred in their homeland."[152]

A Time of Crisis

In the end the system of apartheid as utopian partitioning of equal and independent nations along racial and ethnic lines proved unrealistic and the apartheid leaders began to look for a way to alter the system without sacrificing white sovereignty to a political system dominated by black people. Several factors contributed to this development:

First, apartheid was designed and implemented by the white man and naturally favored the welfare of the white population more than others. Blacks and coloreds were subjected to it by violence and had no say in the matter. For example, the whites reserved for themselves substantially larger areas of land and the best arable farming sites, leaving the black and colored homelands overpopulated and with low standard of living.

Second, despite the pretense of empathy for the black people's sufferings at the hands of Anglo capitalists, racism was the underlying notion for apartheid. White Afrikaners believed that they were superior to the black and colored South Africans. They viewed the blacks and coloreds as "not yet" competent to manage their own affairs and needed therefore to be trained. This "training" was often little short of outright violent enforcement of the white's aspirations. Apartheid policies antagonized the black and colored communities.

Third, the business sector opposed apartheid, as the partitioning put undesirable labor constraints on businesses and their need for cheap labor. The system prioritized white supremacy above profit considerations. Government intervention deliberately hampered competition in the labor market in order to raise the price of white labor and so the living standards of the white middle class at the expense of business profit. This would naturally provoke business leaders such as Harry Oppenheimer. Oppenheimer was the head of the South African conglomerate, which included the Anglo American Corporation and De Beers Consolidated Mines. He controlled supposedly 40 percent of South Africa's gold mining, 80 percent of the world's diamonds, over 15 percent of the world's copper, as well as holding the larger share of the country's cool production. Oppenheimer supported the Progressive Party financially and lobbied for the incorporation of educated black and colored South Africans into the political system. He was no fond of people of color, but believed that the integration of black labor force into the economic system of South Africa was a necessary "evil," especially for the gold-mining industry.[153]

Fourth, factionalism was a chronic problem among the black tribes. The black constituted over 80 percent of the total population of South Africa, but due to cultural differences and bitter rivalry they did not unify to defend their common position. The whites did not hesitate to take advantage of the factionalism among the black South Africans by playing the divide-and-rule game. For example, the apartheid leaders tried to make interracial communication harder. English was spoken as the official language among most tribes. The leaders of apartheid were worried that by speaking the same language the cultural variations among different black tribes could be smoothened over time, enabling the tribes to unite against apartheid. The apartheid leaders poured financial resources on education and radio broadcasts in indigenous language and culture. Of course, this appeared consistent with apartheid's basic tenet to value and to promote the culture and language of each race so that they could develop on their own terms. But if the blacks and coloreds did not have their bellies full and a decent job to provide for basic necessities for their families while resources were poured into radio channels in native language, there is little doubt as to the real design behind this strategy.

Fifth, black homelands experienced a demographic explosion partially through higher birthrate but also because of increasing number of immigrants who moved from other parts of Africa in search of better job prospects. This resulted in stretching the black homelands even further for resources. The problem became most acute in urban areas with a black population, whom the apartheid had not succeeded in deporting. The apartheid system had alienated these urban blacks by denying them the right to political participation. Initially, this did not seem a major problem as the blacks constituted only about 25 percent of urban population, but as the number of urbanized black population mounted so did the black alienation and resentment.

Sixth, several black opposition groups and political parties initiated armed struggle to end the apartheid. Since they were often cut off the white areas, they targeted the black or colored administrators in their homelands whom they called "apartheid collaborators." The idea was to sabotage apartheid by eradicating its collaborators.

Seventh, the relocation of millions of blacks and coloreds to their respective homelands proved an enormous operation. The apartheid government had to build a huge apparatus in order to administer the removals and to develop new facilities and amenities in the homelands. The matters became worse, when the blacks and coloreds fiercely resisted the apartheid. To counter the resistance the government built a large police force. Hundreds of thousands of black and colored dissidents were imprisoned. All of these events put excruciating financial burdens on apartheid. In the end, the cost of maintaining the system became unbearable.

Eighth, sanctions and pressure from the international community was mounting on apartheid. Awakened by the horrors of the racial ideology of the Nazis, and driven to a large extent by an increasingly politicized African-American lobby group who were inspired by Dr. Martin Luther King, the international community mobilized a broad coalition against apartheid. This move on the part of the international community acted as a double-edged sword. It placed external pressure on apartheid as well as it bolstered black anti-apartheid leaders to pressure apartheid from within South Africa. Other external factors such as the liberation movement in Mozambique in early 1970s also encouraged black resistance. As we shall see later, their fight drastically changed the dynamics of apartheid and the partitioning project never became fully implemented.

Ninth, the intellectual and educated class of white South Africa gradually awakened to the realities of apartheid. Faced with the system's many shortcomings and concerned about the global public opinion and the UN sanctions they began voicing their discomfort and gradually more and more white South Africans, both Afrikaners and Anglos, joined the ranks of anti-apartheid activists. The effort to change apartheid became the occupation of Pieter Willem Botha[154*] who took over as prime minister in 1978. Botha was not only a shrewd politician and an efficient administrator, but also a highly educated thinker and political strategist. He quickly put together a team of intellectual reformists to find a solution to apartheid's acute problems. This group drew their political ideology from prominent academics in the United States, Arendt Lijphart and Samuel Huntington, and the French military general, Andre Beaufre.[155]

Lijphart believed that liberal democracy based a straight majority rule—majoritarian democracy—would not function well in societies with deep ethnic divisions because the majority would simply dominate the system by completely blocking out the minority interests and rights. In these societies, Lijphart believed, resistance from the minority groups would inherently create instability. He proposed a "consociational democracy," where separate government structures would be created for each ethnic group and representatives from each of these separate governments would join in a united confederal government. This system would offer each ethnic group representation at the leadership level and at the same time minimize political contact, and thus ethnic conflicts, at the grassroots, argued Lijphart. He hoped that leaders would be more apt than the grassroots to compromise on ethnic considerations in the interest of safeguarding the whole system. Lijphart proposed also veto rights to each group and a shared presidency of the confederal government based on a rotational system.[156]

Lijphart's model required to clearly define the ethnic groups. To that extent, the model was consistent with the apartheid's obsession for categorizing ethnic and racial divides, but it also offered an inlet for political integration of different ethnic groups. Botha adopted a program in compliance with Lijphart's thesis to incorporate the blacks and coloreds into a confederation that would protect the minority interests. He named this a "soft boundaries" approach, as opposed to a "hard boundaries" approach that aimed at total partitioning. Botha talked about South Africa as a "nation of minorities," which needed to create "parallel structures" that could be united in a system of "power sharing," "joint responsibility," and "code-termination" in order to protect "group security" as well as each group's "own culture" and "minority rights." He claimed that it was possible and morally justifiable to "differentiate" between groups and "still accord equal treatment" to each of them.[157]

Huntington believed reform programs in a modernizing multiethnic society such as that of South Africa would lead to high expectations for change. This would produce violent political activities by revolutionaries who demand radical change and conservatives who want to maintain status quo. For a reform program to succeed, Huntington believed, the government needed to find the right balance between introducing gradual change and repressing violent activists during the transition period. He advocated a transitional "enlightened despotism," where the government would take only gradual steps in order not to offend the conservatives, but also resort to "blitzkrieg" to curtail the radicals.[158]

Botha was convinced by Huntington's thesis, but he got the balance wrong by consistently overestimating the threat from the conservative Afrikaners during the reform process, and underestimating the blacks' determination to achieve reforms. As a result, the pace of the reform process was slow and as the black activists vigorously resisted the apartheid, the Botha government increasingly resorted to brute violence in order to silence the resistance. As shrewd as Botha was, under him South Africa turned into a police state while little reform progress was made.

The third of the Botha government's external ideologue was the veteran general, Andre Beaufre, who had witnessed the guerrilla wars in Indochina and Algeria. Beaufre was a military counterinsurgency strategist whose ideas inspired Botha and his team. His thesis was that the first side in an insurgency warfare that psychologically surrendered would lose the war.

Because of this belief, Beaufre devised terrorism as a way of inducing fear among the enemy, hence psychological surrender. Beaufre combined also military combat with a systematic effort to win public support for his military operations, which he called "winning hearts and minds" of the public. According to Beaufre, this effort was more important for the success of military operations than the combat itself. The strategy would, he believed, disarm the enemy of its political and revolutionary ammunition and force him to his knees.[159]

Louw states that a combination of the theses of Lijphart, Huntington, and Beaufre provided a significant strategic roadmap for the Botha government's handling of the reform process. One of the black resistance groups that Botha feared most was the African National Congress (ANC), whose world-renowned leader, Nelson Mandela, became the President of South Africa in 1994. Botha believed that ANC was a surrogate of the godless Soviet Union, who intended a "total onslaught" against Western Christian civilization. He embarked on a fierce campaign to win the hearts and minds of both black and white South Africans by trying to convince them of the merits of Christian consociationalism and the dangers of a communist takeover. A byproduct of this campaign was a clampdown on the South African media. To win the hearts and minds of the people, the government's propaganda machine needed to idealize Christian nationalism and distort the realities of apartheid. The danger of communism was simply viewed as too grave to let the media freely and openly challenge Botha's reform strategy. Ironically, the harder Botha attacked ANC the more black sympathizers joined ANC's cause against the government.[160]

Botha never won critical support either in black or white community to change the apartheid in any meaningful way. His government was deadlocked. He did not want to make significant changes out of a fear for white backlash, but imposing discriminatory laws proved increasingly difficult too due to an awakened black movement. The blacks and coloreds had gained the will and leadership to fight for change. Simultaneously, the white South Africans had begun to realize that the days of apartheid was numbered. Within the ranks of apartheid leaders a desire was smoldering right underneath the surface to negotiate with the blacks and coloreds a way out of the impasse. But real change had to wait for his successor, F. W. de Klerk. In the meantime, black opposition continued to evolve. By the end of 1970s, there were twenty-seven illegal and highly politicized, but democratically organized black trade unions. To control the unions' activities the government passed legislations in 1979 to legalize the unions. The government hoped that by legalizing the unions it could negotiate a settlement with them and dampen their most radical demands. Contrary to the government's intention, the legalization empowered the unions. Union membership quickly rose to over a million and some of the unions became more militant.

A new constitution in 1984 enabled black, colored, and Indian representatives to be elected to Parliament—though with clear partitioning of the Parliament's chambers across the color lines. The new Parliament consisted of a House of Assembly comprising 178 white representatives elected by white voters only, a House of Representatives of 85 coloreds elected by colored electorate, and a House of Delegates of 45 Indians elected by Indians. This system gave the white representatives a clear majority in joint sessions. General affairs such as, taxation, national security, commerce and industry, general law and order, and foreign affairs were to be decided by a multiracial cabinet where white members held a majority. Education, health, and local government were considered "own affairs" and left to uniracial ministers' councils.[161] The ANC rejected the new order and insisted on a nonracial majoritarian democracy, where racial or ethnic origin or the color of the skin did not determine political representation and leadership.

In 1986, the government repealed the ban on interracial marriage and sexual relations. It allowed some black urbanization in white areas, yet continued with stringent pass laws. The pass laws proved some of the most challenging aspects of apartheid to enforce. For example, in 1984, the police arrested 238,894 blacks and coloreds for unauthorized transgression into white areas.[162]

Black Resistance

Black resentment in South Africa was born in the early days of British imperialism, but it solidified as an organized opposition when in 2011 the British-controlled government of South Africa prohibited black landownership and regulated black employment outside the reserves. The leaders of the black community were quick to form the South African Native National Congress—later changed name to African National Congress (ANC)—in response to the challenge from imperialist encroachment in Africa. The early South African Native National Congress observed a moderate ideology, which advocated inclusion of all "national groups," i.e. whites, Indians, and coloreds. They had no intention of ousting the Anglo government. Its primary objective was to advance national liberation and respect for the rights of blacks and coloreds through protests and arguments. It sought to ally itself with moderate whites and averted any policy that in any way would alienate these white allies. During 1920s through to the end of 1950s at least four factors led to the radicalization of this organization:[163]

First, the organization's moderate approach produced little or no result. The imperialist encroachment in South Africa grew stronger through 1920s. The organization, now changed name to ANC, gradually lost its grassroots support, as it insisted on avoiding direct confrontation with the white government. Lack of progress and diminishing popular support convinced ANC leaders that a more radical approach was needed to turn the tide.

Second, a piecemeal fusion between the South African Communist Party and ANC occurred during 1940s and 1950s. The Communist party, founded in 1921, aimed initially at organizing whiter workers, but the communist soon recognized that racial discrimination constituted a greater social conflict in South Africa than the traditional notion of class conflict, as defined by Marx and Lenin. Many communist members joined therefore ANC and advocated a militant uprising against imperialism. Then, a mass migration of Communist party members to ANC occurred, when the government banned the Communist party. The increasing number of communist members altered ANC's moderate approach.

Third, not only the communists brought with them a culture of militancy that resonated with many black radicals who craved for speedy change, but it also provided ANC militants with logistic channels for the supply of arms from the Soviet Union and the People's Republic of China. Not everyone within ANC accepted the Marxist ideology. Anton Lembede was a militant Africanist—that is, a black nationalist—ANC member who rejected communism but upheld national liberation as the primary object of a militant struggle. Under his influence the ANC Youth League was founded in 1943, a division of ANC of which the young Nelson Mandela became a charismatic leader later. Spearheaded by the Youth League ANC adopted a strategy of mass mobilization. Mandela led a defiance campaign in 1952. Civil disobedience campaigns, such as widespread school boycotts, took place in 1955. In 1959, Mandela and other black leaders orchestrated an anti-pass campaign, in which the campaigners burned their passes and crossed borders to white areas facing mass arrests.

Fourth, to consolidate its support base ANC organized in June 1955 the "Congress of People" in Kliptown outside Johannesburg, at which the Freedom Charter was adopted. The charter acknowledged that all people are equal, and that all people have a right to live in peace and prosperity governed by lawful democracy regardless of race, color, or gender. The charter called for equal opportunity in employment, land ownership, and political representation. A faction of ANC led by Robert Sobukwe claimed that the land was the birth right of the indigenous black Africans and that ANC had sold this right for political goodwill and alliance. This faction left ANC and established in 1959 the Pan Africanist Congress (PAC). It excluded whites, Indians, and coloreds, rejected communism, and adopted an uncompromising agenda to return South Africa to its indigenous tribes. Though ANC retained its policy of inclusive membership, the synergy as well as rivalry between the two organizations encouraged ANC to pursue a more radical program. PAC and ANC joined forces in the campaign against the passes. The anti-pass campaign drew widespread support and led to a rally in Sharpeville on March 21, 1960. The police rushed to the scene murdering sixty-nine men, women, and children before dispersing the rally. The government moved quickly to ban both ANC and PAC against the backdrop of strong international condemnation of the Sharpeville massacre. The banning of these organizations forced them under ground or to exile. Both organizations formed their separate internal armed wings to fight the apartheid and both parties assumed intense diplomatic efforts in exile to lobby the international community against apartheid. The ANC proved a more successful organizer of both its military and diplomatic efforts than the PAC. Mandela became the man in charge of ANC's guerrilla operations, while Oliver Tambo led ANC in exile. For his role in organizing armed struggle Mandela was arrested and sentenced to life in prison in 1964.

BLACK CONSCIOUSNESS

Neither the armed wings of ANC and PAC, nor their diplomatic efforts and condemnations from the international community produced any meaningful change in South Africa for the next three decades. Apartheid lacked the will to transform itself at this point. Instead, it redoubled its effort to crack down on black resistance. The PAC was incapable of organizing it-self. The ANC, despite having some early successes in sabotaging apartheid, lack the resources to withstand the government's powerful police force. With Mandela in jail and other leaders in exile both organizations quickly lost touch with the people and were sidelined. With ANC and PAC effec-tively suppressed the task of carrying the torch for anti-apartheid opposi-tion went to the Black Consciousness movement.[164]

The background for the Black Consciousness movement was black stu-dents' dissatisfaction with their school conditions. In 1968, Steve Biko, a twenty-two year old student at the University of Natal, attended the Na-tional Union of South African Students Conference—which represented mostly white Anglo students. The white students were lodged comfortably at the conference while the black students were offered inferior segregated facilities. Biko was angered by ignorant white anti-apartheid students who claimed to speak on behalf of their black co-students. He decided to break off from the white-controlled student union to found the exclusively black South African Students Organisation (SASO). The SASO attempted to find the middle ground between ANC and PAC by being more direct and less fearful of alienating the white population than ANC and at the same time being less exclusive than PAC by allowing some collaboration with white and colored students. Black Consciousness sought to restore the black pride and self-esteem by mobilizing the blacks against the notion that black is, as Biko wrote in 1971, "an aberration from the 'normal' which is white".[165]

In June 1976, thousands of black schoolchildren in Soweto demonstrat-ed against a government decree that ordered black schools to teach half of their subjects in Afrikaans. Not only the blacks considered this an act of oppression, but also this decree contradicted the apartheid's basic tenet of allowing each racial and ethnic group to grow and manage its own affairs independently and along the lines of their own culture and language. Dem-onstrators marched through the streets in anger. The police opened fire, killing a thirteen-year-old student. The killing of the child spread a shock wave through the black and colored communities and soon thousands of people took to the streets to protest. The government did not hesitate to repeat the violence. By February 1977, at least 494 blacks, 75 coloreds, 5 whites, and 1 Indian had been killed. No fewer than 134 of the victims were minors. The government banned SASO and arrested Biko, whom the police brutally tortured to death.[166] Thousands of black South Africans fled the country and joined the military training camps of ANC and PAC in Angola and Tanzania.[167]

UNITED DEMOCRATIC FRONT

The Soweto uprising became a turning point in black resistance. The government had used excessive terror in a hope to strangle the blacks' resistance sensibilities and to enforce their surrender and obedience. This was part of Botha's blitzkrieg strategy to curtail the radicals. Instead, people's anger spread wider and grew stronger. In 1983, a thousand delegates of all races, representing 575 organizations including trade unions, various community groups, women's and youth organizations, collaborated to create the United Democratic Front. Atop their agenda was the creation of a colorblind and united democratic South Africa based on the principles of the Freedom Charter that had been endorsed by ANC nearly thirty years earlier. The Front represented a monumental determination by the blacks to oppose apartheid. Black resistance in mid to late 1980s ranged from passive resistance in the forms of widespread strikes that often halted business and industry or refusing to carry passes or burning the passes as a symbol of struggle, to assassinations and other form of political violence. In 1985, the number of recorded insurgency attacks had risen to 136 causing no fewer than 879 political deaths—up from 175 deaths the previous year. About 240,000 workers participated in 390 strikes in the same year.[168]

THE TRANSITION

By the end of 1980s the situation had come to a stalemate for all parties concerned: the black opposition, apartheid, and the international mitigation. As a leading opposition group, the ANC had realized that armed struggle did not produce the intended result. A new vision was needed to effect change. In the meanwhile, Mandela's reputation as a tough opposition leader had grown significantly during his twenty-seven years in prison. The government had repeatedly offered him freedom, if he renounced violence and cooperated with apartheid, but he had consistently refused to compromise. Botha wanted to negotiate a settlement, by which ANC would embrace the concept of consociational democracy where all racial groups could participate in a universal power-sharing program. Mandela never waved his demand for a majoritarian democracy in South Africa, but by the end of 1980s, he too had come to the conviction that this objective could not be achieved through violence. He agreed to negotiate a settlement. Still in jail, secret talks took place between Mandela and apartheid leaders and between apartheid leaders and ANC leaders in exile with the object of creating a framework for negotiating a possible reconciliation—the so-called "talk about talk".[169] This was a shrewd maneuver by Mandela. An agreement to give up arms and enter direct negotiations with apartheid could have been interpreted as surrender, whereas he could claim partial victory by agreeing to abandon armed conflict and negotiate a settlement first after apartheid had accepted Mandela's preconditions for reconciliation.

Botha's government had failed to engage the black and colored population into a system of power sharing. The growing violence and the unbearable cost of maintaining security in South Africa implied that the only way out of the deadlock was to negotiate with ANC. In 1948, the whites constituted about one-fifth of the overall population in South Africa. By the eve of reconciliation, only about one in ten South Africans was white. Apartheid could no longer justify his grip of power. The cost of continuing the conflict would have been a prolonged period of insecurity and economic decline.

The changing international environment at the end of the Cold War acted two ways. It relieved the apartheid leaders from the fear of a communist intrusion in South Africa, but it also deprived them from their pretext to oppress the black resistance. No longer could the apartheid leaders play on the fear of communism to clamp down on the opposition. For ANC, the changing international environment meant that they could no longer count on support and military supplies from the socialist governments, but at the same time the absence of communist threat meant that the Western countries would be more willing to support ANC in its cause. The Soviet Union pressured ANC to negotiate soon after Gorbachev assumed power.[170] For both ANC and apartheid the end of the Cold War had both negative and positive impacts simultaneously, and for both parties the only viable option was to gather round the negotiation table.

For the international community the South African situation represented an impasse. The UN sanctions, while putting significant pressure on the apartheid government, had failed to produce democracy in South Africa. Both Margaret Thatcher and Ronald Reagan backed away from sanctions. Washington adopted the policy of "constructive engagement" on the belief that meaningful transformations in South Africa could best be achieved only by encouraging the white apartheid leaders to reform the system from inside out. Washington's pressure on apartheid increased considerably only after the Cold War ended.[171]

F.W. de Klerk took over the government after Botha in 1989. Shortly after assuming office, he surprised the world by legalizing ANC, PAC, and South African Communist Party, freeing Mandela from his detention on February 11. 1990, and entering full and open negotiations with ANC. De Klerk was regarded as a conservative apartheid leader who as a former education minister had supported the segregation at South African universities. He was no more of dues ex machina for apartheid, as Gorbachev was for the communist system of the Soviet Union. De Klerk had simply recognized the necessity for a grand transformation of South Africa's system of apartheid. He may not have been the greatest ideologue of the country, but he surely became the apartheid insider who brought with him the internal leadership and the power to change. Although Mandela and the international community played an indispensable role in bringing about change to South Africa, change could not have been possible without de Klerk first pulling the trigger. When Mandela was released from jail, ANC was ill prepared to stay up to the challenge. During three decades of repression the party's internal structure had been almost completely demolished. It needed some time to rebuild itself anew. De Klerk's firm stance during this initial phase was essential for the transition to succeed.[172]

Another argument for the importance of de Klerk's leadership in the early days of the transition was his confrontation with the conservative faction of the NP. The conservative constituency threatened to desert the party, if de Klerk continued the path of negotiations with ANC. De Klerk responded by calling for a referendum of all white voters to determine the support for his policy. An internal assessment of the public opinion prior to the referendum revealed substantial support for de Klerk's approach among the whites and de Klerk was confident that the referendum would go in his favor. The referendum, which was held in March 1992, turned out to be a huge triumph for de Klerk. About 68.7 percent of an 87.6 percent turnout endorsed the continuation of reconciliation process.[173] While some black opposition groups saw the white-only referendum as yet another sign of the NP's attempt to exclude the black voters from the political process, it allowed de Klerk to effectively silence the challenge from the conservative constituency within his party. Without this astute maneuver the reconciliation process might have been blocked.

THE NEGOTIATIONS

De Klerk opened up direct negotiations because he recognized the political imperatives of his era. Apartheid was a lost cause—one that had been drawn up by de Klerk's predecessors as a rosy picture of a utopian society, which never materialized. De Klerk feared that the division in his country, the growing internal opposition as well as international condemnation and sanctions, the poor prospect for an apartheid-controlled economy in an increasingly global economy, and the changing demographics of South Africa would soon or later break up the NP's hold of power and shake up the country's socio-political structure. De Klerk's vision was to unleash the mechanisms for this foreseeable transformation while the NP was still powerful enough to control the transitional process and prevent the most adverse consequences of this transformation for the white South Africans. His aim was to negotiate a power-sharing settlement that would reserve a substantial political leverage for the white constituency. Viewed from this vantage point, de Klerk's agenda differed little, if any, from that of Botha's. De Klerk's approach of legalizing the opposition parties and entering direct negotiations was only a different tactic necessitated in the new political environment in order to achieve the same objectives as those of Botha's. In short, de Klerk demanded power sharing through consociationalism— a system in which each constituency would have its own administrative organ and leadership from which representatives would be elected to a general legislative body, say, a Parliament; a multi-party cabinet with rotational presidency was to be implemented, and restrictions be place on the system to ensure minority interests. These restrictions included the right to veto, a strong second chamber in Parliament representing minorities, and constitutional amendments safeguarding the position of minorities. The ANC stood firm with its notion of full majoritarian rule, where all parties could run for elections and people regardless of color, race, ethnicity, or gender would be equally enfranchised in a unified electoral system. The majority vote would determine the make-up of the legislative assembly and the distribution of the power of government. The ANC embraced the individual rights but rejected a political system based on ethnic group rights. It rejected the rights of veto and a second parliamentary chamber for minority groups. De Klerk called for drawing up a new constitution before the election to prevent a possible block out of the minority interests by a black majority. The ANC wanted the new constitution to be drawn up after the majority had elected their representatives to the Parliament. Finally, the ANC demanded mechanisms—such as new tax laws and affirmative action in employment (but not coercive measures such as the forced land redistributions in Zimbabwe under President Robert Mugabe)—for reallocating wealth that had been amassed unfairly by the white South Africans for generations.[174]

MAJOR PLAYERS AND THE ERUPTION OF VIOLENCE

The ANC was the main, but not the only negotiating partner with the NP. When formal negotiations began in December 1991, no less than 228 delegates from nineteen political organizations participated in the talks.[175] Among these nineteen organizations—including political parties from all ten homelands—ANC, NP, Inkatha Freedom Party, and the Left were the dominant parties (white Right and SAP boycotted the negotiations). Inkatha was the main Zulu party, who like the NP, was skeptical of a majoritarian democracy. The Zulu tribe constituted a minority group in South Africa, and Inkatha feared that through the majoritarian system the ANC would dominate their region and potentially wipe out the Zulu's traditional way of life. Clashes broke out between ANC and Inkatha, leaving over 14,800 deaths—many of whom women and children—during the negotiation process.[176] Senior military and police officers were accused of supplying Inkatha with arms and money and turning a blind eye to the killings.[177] The ANC demanded repeatedly that the government do more to stop the violence.

The atrocities during the negotiation period did not only target the ANC or NP members. The white Right assassinated several black leaders, and the armed wing of PAC carried out attacks on the whites.[178] In April 1993, an anti-communist Polish refugee shot and killed the popular Chris Hani, the general secretary of South African Communist party and leader of ANC Youth League.[179] The assassination of Hani renewed fear for eruption of violence and massacres. Mandela played an incredibly important role in this crucial time to calm down the tensions. He tirelessly called for nonviolence and constantly reassured all parties that the only way forward was through peaceful actions. His leadership kept the process on course despite many violent incidents. It is impossible to tell what direction the process would have taken without Mandela's message of peace. For his peace efforts Mandela earned the Nobel's Peace Prize alongside de Klerk in 1993. Despite Mandela's wholehearted effort to curb in the aggression, the number violent deaths peaked during 1991-94 to around 230 a month on average (as opposed to 86 deaths a month on average during apartheid's most violent period in the mid 1980s).[180]

The breakthrough in negotiations came in September 1992 after nearly four months of standstill. In May, ANC had halted negotiating with NP, as the NP insisted on constitutional guarantees for safeguarding minority interests even if those interests contradicted the wishes of the majority. The ANC had changed its tactics from negotiating with the NP to organizing mass rallies and demonstrations in a hope to enforce their objectives. The ill-fated effect of this was a period of inadvertent anarchy and street fighting, culminating in the killing of 28 people and wounding another 200 in September 1992, in Bisho, the capital of Ciskei homeland.[181] Both ANC and NP leaders realized that the country was at the risk of slipping into irreversible chaos unless a settlement was reached quickly. The ANC and NP rushed back to the negotiation table and shortly afterwards the Record of Understanding was adopted, which set out to elect a constituent assembly to draft a new constitution, create "an interim Government of National Unity (GNU)" governed by an interim constitution and Bill of Rights, and to nominate an independent body to review police actions.[182]

The Record of Understanding became the turning point for NP. Though never admitting defeat openly, the party stopped wrestling for consociationalist democracy, leaving the door wide open for ANC. A number of other tactical moves strengthened also ANC and weakened NP's negotiating position. One of these moves that had inadvertent effect on the NP was the party's change of identity. As mentioned earlier, the main element of NP's demand was to secure the rights of racial and ethnic minorities, in particular those of the whites. Following the changing political landscape, the NP decided to abandon its racial identity and become a nonracial Christian Democrat party. The NP was to become a party for all. This move was seen essential in order for the party to build a coalition with Inkatha and other black conservatives to counter the ANC's demand for majoritarian democracy. But this change of identity forced the NP to play down talks about minority rights, which ultimately left the ANC's negotiating stance uncontested.[183]

In the end ANC got what they wanted: a full majoritarian democracy based on a "one man, one vote" system. The NP's power sharing demand was reduced to only sharing the power within the interim government for a limited period of time—known as the "sunset" period. The sunset period was at first proposed for five years, i.e. until 1996, and the NP had hoped to make power sharing permanent, but in 1994 the NP walked out of the interim government, after it became clear that ANC would not accept anything less a majoritarian democracy.[184] The elections in the same year made Mandela the first democratically elected president in South Africa. By this time it was clear that the NP had made little gains out of the negotiations. On the other hand, the Zulu tribe had threatened to boycott the elections until ANC granted the Zulu king a degree of regional independence.[185]

THE WILL TO POWER AND THE LESSON FOR US

In the end apartheid failed in two ways: firstly, it never succeeded in fully partitioning South Africa and secondly, to the extend it did succeed to partition the country, the white South Africans remained atop the social strata, i.e. South Africa remained horizontally segregated with the white population at the top of the pyramid, contrary to apartheid's philosophy.

Perhaps like many other countries in the world, South Africa is today steaming with many social and economic problems. Of course, the collapse of apartheid offered many new opportunities to black South Africans. The educated class of black South Africans is today graduating from the country's top universities, which were reserved for white during the apartheid era. The black middleclass South Africans prospered from the neo-liberal economic structure, so did many big South African corporations who benefited from unrestricted access to post-apartheid's labor market, the lifting of UN sanctions, and better flow of domestic and foreign capital. But a large underclass of black South Africans remains poor. The affirmative action in the labor market has opened up many public jobs to black South Africans, but the most lucrative corporate jobs in Anglo businesses are still out of reach for many black jobseekers. Sixteen years after the collapse of apartheid only about 5 percent of the farming land has been redistributed to black South African. The unemployment rate among blacks has been rising since the end of apartheid. Though apartheid was dismantled in 1990s, a degree of social apartness still exists in many communities in South Africa. The current government has failed to efficiently combat health problems such as, the AIDS epidemic, in poor sections of the country. The crime rate remains high. In a recent report one in four men admitted to having raped someone, and one in three women claimed that they had been raped in the last year. Violent assaults against both blacks and whites remain high. Ironically, some white South Africans feel they are being persecuted in today's South Africa just as the blacks were persecuted during the apartheid. This is regrettable, but perhaps not quite unexpected considering the deep scar that apartheid left on the minds of many black people. After the demise of apartheid a nation-wide and televised debate took place under the heading "Truth and Reconciliation." The purpose of this debate was to grant parties on both sides amnesty, if they came forward and told the truth. People from both sides of apartheid admitted their misdeeds and asked for forgiveness. This process allowed the vast majority of South Africans to come to terms with their past and move on. Still, there are some groups of rightwing white supremacists as well as radical black activists who never put the past behind them. They continue to attack one another or innocent citizens across the color line. This is particularly distressing because many of whom targeted are a new generation of South Africans who had nothing to do with apartheid. Many whites live today in houses fortified with security fences and cameras. The country is also suffering from a major brain drain, as many educated whites are immigrating to England, Australia, and America. The combination of white emigration from South Africa and higher birth rate among the black population has a noticeable effect on racial distribution in the country. According to a consensus, the blacks and whites constitute respectively 83 percent and 9 percent of the population in 2010, whereas the figures are estimated to be 87 percent blacks and only 6 percent whites by 2035.[186]

Yet the point is that South Africa succeeded in transforming itself to a better society despite a long history of racial conflicts. Today's South Africa is not a perfect society, but few people would argue that segregation based on racism is any better. With a death toll averaging to about 230 a month and many more wounded in brute violence during the negotiation years, the prospect for a South African democracy seemed implausible. Yet it did happen, and indeed, it happened relatively fast. For a country that had been partitioned for over four decades, for a people that had never lipped the taste of democracy, and for a majority who had been brutally suppressed and marginalized to embrace a full-fledged liberal democracy within only four years of negotiations, it is pretty amazing to say the least. On one hand, this phenomenal achievement was possible through a heroic struggle for freedom by the blacks and a desire to finally end the struggle in harmonious coexistence with their white neighbors, sharing the same land, air, and water. On the other hand, what made this achievement possible was that decades of failed attempt to partition different racial groups taught the white South Africans that they could never subjugate a people determined to fight for their liberty. Eventually, they realized that the only way they could live in peace and harmony was to dismantle apartheid. The negotiation years of 1991-4 were perhaps the most volatile period in South African history. But the will to live in peace and democracy on both sides, coupled with strong ANC leadership, in particular Mandela's leadership, helped avoid a full-blown civil war and ethnic rinsing that has been so commonplace throughout the history.

The NP had a formidable military force at its disposal. The chief of the South African army believed that the NP negotiators should apply their military muscle to win favorable terms[187], but de Klerk refused to use the iron feast out of a conviction that a lasting peace could only be reached through non-coercive means where all parties came to full agreement. De Klerk had learned that the application of force was no longer effective.

Indeed, the application force could neither impose apartheid, nor democracy. It is hard to believe that any armies of the world would have been able to enforce democracy in South Africa through its four decades of apartheid. Though international encouragement and guidance were important elements during the transitional period, real change had to wait till the conditions were ripe: a will to live in peace and democracy amongst the population on all sides and a strong internal leadership.

PART III

CHANGE AND POLITICS IN IRAN

7. The Evolution of National Aspirations and Origins of Enmity, Example: Iran

The history of Iran is a rich complexity of internal strife and foreign intrusion. Understanding Iran requires a thorough examination of how the individual and national aspirations of the Iranian people, internal or external threats, socio-economic aspects, and cultural traits, played out in the historical context to shape the county.

Many Iranians feel strongly that the current image of their country as a brutal and regressive terrorism-sponsoring outcast does not do justice to what Iran has stood for in its very long history. It is true that the Iranian government has for the last two or three decades supported Hezbollah and Hamas and recently the Shia insurgency in Iraq. Hamas and Hezbollah are paramilitary organizations in Gaza and Lebanon, classified as terrorist organizations by the US, Israel, and other Western countries. But Iran has initiated by far fewer wars over the past two millennia than the colonialist European powers did during their few centuries of colonial rule or the United States in its 300 years of history. Iranians have been portrayed in the Western media as being so crazy they would use nuclear devices to attack Israel and the West, as soon as they could. No one has ever bothered to ask why they have not already used conventional means to attack other countries, if they really are that crazy.

This is not to say that Iran should be allowed to pile up a nuclear arsenal; nor that everything Iranians do is reasonable. But even the current Islamic regime of Iran is not as mad as some "rogue states" whose records on human rights and war are not publicly questioned. But for the past few years, the Western media has unduly depicted Iran as the pariah state of the Middle East, while supporting, for example, the former militaristic Pakistani president, Mosharaf, or the dictatorial King Abdul of Saudi Arabia.

Despite innuendos from the Bush Administration and others, none of the individuals who committed 9/11, the 7/7 bus explosions in the UK, the train bombing in Spain, or attempts to commit similar acts in the West were Iranian nationals. Neither have any of the so-called "home-grown" terrorists in the West been of Iranian descent. Iranians have not been responsible for the atrocities perpetuated in the West over the last decade. Yet many Iranians are often personally treated as potential terrorists.

Why have Iran and the West been so hostile to one another in recent history? Is Iran dangerous to the world peace? Is there momentum for change in Iran? And is there a justification for a US-led regime change in Iran?

Iranian history can be traced back to the glorious days of the Persian Empire. The Persian king Cyrus wrote one of the first "bill of human rights," freed slaves, and spearheaded economic and technological developments over two and half millennia ago. The Persian Empire became the mightiest power the world had ever seen, but the defeat of the Persian king by Alexander the Great from Macedonia put ancient Persia on a slippery slope. Soon the country lost all its glory and much of its territory. A combination of the Iranian people's hospitality towards foreigners, their lack of guile, and the corruption of a central government headed by frail shahs allowed the Muslim invaders, and later the Europeans, to sway the internal affairs of Iran in their favor. Iran's territorial integrity was violated numerous times. Its mainland became the battleground for the great European powers, whose rivalry (known in Britain as "the Great Game") dislocated the Iranian society and its delicate economy. They stripped the nation's natural resources and Iranians began to resent the European encroachment.

To see how this history played out, we have to go back a hundred years, when the European quest for dominance and resources gained momentum.

THE QUEST FOR DEMOCRACY AND THE ORIGINS OF ENMITY BETWEEN IRAN AND THE WEST

The history of Iran's political evolution took a major turn with the Constitutional Revolution of 1906. The 1906 Revolution was a popular response to the growing foreign encroachment in Iran, and it ended up ushering in democracy. The shahs of Iran had been selling the country to European powers bit by bit, and this had to be stopped. Interestingly, democracy was seen as the only political model that could give the Iranian people leverage to stop the wholesale of the country. As the proceeding readings show, both democracy and the politicization of Islam were direct responses to the threat posed by the imperial West.

The 1906 revolution occurred under the Qajar dynasty, which in its weakness was obliged to grant concessions after concessions to both the British and Russians in an attempt to appease them. Additionally, many of these concessions were designed to procure the much needed cash to help the government fulfill its obligations, for example, to pay the army troops or pay off foreign loans. Poor financial management had drained the Imperial Treasury of Persia of resources and lack of funding had crippled the Iranian army. For the most part, the army constituted a brigade of untrained peasants with rudimentary armaments.[188] If giving concessions to the British and Russians was a way of countering foreign threats, for its internal security, the government relied on regional lords. The shah bribed these lords dearly for their loyalty.

The Qajar shahs also granted concessions far too easily for their own personal benefit, as they received handsome bribes in exchange. The Qajar shahs simply inherited their posts and had no incentives to improve the lot of the Iranian people. The Islamic clergy, *ulama*, held the authority over the day-to-day problems of the average Iranians. They were in charge of education, justice, weddings and divorce, writing wills, transfer of properties, and so on. The ruling Qajars usually provided the ulama with scholarships and pensions, but most of the ulama's income came from the Islamic tax or donations.

Consequently, the ulama controlled most aspects of public life, and they operated for the most part independently from the royal court.[189] Sporadic attempts by the Qajar dynasty to modernize the education and judicial system after the secular European models met with swift opposition from the ulama, as the clergy sought to protect their authority. All the Qajar royalists had to do was see to the nation's security, but instead their focus was personal pleasure, to the exasperation of the people.

The biggest concession was awarded to the British investor Baron Julius de Reuter in 1872 under Mirza Hosain Khan's premiership. Hosain Khan was an ardent reformist, who argued that Iran could become modernized only if the British took full control of the economy of the country, but he was also bribed significantly by Reuter. The terms of this concession offered Reuter exclusive rights for railway construction, essentially all mineral extraction, banking, and so on. It amounted to no less than a wholesale of the country to a foreign subject, as no substantial area of the economy would remain under the Iranian control after this agreement.

The growing foreign encroachment eventually backfired, leading to the emergence of Iranian nationalism and escalating wrath in political circles towards the Western powers. The Reuter concession ignited the first significant popular opposition against the government. The ulama joined the ranks of the bazaaris (merchants, who constituted a powerful class in the Iranian society due to their financial resources and grassroots contacts), anti-British government officials, and other political dissidents to force the shah to annul the agreement. Russia too pushed for the concession to be withdrawn, as it gave the British such an advantage. Nasir ad-Din Shah, who held the throne at that time, rescinded the concession, dismissed Mirza Hosain Khan, and Reuter lost tens of thousands of dollars in the process.

What followed soon after the Reuter incident was the adoption by the British government of a more aggressive policy in pursuit of concessions in Iran. Until Reuter, British subjects and companies pursued privileges on a private basis. Protection from the British government was sought only at times of disputes, but now the British government through its diplomatic delegation assumed a more proactive role in advancing the interests of British companies. With the arrival over a decade later of Sir Henry Drummond Wolf as the new British Minister to Iran, the annulled Reuter agreement was renegotiated, and Reuter achieved the rights to establish a national bank, named *The Imperial Bank of Persia*, with exclusive rights to issue notes. In return Russia extorted the rights to build roads in northern Iran as well as establishing a smaller banking operation, which they primarily used as an instrument to sway prominent Iranian government officials by lending them money on favorable terms.

The anti-British, not to mention the anti-shah, sentiment came to a head when Naser ad-Din Shah granted in 1890 a British corporation a monopoly for fifty years over the entire production, purchase, and sales of the Iranian tobacco.[190] The tobacco industry played a significant role in the Iranian economy a hundred years ago, and the concession to the British tobacco company sparked bitter riots all across the country.

Jamal ad-Din al-Afghani (1839–97) was an Iranian pan-Islamist and political activist who pioneered politicalized Islam as an instrument for countering the growing influence of colonial power in the Islamic world.[191] He mobilized a broad coalition of religious and radical dissidents against the tobacco concession and against the Shah himself, but he was sent to exile.

When the protests grew stronger, a *fatwa* (Islamic decree) was issued to boycott all purchase and use of tobacco. To the astonishment of the royalists and their European friends, the fatwa was observed on a national scale, including by many non-Muslims and to the shah's fury, even by the women in his own harem. The tobacco merchants closed their shops. Consumers destroyed or hid away their water pipes. As one foreign observer noted: "I have been informed by persons long resident in [Iran] that they have been astonished at this assertion of power on the part of the [ulama], both as regards their opposition to the Government and the implicit obedience which the people have yielded to their commands with regard to an article which is not forbidden by the religious law and the use of which is now declared to be a more heinous offence than indulgence in the articles forbidden by the Koran itself."[192]

This incident marked the beginning of the Islamic political power in Iran. The opposition to the tobacco concession changed the nature of the Iranian politics. The fatwa not only forced the shah to abolish the Tobacco Concession but also decisively shifted the balance of power in favor of the ulama and their followers, and laid the foundation for the 1906 Constitutional Revolution. Wolf's policy of aggressively pursuing concessions had finally backfired.

Smoldering Opposition

With the annulment of the tobacco concession a period of relative tranquility emerged. But below the surface the opposition to despotism continued to smolder in secret societies. The mobilization and leadership from within the Iranian societies eventually broke down the shah's grip on power and led—between October and December of 1906—to the creation of the Iranian Parliament, Majles, and the Constitutional government. The British stayed on the sideline in the beginning of this movement, but alarmed with growing Russian influence, they intervened and financially supported the operation of many secret societies. Several international incidents also encouraged the Iranian revolutionaries. Russian defeat in 1905 Russo-Japanese War, followed by a Russian revolt and Britain's humiliation in the Boer War a couple of years earlier, emboldened the Iranians who saw the European powers being too busy to impede their revolutionary aspirations. Furthermore, the Russo-Japanese war in 1905 had led to diminishing trade which, coupled with Russia's reluctance to provide further credit to Iran, caused a sudden inflation in the prices of basic necessities.[193]

By 1905, discontent among the merchant class, the ulama and other segments of the society had come to a head. The desire to have a say in matters of politics, economic hardship, deep-seated concern for the loss of sovereignty, and a fear especially expressed by the ulama that Islam could cease to exist under the influence of foreign cultures offered the platform for popular uprising. Thus the Constitutional Revolution was a democratic movement fueled with economic disparity, nationalism, and a desire to maintain religious integrity, but it was the shah's wholesale of the country that translated complex grievances into a unified revolt.

The Majles, as a representative body elected by the people, was the first of its kind in the Middle East. Chief among the Majles's first moves were the rejection of a proposed joint Anglo-Russian loan of £400,000 to the royal court and the dismissal of the Minister of Customs, a disreputable Belgian subject, M. Naus, who had been instituted by the shah to manage the Iranian custom operation and was suspected for misappropriation of funds.[194]

However, as it will emerge later, a coalition of royalist despots assisted by Russia, Britain, and later America, succeeded in the following years to thwart the Constitution and to turn the Majles into a chamber of marionettes supportive of the authoritarian rule. In the meantime, the Constitution empowered Iranian institutions such as the Finance Ministry and encouraged free exchange of opinion. In October 1907, less than a year after the ratification of the Constitution, publication of most books, newspapers, and satirical journal other than those criticizing Islam was legalized.

DEMOCRACY IRANIAN STYLE

To underscore the theme of this book, it was the Iranian people, not the international community, which ushered in democracy. Internal mechanisms and Iranian willpower were at work. A coalition of baazaris, ulama, secular intellectuals from left and right had united in a common goal, that is, to strip the shah of absolute power and to establish a parliamentary democracy, though still under religious control. Democracy was not imposed on Iran from outside, as it is being attempted today in Iraq or Afghanistan.

Even though it was purely Iranian aspirations, leadership, and mobilization from within the Iranian society that brought about democracy, true democracy proved to be far in the distance for Iran. It was a dream without a foundation, an imitation of a Western model but Iranians lacked the capability to make it work. It came with a smack and disappeared with a puff.

Factionalism, favoritism, and self-centered interests shattered the unity that had proven essential in bringing about the democracy. Although the political divisions never produced anything even remotely resembling the level of violence and social disorder that is prevalent in countries like Congo, Nigeria, Iraq, or Afghanistan, disunity caused substantial political chaos which effectively derailed parliamentary exertions. The problem for Iranian democracy was not so much violence but greed, lack of communication, and unwillingness to compromise.

During the first half of the twentieth century, the Iranian parliament employed two American financial experts to balance the books of the central treasury. Iran also engaged a number of experts from various European countries to work the oil fields, the customs houses, etc. Parliamentary members believed that the West had ready-made solutions for all of Iran's social and political problems. They incessantly sought Western expertise and advice, and believed that the West would act in the best interests of their Iranian friends. If Iranians could previously hide their incompetence behind the veil of a totalitarian ruler, now with democracy they were exposed, and they failed the test.

Finding Iranian political institutions and society deteriorated by corruption and internal rivalry, the European powers spared no chance to influence the affairs of the country in their own favors. European tactics in Iran in this period were those of the Great Game. In August 31, 1907, the two powers signed the Anglo–Russian Convention, which divided Iran into three imaginary spheres of influence without consulting the Iranians: the vast area of the northern part of Iran including Tehran and the resourceful Caspian Sea as the Russian Sphere of Influence, the south-eastern part of Iran which offered access to the routes to India and strategic ports in Persian Gulf as the British Sphere of Influence, and the middle part of the country as the Neutral Sphere where the two powers agreed between them not to press Iran for any concessions.[195] The purpose of the Neutral Sphere was to create a buffer zone so as to avoid potential confrontation between them. The imaginary but well-defined boundaries of the spheres of influence contained the powers from expanding beyond the designated borders, but gave them free hands to press for privileges within their regions.

In January 1907, just a week after signing the Constitution, Crown Prince Mohammad Ali, succeeded the throne.[196] Mohammad Ali Shah wished to eliminate the Majles and become a totalitarian king in Iran. At the same time, the program that the Majles had initiated in order to build up the Iranian economy and institute law and order threatened the interests of Britain and Russia. To counter this threat, the colonial powers worked closely with Mohammad Ali Shah to dismantle the Majles. In particular, Russia played an aggressive role in destroying the people power in Iran. Many dramatic scenes played out between the Majles and the great powers within five years of the inception of Majles, ranging from threatening invasion, confiscating Iranian property, bullying, to bribing corrupt royalists and parliamentarians, but the Majles remained defiant and pressed ahead progressive legislations. After five years of democratic order in Iran, Russia decided to intervene militarily to restore the rule of dictatorship by force. Thousands of heavily armed Russian troops poured into Iran, laying siege around the capital city, Tehran. The fiercest struggle occurred in Tabriz—a city in the northern province of Azerbaijan—where the royalist and Russian troops laid siege on the city for several months to starve the residents. A massive carnage resulted when the troops finally invaded the city.[197] It was common for Russian army leaders at the time to allow their troops loot, rape, and kill civilians in enemy territories as a reward for the pain they (the troops) had to endure during the course of the war.

The siege on the capital created panic. Some Iranians defected to the enemy camp out of fear, while others heroically defended the Constitution. With only hours left before the fate of the constitutional government was to be determined, the Majles rejected two Russian ultimatums, which threatened full-scale invasion if it did not surrender. In the parliamentarian discussions about the ultimatums, a cleric who was a deputy in the Majles rose and said: "It may be the will of Allah that our liberty and our sovereignty shall be taken from us by force, but let us not sign them away with our own hands."[198]

Desperate to save the country, some deputies contemplated granting American companies concessions to build roads and railways in a hope that the promise of lucrative economic interests would engage the American government as an opposing force to the Russian aggression.[199]

Other deputies began to tremble and called for acceptance of the second ultimatum. When news spread out that some deputies were ready to throw in the towel, a group of about 300 women marched to the Majles and demanded to see the president with the message that they would kill their husbands, sons, and fathers if the men of their country gave in to the Russian demands.

But faced with 50,000 heavily armed Russian troops determined to crush Iran, a portion of which was already in the Iranian territory just north of Tehran, mere bravery and resolve could not save their lot. Without an iron fist matching that of the Russian army, their cause would be a dead one from the start. If they fired a single bullet on the Russian troops, as Morgan Shuster—an American financial expert whom the Majles had hired to help reconstruct the Imperial Treasury of Persia—remarked, "The 50,000 Cossacks who would be poured into [Iran] when the snows melted the following spring would crush out the last spark of Persian liberty and leave, perhaps, not even widows and orphans to mourn at soldiers' graves."[200] So they opted for passive opposition and hoped that somehow justice would prevail in the end.

On December 24, 1911, the pro-Russian elements of the Cabinet executed a coup d'état. A de facto government was installed promptly. Shuster's work in Iran had uncovered the extent of British and Russian abuse in the country, and the Russians were keen to remove him from office. He was dismissed immediately and soon left the country, only about eight months after his arrival. The Majles reopened later, but only under the control of foreign agents.

Back in the capital, the Russian and British legations threatened the government with severe measures if anyone other than the Belgian Customs Administrator, Mornard, was allowed to fill in the position after Shuster.

Mornard had for a long time acted as a loyal puppet for the two powers.[201] The Russians also banned Iranians from hiring foreign experts to run the affairs of their country without the Russian and British consent.

THE WORLD AT WAR

Much of the political landscape changed soon after the fall of Majles. Germany had joined the Great Game in the Middle East. On August 19, 1911, Germany and Russia had struck the Potsdam Agreement—by which Russia had promised not to obstruct the Baghdad Railway, hence strengthening Germany's geopolitical clout in the Middle East.

With the advent of World War I Germany was desperate to find an ally in the Middle East to balance off against the Allied Forces. Iran had declared neutrality, yet its territory soon became a battleground in the war. Germany provided money to Iran and invited to Berlin Hasan Taqizadeh, who was the prominent revolutionary and constitutionalist leader from Tabriz. In Berlin, he was equipped with nationalist propaganda and encouraged to fuel a national resistance against Britain and Russia. Taqizadeh was of the opinion that to promote prosperity and independence, Iran should thoroughly follow the Western democratic models.

After the Russian Revolution in 1917, the Bolsheviks renounced the tsarist imperialistic aspirations, liberated northern Iran, canceled Iran's debts and most of the unequal treaties, and called for a renegotiation of the fishery concession. In 1921, the two countries signed a friendship agreement, known as the Russo–Persian Treaty. Iran recognized the Russo–Iranian border of 1881, which included territories acquired by Russia following Russo–Iranian wars in the previous century. Diplomatic and trade relations were normalized.

In the meantime, the war was taking its toll on Iran. Deprivation and hunger became prevalent. Destruction of arable land and trade routes coupled with increasing foreign troops' demand for food created a severe famine in 1918–19, killing up to a quarter of the northern population. Nationalist movements gathered strength in different parts of the country. Kuchek Khan, a local leader of the Caspian province of Gilan, led a democratic movement in the North. They operated from the heart of the forests (hence the nickname *jangalis*, "forest dwellers").[202]

When the war ended, British leverage in Iran grew. A puppet government headed by Prime Minister Vosuq ad-Dauleh was appointed. Under massive pressure and bribery, the Prime Minister signed the Anglo–Persian Treaty of 1919. In exchange for British military advisers and arms, Iran was to provide Britain concessions to develop transportation and communications networks and to reduce the tariffs on British goods. A substantial loan from Britain would pay for the military advisers and arms from Britain. Before the treaty was ratified by the Majles, Britain began acting as if the treaty was already in force by sending military advisers and arms to Iran and taking control of the Iranian economy. Fearing that the treaty would give a monopoly to Britain, American officials inquired if American advisers could ever be sent to Iran. The British Foreign Secretary, Lord Curzon, replied that they could, provided they met British approval. However, the British tried to keep four French law professors from entering Iran.[203]

New tariffs put Russian goods at a huge disadvantage, leading to a virtual halt of Russo–Iranian trade. Iran's trade deficit with Britain mushroomed. The treaty, which was already in force but never ratified, eventually backfired. Many secret societies opposed to the treaty appeared all over the country. The puppet government moved swiftly against the dissident groups.

A new ideology was needed to bolster the opposition. This was supplied from the North. The Bolshevik communist ideology gave new impetus to popular resentment. In 1920, Kuchek Khan declared the establishment of a Soviet-style socialist republic in North and joined a coalition of Armenian, Azerbaijani, and Kurdish guerrillas backed by Soviet Red Army to march on Tehran. Other democratic leaders such as Shaikh Mohammad Khiabani, who had led the 1905–11 constitutionalist movement in Azerbaijan, entered the scene to oppose the government's submission to the British policies. Khiabani was later killed in an attack by the Persian Cossack Brigade.

Communism, Islam, and nationalism all played a role in fighting the British encroachment. At this point concerns were widespread in the population that Iran was on the verge of becoming a British colony. In an effort to diminish calls for social reforms, the conservative nationalists joined the anti-British movement; hence a united front against British influence was formed. Vosuq ad-Dauleh was forced to resign in June 1920. A new government under Moshir ad-Dauleh, a moderate nationalist, resumed power. Moshir ad-Dauleh suspended the Anglo–Persian Treaty and demanded the departure of the British as well as the Russian troops who had remained in Iran after the end of World War I. Britain and their Iranian allies moved fast to overthrow him and appointed Sepahdar as the new head of the government.[204]

A TOTALITARIAN RULER WHO REVERSED THE BRITISH ENCROACHMENT

Iran's democratic system was still too feeble to end decades of chaos. By early 1921, the British found a strong and authoritarian ruler to restore the stability in Iran. In February 1921, the chief of the Cossack Brigade, Reza Khan, executed a coup d'état and declared himself the Minister of War. He consolidated his power and became in 1925, the new shah of Iran under the title of Reza Shah Pahlavi. The Pahlavi dynasty lasted until 1979, when it was finally ousted by the Islamic Revolution.

Reza Shah effectively silenced the opposition and centralized decision making. But he was also a strong leader who aspired to build a powerful army and to develop the country by building roads and promoting trade. He built the trans-Iranian railway stretching over 865 miles from the Persian Gulf to the Caspian Sea and a branch running to Tabriz. Several laws and decrees diminished the control of the ulama over education. In 1934, he established the University of Tehran. He built bridges, tunnels, hotels, hospitals, and casinos.

Literacy rose under his reign. Agricultural reforms were undertaken to promote economic self-sufficiency. Electric power was extended throughout Tehran and other major cities. Numerous companies popped up in urban areas. Sports flourished and were funded by the government. The government also sponsored the country's first Boy Scouts and Girl Scouts. The shah sought to advance women's participation in society. He forcibly banned the Islamic head covering for women, *hijab*, and encouraged women to pursue higher education and careers outside their homes. The armed forces grew from 40,000 to 90,000 men. Several gunboats, tanks, and fighter planes were purchased. The wheels of industrialization and commercialization began to spin with stunning speed. Sugar refineries, spinning mills, soap factories, food processing, and weaving mills were built. Speedy progress became indeed the hallmark of Reza Shah's reign. Iran grew more independent. Western influence dwindled. Reza Shah raised tariffs on many goods and renounced tariffs that had been negotiated under pressure. The

British bank's privileges to issue notes were withdrawn in 1930. In 1931, the British-owned Imperial Airways was refused permission to fly over Iranian airspace. The concession was instead offered to the German-owned Lufthansa Airlines. Oil resources had been found in Iran some time earlier and a concession to extract the oil had been granted to a British company, formerly known as Anglo–Persian Petroleum Company (APOC)—the predecessor of BP. The shah unilaterally canceled the British oil concession, which offered Iran a 16 percent share in profit, and demanded 20 percent instead. APOC conceded. To curb Britain's leverage, experts from other European countries such as, Italy and Germany were hired for projects in Iran. But Reza Shah was vigilant not to allow any foreign country too much power.[205]

Reza Shah was inspired by Atatürk's success in modernizing Turkey. In the early 1920s he had increased his power base by courting the Muslim clerics. He had even allowed violent persecution of a rival minority religion, Bahai, to appease the ulama. The persecution led to the murder of many Baha'is. As the new shah, he soon followed Atatürk's example to secularize the country. He eliminated the shari'a law in 1939–40, and introduced a judicial system after the European model, in particular after the French system. Traditional beards were discouraged and Western style dress for men and women introduced, but he also rejuvenated Iran's ancient glories and culture to generate a distinct sense of Iranianness.[206]

Reza Shah's progressive policies came with a high cost. He used forced labor or refrained from remunerating suppliers in order to complete projects cheaply. The reign of terror alienated many Iranians. Instead of national unity, disunity and corruption intensified. As Arthur Millspaugh, an American financial expert in Iran, noted, "[Reza Shah] did things to the people and for the people. Little was done by them."[207] (This is an interesting comment to throw at the hawks in Washington, who advocate sending in the US military to do things for other nations.)

Despite the progressive trends in the culture and economy under Reza Shah, financial mismanagement and corruption lurked as the most perilous threat against the country's sovereignty. Foreign powers used the financial chaos to gain influence over Iran. Public funds circulated in corrupt hands. Taxes were often not collected or remained in the tax collectors' pockets. Hence the treasury ran virtually empty. Without reserves the country was vulnerable to economic fluctuations. Periodic crop failures could, for instance, trigger a famine which the government was unable to remedy.

The pace of Reza Shah's developmental projects necessitated streamlining the country's financial management. It was under these conditions that Millspaugh was commissioned in Iran, but he grew gradually frustrated and pessimistic about the Iranians' ability to govern their country. His predecessor, Shuster, had been passionately sympathetic to the Iranian cause. In Iran's defense Shuster had written a decade earlier in his book *The Strangling of Persia*: "With the knowledge of the facts of Persia's downfall the scales drop from the eyes of the most incredulous, and it is clear that she was the helpless victim of the wretched game of cards which a few European powers, with the skill of centuries of practice, still play with weaker nations as the stake, and the lives, honor and progress of whole races as the forfeit."[208]

Shuster believed that without foreign harassment and meddling in the country's internal affairs, Iranians would be able to develop a full-blown democracy along particular lines of their customs and character. Millspaugh maintained that what obstructed progress for Iran was not just foreign influence but the Iranian culture. He wrote in his book *Americans in Persia* that, "...[Iran] cannot be left to herself, even if the Russians were to keep their hands off politically."[209] With these words, he advocated American intervention in Iranian internal affairs. American engagement, he hoped, would end the dictatorship and rescue "the long-suffering and innocent masses [from] further exploitation and impoverishment."[210] He wanted to do things to the people and for the people of Iran.

Millspaugh's book was widely read in Washington and informed America's foreign policy towards Iran. Among other things, in 1953, the CIA orchestrated a coup d'état against the Iranian government, which exasperated the Iranian people and eventually helped bring Khomeini to power on an anti-American platform.

THE LESSON FROM IRAN'S RELATION WITH RUSSIA AND BRITAIN

Up until World War II, Britain and Russia was the focus of the Iranian people's animosity on account of these countries' adversarial policies. These countries were the aggressors, not Iran. The Iranians' guilt was their credulity, ineptitude, disunity, and lack of vision, but they represented no threat to Britain or Russia. Iranians were incompetent, but a nation's incompetence does not justify another nation's abusing it. Especially, the Russians' treatment of the Iranian people was abysmal. The changing political landscape post World War II eliminated Russians' influence in Iran, and today Russia is one of the most important trading partners of Iran. Iran also normalized its relations with Britain, and the Islamic Republic under former presidents Hashemi Rafsanjani and Mohammad Khatami made several efforts to improve the two countries' relations. Relations with Britain worsened only after Tony Blair's government joined the Bush Administration to threaten Iran with an invasion.

Post World War II, the United States became increasingly involved with Iranian affairs. Some US policies antagonized the Iranian public. But is there any reason for Americans to worry about a potential Iranian retribution on account of the animosities between the two nations? The history of Iran's reconciliation with Russia and Britain demonstrates that Iran is not a vengeful nation—not even under the Islamic Republic. Washington's propaganda machine is trying to promote the fear of Iran, but it is absurd to suggest that a weak country such as Iran, with a few primitive missiles and unsophisticated aircraft technology, could pose any serious threat to the West. Iran has only attempted to retaliate against what it has viewed as ongoing US assaults. As soon as the US threat is eliminated, friendship can be restored. Peace is always in the hands of the powerful—i.e., the US—as it is always the powerful that have the potential to abuse their power.

The CIA Coup in Iran

The first decade after the end of World War II was characterized by a weak monarchy. Reza Shah's son, the twenty-year-old Mohammad Reza Pahlavi, assumed power after his father's abdication. Under lack of clear royal authority the Majles blossomed and political activism became more vibrant. In 1951, Mohammad Mossadegh was democratically elected prime minister. Mossadegh was a lawyer, an author, and a passionate nationalist, who galvanized the masses and became the most popular government head in the entire Iranian history. He set out to minimize the role of monarchy and to elevate the power of Majles and government, demanding that the shah should only reign, not rule. Mossadegh worked hard to empower the judicial system, promote free and fair elections, and raise the living standard of the average Iranian. His most significant achievement was the nationalization of the Iranian oil. The British petroleum company, Anglo-Iranian Oil Company (AIOC)—predecessor of today's BP (which changed name from APOC)—had early in the century bought from the shah the monopoly rights to extract the Iranian oil. The AIOC operated as if the company had colonized the entire country. It coerced Iran's central government to win favors and employed Iranian laborers under conditions resembling slavery. Workers were cramped into rooms with little or no sanitary facilities. Many slept on the floor. They were forced to work long hours with scanty compensation. As if the company had not enriched itself enough already, it implemented creative accounting to minimize the amount of pay-outs to the Iranian government. Mossadegh sought to renegotiate AIOC's contract numerous times, but AIOC refused.

The nationalization was the first of its kind in the Third World. It would cause a major blow to Europe's stronghold in the region, unless Britain could find a way to counter Mossadegh. Following the nationalization, Britain imposed sanctions on the Iranian oil, froze Iranian assets, and threatened with invasion. When all their tactics failed, Britain turned to America for assistance. The United States was at first sympathetic to the Iranian cause. President Truman believed that the British were too gluttonous and supported Mossadegh against what he saw as British lingering colonization mentality. But Mossadegh made a number of strategic mistakes. Once a new deal was massaged under US pressure with AIOC, Mossadegh refused to accept it despite the fact that he had desperately sought to renegotiate the contract with AIOC earlier. Playing on post-war communist scare, Mossadegh began to flirt with the leftist party (Tudeh) in Iran in order to press Washington negotiate better terms for Iran. When no better offer was forthcoming, he threatened to walk out on the negotiations. Mossadegh failed to recognize that Iran lacked technical expertise and marketing know-how to extract and sell the petroleum without involving foreign companies. He also had a personal handicap that tarnished his image in the West. Like a crybaby, he showed excessive passion for the Iranian cause. When he spoke to the parliamentary members in the Majles, he sometimes acted as if he was on the verge of fainting under pressure or because his heart was so full of sorrow for the injustice that Iran had suffered. When visiting Washington, he copied Winston Churchill by doing business from bed in his pajamas, claiming he did not feel very well. His personal behavior was often interpreted in Washington as weak or irrational leadership, but in Iran he was seen as a rare politician capable of showing human qualities and empathy for his people. His greatest mistake was perhaps that he overestimated Washington's support and underestimated the Anglo-cultural bond between Britain and the United States.

The tide turned in Britain's favor with the election of Dwight Eisenhower in 1953. President Eisenhower commissioned Kermit Roosevelt, the grandson of Theodore Roosevelt, to plan and execute a coup d'état against the government of Mossadegh. Mossadegh was ousted, the shah placed firmly in power as a despot backed heavily by Washington, and a consortium of American, British, French, and Dutch oil companies put in charge of the full cycle of exploration, excavation, and marketing of Iranian oil. Americans and the British reaped 40% each of the profit, while the French and the Dutch received each a 20% share of profits from the Iranian oil. The coup altered the nature of Mohammad Reza Pahlavi's reign. He dealt swiftly with the opposition and became an absolute dictator. His secret service, SAVAK, soon gained a reputation as a ruthless anti-opposition organization. Mossadegh was put under house arrest until his death. A decade later, President Lyndon Johnson told the shah in a private meeting that America would support the shah's treatment of the opposition. To counter the growing influence of the Soviet Union in the Arab world, the United States unconditionally backed the shah politically, financially, and militarily. Iran became a regional superpower. Its economy grew strong and its military jets brawled in the skies of the Middle East. The shah had virtually a free pass to show off power and to treat the Iranian people in whatever way it pleased him and America sat on the fence and watched.

The CIA-led coup is by the Iranian people considered as the worst and most emotive atrocity the US has ever committed against their country. This is because Mossadegh was a popular leader who seemed to care genuinely about his people, despite all his flaws. The coup made the world's foremost champion of democracy, the United States, look hypocritical. The coup plan had engaged the Iranian military and royalist court, but the anger against foreign involvement would always be stronger—just as communist Americans were regarded surrogates of the Soviet Union during the McCarthyism era and dealt with heavy-handedly.

The coup marked one of the first examples of an event, where Washington intervened in internal affairs of another country without taking into account the significance of internal political and cultural mechanisms, and it left a strained legacy between Iran and the US for decades. The CIA used the theory of communist threat as justification for the coup. There was, however, no evidence of an imminent communist take-over in Iran. As part of the coup plan, Kermit Roosevelt stirred up the Iranian communists to riot, and then he sent out the military to crack down on the riot and use the chaos as pretext for seizing the government power. The communists were, of course, completely oblivious of Roosevelt's plot. Roosevelt would not have encouraged a communist riot, if he truly believed that Iran was on the verge of a communist revolution or that the Iranian military was incapable of countering a possible communist takeover of the country.

Many in the intelligence community have since questioned the legitimacy of the coup. In 2000 both President Clinton and the Secretary of State, Madeleine Albright, expressed regret for the CIA's involvement in the overthrow of Mossadegh's government. But before this apology came, there was revolutionary spirit in Iran in 1978-79, and the revolution's father, Ayatollah Khomeini, knew where the nation ached and how he could use it to oust the shah and cut off America's hands.

THE ISLAMIC REPUBLIC OF IRAN

Compared to Americans, the Iranian people are far more secular. Yet Iran became the country, where religious elite stole the power from the people. Khomeini came to power on three chief vows: first, to bring freedom back to Iran; second, to channel the oil money back to the people and to stop squandering resources on building up a large weapon arsenal, or what he called *ahan pareh*, pieces of metal; third, to cut the influence of foreign powers. Although Khomeini always maintained the concept of *Velayat-e Faghih*— a form of Islamic government operating under the supervisory role of senior clergy—few Iranians who participated in revolutionary demonstrations against the shah realized what they were buying into. Among those who partook in the revolution were secularists, leftists, atheists, feminists, gays and lesbians, and basically people from all walks of life whether or not they viewed themselves Muslims. Right after Khomeini's return to Iran, a referendum was organized on two simple options: whether Iran should form an Islamic Republic or a different form of government. In the heyday of revolution, a great majority voted in favor of Islamic rule, but even then few people truly knew what an Islamic Republic would mean.

Khomeini failed to deliver the first two of his three promises. With the Islamic Republic freedom regressed even more than under the shah.

Khomeini's "guardian forces" and secret service dwarfed by far the shah's SAVAK in brutality and use of arbitrary force. Sadegh Khalkhali, an Islamic mullah, was placed in charge of the judiciary. He equated justice with execution. At an incredible pace, a vast number of former military officers, dissident groups, and whoever considered antirevolutionary or "an enemy of God" were slaughtered. On one occasion, a minor was mistakenly executed. When confronted, Khalkhali lightly brushed aside the embarrassment by saying that if the boy was innocent, he would go to paradise! It took the Shah about 3,000 deaths in the span of one year to capitulate and flee the country. Thanks to Sharia law's liberal outlook on the death penalty with or without formal conviction, the Islamic Republic murdered many times that number within the first two years of its existence. The government purged the system of foes with remarkable efficiency. Homosexuality became punishable by death. Bodily mutilation was introduced as a penalty for lesser crimes. Women were forced to cover their whole bodies from head to toe and stringent dress codes were introduced for men too. Khomeini warned that while the Shah still in power, Islam was in jeopardy. So many people had to die and many more to suffer for Khomeini's Islam to survive.

Khomeini did not deliver on his pledge to redistribute the oil money to the people, either. A war broke out between Iran and Iraq and more money was spent on weaponry and warfare. The Iranian economy contracted fast and other than those who joined the vigilante groups or the guardian forces to maintain calm in the cities, the poor became poorer.

The Iran–Iraq War was initiated by Saddam in 1980, not Iran, although when Saddam was ready for truce a year later, Khomeini refused, ordering the war to continue till the Iraqi people were freed from the Baath regime. Saddam's motive behind the war was partially old border disputes from the shah period and partially Khomeini who agitated a similar Islamic revolution in Iraq. Finding Iran weakened by post-revolutionary turmoil, Saddam decided to strike. Iran's Arab neighbors worried about the impact of the Iranian revolution in their own backyards, and supported Saddam during the war. Khomeini's anti-Western stance helped to rally Europe and America behind Saddam. When he used chemical weapon against Iranian troops or targeted Iranian civilians in big cities with his deadly missiles, the West looked the other way. Khomeini accepted ceasefire in 1988, only after the war drove the country to the verge of a complete break-down.

Khomeini did, however, deliver on his promise of cutting foreign influence out of Iran, but he did it not with smart diplomacy, but with raw tactics and affront. This was a time for the 1953 coup against Mossadegh to backfire and if the Iranians believed they had been held hostage by the shah over two and half decades following the coup that was organized by CIA operatives, the American Embassy in Tehran was about to get a taste of the same thing. Shouting death to America, a group of extremist students stormed the American Embassy in October 1979 and took its personnel hostage. Some of the personnel were released on humanitarian grounds, but 52 of the staff were kept hostage for 444 days. The students had acted on their own on a suspicion that the embassy might devise another coup against the Islamic revolution, but Khomeini moved quickly to endorse the action and demanded the arrest and extradition of the shah, who had fled Iran. For Khomeini, the hostage taking was an expression of the Islamic Republic's determination to withstand the mightiest power on Earth.

The hostage crisis left a terrible scar on the relations between the two countries, from which they yet have to recover. President Carter's poor handling of the crisis cost him a second term in office—among other things, Carter arranged a failed rescue attempt, where a US helicopter flying secretly through the desert in Iran to free the hostages in a Rambo-style action crashed in stormy weather, killing its crew. Needless to mention the incredible pain and agony the hostages and their families suffered during this period. But when President Carter lost the election as a result of the crisis, the Islamic Republic hailed it as the Iranian way of enforcing regime change in the United States. On the flip side, the hostage crisis was one of the main reasons why the US sided with Saddam or turned a blind eye to his war crime during the Iran–Iraq War, which cost the Iranians dearly in casualty and otherwise.

Every bit of hostility between the US and Iran can, in one way or another, be traced back to the 1953 coup and the 1979–1980 hostage crisis. Many Iranians—including some of the students who invaded the American Embassy—have since regretted the incident, acknowledging that it was damaging for Iran, and as mentioned above, the Clinton Administration regretted the US involvement in the 1953 coup. Both countries would have been better off had the coup and the hostage crisis never occurred. Exhibiting the Islamic Republic's determination against the US helped Khomeini unite the Islamists in Iran in a fragile period right after the revolution, but it harmed Iran's image and reputation abroad. As much as it united the revo-lutionaries, it divided the nation. The first Prime Minister of the Islamic Republic, Mehdi Bazargan—who had until the hostage crisis been a faithful revolutionary himself—resigned as his effort to release the hostages failed. Neither was the Shah ever extradited to Iran. The incident also isolated Iran politically and economically, as crippling sanctions was levied against the country. Iran and the US are still dealing with the impact of the coup and the hostage crisis.

Since the bitter memories of the coup and hostage crisis continue to haunt both nations, it is important to have an open and honest debate about the full effects of these two incidents. This discussion is omitted from this section in the interest of the focus of the chapter. An in-depth assessment of the coup versus the hostage crisis is provided in an appendix to this sec-tion for the interested reader. Here it suffices to point out that while both incidents were highly regrettable, the coup against the Iranian government was a much worse action than the hostage crisis because it violated Iran's sovereignty, led to 300 deaths, and altered the Iranian society in ways that the hostage taking never did.

8. The Politics of the Islamic Republic

Iran's relationship with the US and the rest of the West grew more con-
voluted under the Islamic Republic. Khomeini believed that Westerniza-
tion was threatening the existence of Islam. On the eve of the revolution,
Iran was by and large a secular country. Khomeini was acutely aware of
the threats to Islam coming from both within and without the Iranian society. The danger of a large secular segment in the population was that it
could potentially be infiltrated by the Western intelligence agents to stir
up a revolution against the Islamic regime. To counter the Western threat,
the Islamic Republic copied a foreign policy tactic commonly employed by
world powers: to seek influence outside one's own country under the flag
of assisting the oppressed, and brandish that influence in the face of threat
to deter the enemy. At first, the leader of PLO, Yasser Arafat, was invited to
Iran, where substantial amount of cash exchanged hands, but Arafat refused
to accept the Islamic Republic's hardline anti-Israeli stance.[211] With Arafat
out of the picture, the Islamic Republic sought other and more extreme
groups. Hence while the Iranian economy was in shambles and the poor
lacked basic necessities, the Islamic Republic extended financial assistance
and weaponry into Hamas and Hezbollah. Iran's support for Hamas and
Hezbollah further deepened the antagonism between Iran and the West.
Iran has since modulated this policy depending upon variations in hostility between the country and the West. When the country faced the threat
of an imminent US invasion under the second Bush Administration or the

increased Israeli hostility in the same period, it stepped up its support not only for Hamas and Hezbollah, but also for insurgents in Iraq as a manner of weakening the US's capacity to invade Iran.

Several incidents defined the US-Iranian relationship in 1980s. In 1983, Lebanese suicide attackers drove trucks loaded with five tons of explosive through Beirut barracks where international peacekeeping forces stayed, killing 241 US marines. Intelligence sources implicated Iran and Syria in the attacks, although both countries denied involvement. Two years later, it was revealed that Iran had secretly purchased American weapon via Israel (the revelation of which went under the name Iran-Contra Affair and became the biggest scandal of the Reagan Administration[212]). In 1988, as the Iran–Iraq War was drawing to a close, an Iranian vessel was sunk by US marines in response to Iranian mine attacks. An Iranian passenger plane was shot down accidentally in the same year by the US forces in the Gulf, killing 290 passengers and crews.[213] None of these events were helpful for the US–Iranian relations. After the Iran–Iraq War, the wartime speaker of the Majles Ali Akbar Hashemi Rafsanjani became the president of Iran. Rafsanjani was a pragmatic leader, who initiated an economic reform program to lessen the government's hand in private enterprise. He also attempted to normalize Iran's relationship with its neighbors and the West.

Major democratic reforms, however, had to wait till the election of the reformist leader, President Seyyed Mohammad Khatami. Khatami was an ambitious cleric with a broad vision for Iran's future. He was highly educated. He had lived in Germany before the revolution and understood the Western culture, but at the same time, he was an insider of the Iranian politics. Firstly, he was a Muslim cleric. Secondly, he had already held a position as the Minister of Culture under the Islamic Republic. Khatami was a force within the system, who appreciated the cultural dynamics of the Iranian society, but he was a progressive leader who wanted change. As the Minister of Culture, he had already left a track record as a liberal thinker who had tried to reduce censorship. He clearly represented a threat to the conservative establishment in Iran, and for this reason, commentators were surprised by his election victory in 1997.

As a progressive leader who was at the same time internal to the Muslim ideology, he had the best chance of both preserving the religion and making changes. He was swept to power by about 70% of the voters. Two-thirds of Iran's population was under the age of 25 in 1997, and Khatami had succeeded in galvanizing the young and the female constituencies. The fact that an overwhelming portion of the electorate wanted to minimize the power of the conservatives in Iran proved that the Islamic Republic had failed. The first Prime Minister of Iran under the Islamic Republic, Mehdi Bazargan, had once famously replied to Khomeini's warning about Islam being in jeopardy by saying that "the only the danger to Islam is the experience of living in Iran under the Islamic Republic." Now, this discontent expressed itself in bringing to power a leader that promised change. Khatami wanted to increase the role of women in society. He argued strenuously against coercing Islamic way of life on those who did not want it. He wanted free press, and he believed that real Islam promoted peace, not violence. And for all of this to happen, Iran needed to cultivate a new system of governance: democracy. He believed that democracy was compatible with Islam and he aimed at making the Islamic Republic democratic, not by revolution, but through incremental reforms.

The fact that a trained Islamic cleric such as Khatami interpreted Islam in ways that would embrace democratic principles demonstrates at least that such a reading of the Islamic tenets is possible. Convincing other Muslims to follow in his footsteps becomes a matter of logistics and determination, not necessarily a matter of principle.

To make the Islamic Republic democratic without discarding religion altogether, the Islamic leadership must be willing to change its outlook. Turkey represents an example of an Islamic country on the path to democratization. But Turkey imported the Western ideals of democracy blindly in an effort to accommodate modernization after the Western model. Secularism was adopted militaristically and democracy in Turkey never evolved through an open debate across the social strata. Turkey has achieved a relatively stable society with a booming economy, but not without harshly suppressing dissension. The Turkish democracy is also threatened by the Kurdish minority group, which demands sovereignty. The country has been an applicant to the European Union for the past few decades, but as a result of internal conflicts, it has not been able to meet the EU's prerequisites for entry to the European open market. While Turkey looks just like any other European country on the surface, it has constantly been humiliated by the EU.

On the other hand, Khatami's reform process seemed promising. Under his presidency, the Iranian society opened up inwardly and outwardly.

Khatami understood that the mistake of the Pahlavi shahs was that speedy modernization projects had been forced down on people from above. As a result, the Iranian economy had boomed, sky scrapers had been built, and the country looked Westernized, but the culture had remained stagnant or changed only superficially. Khatami recognized that cultural evolution was a precondition for democracy. To rebuild the culture he needed to unleash the forces of social criticism. Under his government, a wealth of publications flourished. Dissident newspapers and books helped create a vibrant atmosphere for debate and free thinking. Khatami did not offer a ready-made solution for how the Iranian way of life should be organized. He wanted the people to take ownership of their political institutions and to devise new ways of arranging power.

Khatami sought to rebuild Iran's image internationally. He proposed dialogue among civilizations as an answer to Samuel Huntington's concern about a future clash of civilizations. In a major speech in the UN, Khatami elaborated how he envisaged that dialogue could open up divergent societies to one another for the benefit of cultural exchange and mutual understanding. Slowly but systematically, Khatami's government approached the West. Better trade and cultural ties were established with Europe. The British Council sent an envoy to Tehran in 2000. Creating better ties with the US proved much harder. The conservatives opposed Khatami's overtures to the US every step of the way, but progress was made. The Clinton Administration established an unofficial channel for dialogue with Khatami's government. Collaboration between Iran the US peaked immediately after 9/11, when Iran rendered assistance to the combat efforts of the US forces against the Al Qaeda and Taliban militias in Afghanistan.

Just as the sun appeared to be rising up on the US-Iranian relationship and Iran was becoming the US forces' most important ally in Afghanistan, President Bush had a speech in which he surprisingly called Iran an axe of evil alongside North Korea and Syria. Many pondered why the president's attack came exactly at a time when hostility between the two countries seemed finally to have alleviated and a new environment of collaboration and mutual respect was prevailing between them. The speech was a major blow against Khatami and his reform process and a boost for the conservatives who had strenuously argued that Iran should not rely on or trust the West. The conservative hardliners believed that the US was only interested in positive relations with Iran on its own terms. Mossadegh had turned to America, but been betrayed. Khatami had renewed efforts to build constructive relations with the West and the result was being branded an axe of evil. It had taken Khatami several years of fighting against Iran's conservative faction to improve Iran's foreign relations. Suddenly, the conservatives seemed to be winning the argument.

President Bush's accusations and attacks helped the 2005 presidential candidate, Mahmoud Ahmadinejad, who argued that the Islamic Republic should go back to the principles laid down by its founder Ayatollah Khomeini and take a tougher stance against the West. Democracy is always plagued by threats to national security and the Bush Administration's threat of making Iran the next country for US incursion after Iraq helped take the lifeblood out of the reform process. Iran was one of the first countries in the Muslim world which strongly condemned the 9/11 attack and offered the US assistance to defeat Al Qaeda in Afghanistan, but a chain is only as strong as its weakest link and the strength of the US-Iranian relations failed the test in the panic of post 9/11.

Domestically, Khatami's presidency was paralyzed by a lack of institutional power. The Iran expert, Zhan Sahib offers a comparative analysis of the politics of change under Khatami versus the transformations in the Soviet Union under Gorbachev. According to him, "Khatami, although enjoying popular electoral legitimacy, did not enjoy the institutional power that Gorbachev did. This limited his ability to reshape through bureaucratic means the dynamic between the revolutionary and republican institutions. Therefore, Khatami's politics of change was greatly dependent on his skill and leadership in handling and managing the various elite factions in various [Islamic Republic] institutions...The overall strategy, as conceived by many of Khatami's closest advisors, was to use popular pressure from below in factional struggles behind the scenes at the top levels of the republican and revolutionary institutions in order to advance the politics of change. This active use of popular pressure from below was needed since Khatami was attempting to re-define the power and prerogatives of revolutionary institutions whose real power was greater than that of the republican presidency. Khatami found institutional change more politically challenging than did Gorbachev who headed the revolutionary institution which enjoyed theoretically absolute power."[214]

Institutional change takes time and the slow pace of reforms disillusioned Khatami's constituency. In the end, Khatami suffered from all fronts:

the conservative opposition to his reforms, the threat of invasion by the US, and eventually the discontent from his own constituency. The process Khatami started was never completed, yet it changed the Iranian society in ways that will never return to the most oppressive days of post-revolutionary era. The anti-Ahmadinejad demonstrations in 2009, where several millions of people took to the streets to protest the allegedly rigged reelection of Ahmadinejad to a second term in office, clearly exhibits that the cultural transformations under Khatami's government has had a lasting effect after all. Such display of opposition would never have taken place during the Khomeini era. Although Ahmadinejad's government cracked down the demonstrations in the end, there is no doubt that the spirit of freedom survives right beneath the surface.

A VILLAIN OR A SAVIOR?

Ahmadinejad won the presidential election in 2005 amid serious threat of a US invasion. He quickly set out to undo the achievements of his predecessor. Press freedom was reverted to pre-Khatami period and the moral police saw its hand strengthened again. Ahmadinejad is considered by most observers as a populist with an uncompromising style and cinematic stage behavior, who seems to enjoy media attention. Why would he so bitterly oppose the freedoms that the Khatami government had helped to secure for the average Iranian, if he is a populist?

Ahmadinejad's handling of the economy has been catastrophic. He himself has admitted that he does not understand the economy. Under Khatami, the economy grew by about 6 to 7% annually. Ahmadinejad's economic policy, or rather lack of a well-crafted policy, has reversed this trend, causing soaring inflation and unemployment. Sporadic cash injection in rural and poor areas during his first term in office inflated the commodity prices. The official rate of unemployment in 2010 was over 20%. However, analysts believe the real unemployment figure is more than a third of the workforce. Half way through Ahmadinejad's first term in office, a group of about 70 leading economists and university professors in Iran wrote an open letter to the president's office, warning about adverse impacts of Ahmadinejad's sporadic cash injections on the national economy. Despite the admonition, Ahmadinejad obstinately continued cash hand-outs in the first two years of his presidency, as if the government budget had no end, but why?

Ideologically, Ahmadinejad is known as a religious zealot, who predict-ed in 2005 that Mehdi would reappear within two years by which time he would be able to step down with clear conscience and hand over the leader-ship of the Islamic Republic to Mehdi. Mehdi was the last of the twelve Shia imams (descendents of Prophet Mohammad). The Shia believe that Mehdi disappeared in the ninth century and that he is still alive and in a state of occultation, awaiting reappearance to carry the torch for Islam and save the earth when the world is in a state of widespread apostasy and immorality. But why did Ahmadinejad believe that Mehdi would reappear within two years of the start of his presidency?

Ahmadinejad adopted a tremendously tough stance against the Bush Administration, opposing the US president in every possible way. At a time, when Iran was under serious threat of invasion, instead of trying to defuse the situation, he adopted an extremely harsh rhetoric against Wash-ington and its ally, Israel. Many Iranian intellectuals, including the former president Khatami, warned that such rhetoric could lead Iran to dangerous paths. At a time when most of the Iranian populace desperately wanted to keep calm, so as not to escalate the possibility of a US invasion of the coun-try, he notoriously proclaimed that "[Israel] must be wiped off the world map." He returned the rhetoric coming from Washington with branding the US government an "arrogant power." To most people, Ahmadinejad's behavior seemed reckless. He is a president of relatively weak country. In the face of a major threat from the world's mightiest power, especially at a time when the Bush Administration had left a clear track record of military interventions in Iraq and Afghanistan, would it not have been suicidal for Ahmadinejad to act the way he did? Why did he act aggressively at a time when intuitively it seemed wise for him to stay calm and calculating?

Ahmadinejad's acrimonious behavior has been interpreted in a variety of ways. As the Iranian scholar Ali Ansari points out, "foreign representations of Ahmadinejad have tended to portray him as a villain of extraordinary pro-portions and existential consequences, complete with forked tail and horns: the personification of evil."[215]

The Iranian journalist, Kasra Naji, has portrayed Ahmadinejad as a sim-ple-minded and naïve but frank president: a man of conviction, but one that does not understand the game of politics; not a villain but a dummy, yet an honest dummy who would potentially put Iran on a dangerous path owing to his foolishness but not evilness. Naji does not use words, such as honest and frank about the presidents, but he depicts him as a simple-minded man who speaks his mind. Referring, among other things, to Ahmadinejad's letters to the US president, George Bush, where he seemed to be inviting Bush to convert to Islam, or the Holocaust Conference in Tehran in 2005, where Ahmadinejad proposed a revision of the history of Holocaust, Naji writes, "...here was also a man who wrote incoherent letters to heads of state, who invited neo-Nazis to speak at high-profile events, who was lampooned and ridiculed the world over for believing that he was an agent of the divine, preparing Iran for the arrival of the messianic Missing Imam. Here was a leader whose grasp of geopolitics was rudimentary, a man who seemed not to understand economics, a man who would drag Iran to the brink of an unwinnable war with the West."[216]

In reality, Ahmadinejad is neither as villainy as portrayed in the West nor as foolishly honest as pictured by Naji. Understanding Ahmadinejad requires understanding the circumstances in which he came to power, where Iran faced an imminent threat of invasion by the United States. This chapter sees Ahmadinejad as a great manipulator and a political strategist, who tries desperately to avert a US invasion. His policies during the two first years of his presidency would have a lasting negative impact on Iran's image, economy, and international standing, but the most acute situation which required full attention between 2005 and 2007 was the threat of invasion and as the president, Ahmadinejad's principal assignment in this period was to prevent a war with the US at whatever cost necessary. He was prepared to sacrifice all other economic and political considerations in order to save Iran's sovereignty. Naji accuses Ahmadinejad of simply not understanding that, "by laying himself open to the charge of anti-Semitism—a term laden in the West with terrible memories—he was weakening his own position internationally and undermining his country's interests. What he could not see was that by playing the Holocaust card he was making the American and Israeli hostility to Iran appear reasonable and justifiable."[217]

Naji, however, misunderstands the nature of the American and Israeli hostility to Iran between 2005 and 2007. He believes that America and Israel would have looked more favorably at Iran or less inclined to attack the country had Ahmadinejad maintained calm, but this is the opposite of the case. During these two years, the Bush Administration seemed certain to attack Iran. It appeared as though the decision to invade Iran had already been made, in spite of both US domestic and international outcry against a war with Iran. Whether or not this was a bluff, it certainly appeared very real. Iran had been surrounded by the US forces in Iraq, Afghanistan, and the Gulf region. The US military had contemplated plans for a full-scale invasion. Although many prominent military commanders advised against it, the Bush Administration seemed determined to attack Iran. Most international commentators believed that Iran was part of the larger US scheme to penetrate deeper into the Middle East, starting with Afghanistan and Iraq, then Iran, Syria, and possibly elsewhere. European surveys showed that the Bush Administration's policies were regarded as endangering the world peace. The anti-war sentiment ran high, especially in 2006, calling for the Bush Administration to keep its hands off Iran. The whole world had rallied in 2003 to stop the invasion of Iraq, but the Bush Administration's resolution had proved unshakable. Months before the invasion of Iraq, Saddam unconditionally agreed to allow the UN weapon inspectors full access to all Iraqi weapon sites. The Bush Administration rejected Saddam's gesture, insisting on regime change. The more Saddam showed fear and caved in, and the more the international community cried out against going to war, the more the US Administration showed its determination to removing Saddam from power. On the other hand, the Bush Administration threatened North Korea with military strike as punishment for the country's pursuit of nuclear weapon, but North Korea responded swiftly that any military action against the country would lead to a full scale war between the two countries. North Korea's tough stance shocked much of the world, but President Bush quickly made a U-turn, offering North Korea a diplomatic resolution. All of these indicated that the invasion was not contingent on Ahmadinejad's affability towards the US; it seemed imminent. The point is that the Bush Administration was not concerned with world opinion. Making its war efforts look reasonable and justifiable was, for the Administration, of secondary importance. In this environment, Ahmadinejad could not simply remain quiet, hoping that his calm would appease the White House. This was not a time to reason, but to act. Ahmadinejad was facing the mad-bull phenomenon: if you are in the ring with a mad bull, you cannot simply stand still hoping that the mad bull will not attack you. You would not plead for help either, if you believe that the onlookers will not jump in and save you. You copy the bull's madness and wave your arms and legs frantically and yell.

North Korea seems to have some nuclear firepower to back its rhetoric. Since Iran does not currently have significant power to counter Western aggression, Ahmadinejad's tough talk and suggestion of the ability to retaliate in some measure were all the weapons he had. At best, Ahmadinejad could make it look like attacking Iran would set off unpredictable trouble for the whole region.

The Middle East expert Kenneth Pollack had discussed convincingly in his book in 2005, *The Persian Puzzle*, that the Islamic Republic was an adversarial regime, but not suicidal. Pollack showed that the Islamic Republic had in the past been at least rational enough to act reasonably, when threat to its existence had become imminent. While Pollack was arguing against invading Iran, he was giving away a strategic secret about the mindset of the Iranian leadership: that it would back down, when faced with existential threat. For a US Administration determined to attack Iran, Pollack's insight offered an important piece of knowledge. Ahmadinejad saw it his job to reverse this notion. He could not act rationally because rational acts are predictable and the Bush Administration could calculate Ahmadinejad's next move. He needed to cast himself as irrational; as someone who would do anything; as someone, from whom the West was better off staying away. Only reckless behavior would pay off. In other words, he needed to *appear* mad to avert war; in this way he could avoid committing an actual act of madness. Of course, the West then used his theatrical madness to argue that the Islamic Republic should not be allowed to develop a nuclear arsenal. The reality is, this was a desperate time requiring desperate measures. The Bush Administration had adopted an extremist foreign policy approach, and Ahmadinejad needed to go to the extremes to counter it.

In this period he needed to show no fear. He boldly attended to the UN assembly in New York under heightened hostilities. He wrote letters to Bush inviting him to Islam as a sign of defiance at a time when Bush was believed throughout the Third World to be waging a war against Islam. In this way, Ahmadinejad countered the threat from Bush with psychological warfare. He toured Iran and provided cash hand-outs, perhaps as a way of buying popular support for his government. The cash hand-outs had a crippling impact on the economy, but this was a time of extraordinary threat to Iran's national security, which justified any short-term measure. He needed to attract the Iranian zealots in order to strengthen his government and to bolster Iranians' confidence at the time of looming threat. Hence, he would attempt to reverse the people's natural fear for a foreign attack with the promise of the pending arrival of the messianic Missing Imam, Mehdi, whether or not he believed it himself. Everything he did in this period must be interpreted in the light of imminent threat of invasion.

Even in the US, civil liberties were suspended in the wake of the 9/11 attack. It makes no sense to believe, as Naji does, that as the president of Iran under imminent threat of a foreign invasion, he would simply relax and focus on the economy or other aspects of social life.

Furthermore, when Naji accuses Ahmadinejad of not understanding the world outside Iran, he only refers to the Western world. Ahmadinejad did not even appear to be attempting to win the hearts and minds of the Western people. Westerners had proven incapable of stopping the Bush Administration's invasion of Iraq. Ahmadinejad's tactic was hailed on the Arab Street.[218] While the US-backed Arab leaders fiercely opposed the regime in Tehran, many Arab people viewed him as a hero who stood up against the West's "unjustified attacks on the Muslim world." To deter the enemy, Ahmadinejad needed the possibility of an Arab uprising, if Iran was attacked. By deliberately putting himself in the firing line and making himself look like the victim of Western assaults against his person and his country, he drew the sympathy from the Arab world.

Whatever judgment one may adopt about Ahmadinejad's seemingly inexplicable behavior, it is clear that it worked for the most part. People in the Arab Street rallied behind him, the people in the West screamed at President Bush (even though Bush would not listen in the beginning, it worked in the end), and the Bush Administration eventually backed down. If the above analysis is correct, Ahmadinejad, far from being naïve and reckless, was a shrewd strategist, who succeeded in averting the war with his bare hands. Iran was on the verge of a war. The Bush Administration framed it sometimes as a charity incursion to free the Iranian people from the Islamic Republic, but no Iranian wanted the war. Even the son of the shah, Reza Pahlavi, who has for the last 30 years run a campaign in exile against the Islamic Republic and has made no secret of his desire to reintroduce the monarchy in Iran, published a video on YouTube saying "Don't bomb my country!" Iran's Jewish community weighed in against the war too. Iran has about 25,000 ethnic Jews—a small number, but the largest in the Middle East outside Israel. The Iranian Jews oppose Ahmadinejad for obvious reasons, but they would rather live in a stable and peaceful Iran than under the chaos of a US invasion.

Ahmadinejad would go on to crack down violently on peaceful demonstrations against his allegedly rigged election in 2009. He has a long repertoire of human rights abuses, misbehavior, and questionable policies. But his ostensibly bizarre strategy during that period of imminent threat of invasion, when nothing else would work, saved Iran much death and devastation that would have followed from a war with the United States. A war with Iran would have also damaged America's international standing and further drained the US military of power and resources. This might have had catastrophic ramifications for the US national security, far beyond the current threats the US is facing. Ahmadinejad is no lover of the United States, but inadvertently he saved America from a devastating war at a time the American president was putting this country on a suicidal foreign policy path. In fact, some of the President Bush's rhetoric too appears insane, when viewed out of the context of its time (or perhaps even within the context of its time). President Bush himself used aggressive language to frighten the opposition—what the opposition called "fear tactics." President Bush and Ahmadinejad were two of the same type. The reasons why Ahmadinejad appeared madder than Bush were that, one: Ahmadinejad was in a weaker position and his enemy, the US, stronger—he compensated his weakness with more aggressive rhetoric—and two: Ahmadinejad was unchecked, while the Bush's office was organized under a democracy and the US president was after all answerable to the democratic system.

The verdict must then be that, in stark contrast to popular perception, enemy number one to America was not Ahmadinejad, but the US's overly aggressive Iran policy in 2005 and 2006. If history judges a leader by his achievements, and not only by his rhetoric, Ahmadinejad prevented a war while the Bush Administration desperately wanted it. And if averting a deadly war is the most urgent job of any president, Ahmadinejad's accomplishment speaks for itself.

Understanding Ahmadinejad's softer image than the one often served by the media is good news for the world. It means that he is not an existential threat to the world, as many people who lack knowledge about him seem to believe. But, of course, it does not mean that everything that he did or said during this period was right. Sometimes he went too far, which brought the Islam Republic down to its lowest moral decadence. The Holocaust Conference was one such example. Threatening to wipe Israel off the world map was another. Naji has brilliantly explained the semantic nuances in Persian language that distinguishes the meaning of the sentence "this Jerusalem occupying regime [Israel] must vanish from the page(s) of time," which is what an exact translation of Ahmadinejad's words would read, from the sentence "this Jerusalem occupying regime must *be made to* vanish from the page(s) of time," which was how his words were interpreted outside Iran (Italic added).[219] The second sentence seems to advocate a more active role in destroying the state of Israel. Ahmadinejad has since modified his words, although still offensive, saying that "he predicts that the Zionist regime will soon be dissolved."

It is also important to put his statement into context. The candidate Hillary Clinton famously proclaimed during her 2008 presidential campaign that "[America] could obliterate Iran." For the world's largest military power to threaten to obliterate over 70 million people in Iran is immeasurably worse.

Nevertheless, Ahmadinejad's words further damaged Iran's reputation in the West. Unfortunately, his personal image and his mistakes and failures are continuing to damage Iran long after the threat of war has seized to exist, and the legacy he is going to leave behind will continue to haunt Iran well into the future. Had he served just one term, he could have gone down in history as just the figurehead that Iran and the rest of the world needed at a desperate time to avoid an ugly war. But in the process, he distorted his personal image to the level that it is no longer beneficial for the country. Yet, this book argues that the solution to Ahmadinejad is not a US-led regime change in Iran, but *the power to change* coming from within the Iranian society. What Iran needs now is a president with the same vision as Khatami, but with freer hands to reform the Islamic Republic.

IRAN'S NUCLEAR PROGRAM

Iran has clashed with the West over the last decade over its nuclear enrichment program. The country insists that its nuclear program is exclusively for peaceful purposes. The West suspects that Iran is trying to develop WMD under the guise of nuclear energy production. And some critics of the Western Iran policy suspect that the West is only seeking a regime change in Iran under the cover of preventing proliferation of weapons of mass destruction. The mistrust between Iran and the West that has been building up on both sides over a century expresses itself through the nuclear standoff. Right before Ahmadinejad ascended to power, the EU3, Britain, France, and Germany, engineered a joint proposal to allow Iran develop nuclear reactors for peaceful purposes but in compliance with the UN Non-proliferation Treaty.[220] The proposal would stop all uranium enrichment activities in the country. The Western countries would supply the enriched fuel necessary for reactors to generate electricity or for legitimate research and medical purposes. The Iranians rejected the proposal immediately. The proposal would mean that they would be dependent on Europe for their energy needs indefinitely. From the Iranian perspective, by holding the key to Iran's access to nuclear energy, the West would be able to enforce its way squarely on the country, if the day comes when fossil fuel is no longer available. Western countries have been dependent on Middle Eastern petroleum more than a century, but the West has had the political leverage and military strength to enforce a steady flow of oil westwards. As a weak country, an agreement that put the Islamic Republic at the mercy of a stronger power for its energy needs is synonymous to risking its long-term sovereignty. The Islamic Republic and the West have long lists of grievances against one another, and the countries that will be able to control Iran's access to energy, when Iran's petroleum reserves are ended in future, will be able to set the political agenda.

The Western media portrait of Iran's position is that different Western countries have extended a hand of friendship, offering Iran a way out of the gridlock, while Iranian authorities have been evasive and stubbornly seeking to build nuclear weapon. But the media fails to understand that the nuclear standoff is a real impasse caused by actions of both sides, and not just an expression of Iranian evasiveness. From the Western perspective, Iran has nothing to worry about, if it is not in pursuit of nuclear weapons. But even if Iran is truly not pursuing WMD and is only interested in peaceful nuclear energy, no easy solution can be found to this problem unless one realizes that there is much more involved in the nuclear standoff than a mere cat-and-mouse game.

If history has taught the Iranian policymakers one thing, it is that they cannot rely on Europe for issues so significant to their national security, such as access to energy. America would not rely on Europe for its national security; why should Iran? As the historian, Nikki Keddie, points out, Iranian leaders early in the last century never built a capacity to defend Iran's interests. They relied instead on foreign protection. As a result, the British, Russians, and other European powers frequently intervened in the internal affairs of Iran, constantly threatened its central government to win concessions, and nearly colonized the country. The modern history of Iran is filled with broken promises by the European powers as well as frustrated efforts by the Iranians to live in peace with the Europeans. This is past history, but the wounds seem fresh still. To understand what history can do one needs look no further than the Europe itself. Not only the EU is still plagued with mutual mistrusts and memories of past misdeeds on the account of bitter European rivalry in the past few centuries—there is a large repertoire of examples to back this claim—, but also interestingly Norway is one of the two or three countries in Europe, which did not join the EU as a fully integrated member state because its history of being trampled by the Danish and Swedish kings until 1814 still scares its people to join the club of big powers. Iranians have only themselves to blame for their long history of weakness. Incompetent kings, corrupt central government, lack of democracy, and regressive culture enabled the Western powers to suppress Iran's population and extort its government for favors. Nevertheless, history's lesson for Iranian policymakers of the modern generation is that giving away their right to enrich uranium without securing mechanisms that guarantees the flow of nuclear fuel to their reactors will be the same as giving the West a blank check to withhold the fuel in case of a future dispute to pressure Iran. No such guarantees can be made indefinitely. Iran does not have the capacity to defend its rights, if promises are broken in the future. The country has been put under sanctions and its assets have been frozen in foreign banks. The country has been under the threat of coup, invasion, and isolation. The Islamic Republic bitterly remembers its role in assisting the US forces in Afghanistan post 9/11, only to be named an axe of evil. Iran's history does not leave much room for trust. From the Western standpoint, Iran's recent aggressive behavior seems counterproductive to its nuclear ambitions. The more aggressive the country is, the more the West is convinced that Iran should never be allowed to gain nuclear technology that can potentially be used in weapon development. From the Iranian perspective, the Western behavior seems counterproductive to Western ambition for curbing in the Iranian nuclear program. Sanctions and threat of invasion simply convinces Iranian policymakers that they cannot rely on the West and encourages them to pursue their nuclear program more vigorously. In any way, excessive pressure on Iran to sign a deal will not necessarily produce a legally solid foundation for nonproliferation, as Iran could in the future back away from the deal citing that it signed the dotted line under duress. The Islamic Republic knows, as indicated above, that if it gives in to pressure, there is no reason for the West not to use its leverage again to score other wins in the future, such as to curb in Iran's support for Hezbollah or Hamas, Iran's trade relations with Chavez's Venezuela, etc. Whatever one may think about the behavior of the Islamic Republic, it would never voluntarily put itself in a situation that would force it to abandon its ways. If Iran is truly intending to build WMD, the West's effort to isolate the country, makes it more insecure and more fixated on getting a fat boy of his own. As Ahmadinejad has pointed out clearly, "[we] know well that a country backing down one iota on its undeniable rights is the same as losing everything..."[221] Even if the Iranian nuclear program is truly for peaceful purposes, Ahmadinejad understands that curbing in on this issue means nothing less than opening up the flood gates for more US pressure.

The EU and the United States secretary of state, Hillary Clinton, have repeatedly refused talking with Iran about any other issues other than the nuclear question. But the Islamic Republic knows that if the US succeed in pressuring Iran on the nuclear issue, it would be irrational for the US not to use its leverage to pressure Iran on other issues, such as its support for Hezbollah or Hamas. If the West is going to have an agreement that can be used to pressure Iran on other issues in the future, it needs to be prepared to talk about all issues with Iran. Any deal would have to be a comprehensive deal, taking into account all Iran's legitimate national interests and security needs, which will enable and encourage the country to play a more positive role in the region.

The West has insisted numerous times that Iran should halt all enrichment activity immediately as a confidence building measure. If the negotiations are going to have a chance of producing an agreement, the West too must make a bigger effort to build mutual trust. The so-called all-options-on-the-table or the threat of covert or overt action to topple the regime in Tehran is not exactly a language designed to gain the opponent's trust.

The question that Washington has been grappling with is how to bring Iranians to the negotiation table. President Obama has acknowledged the need for a diplomatic solution to the problem although he has maintained all options on the table. Lessons from Iraq and Afghanistan are finally beginning to sink in and the White House is keen to avoid a military confrontation, at least in the short term. Yet, President Obama's handling of the nuclear situation cannot go without a critique.

President Obama extended a hand of friendship to Iran. He addressed Khamenei in writing, made statements about the US–Iranian relations on the US TV, and sent a video New Year message to the Iranian people, but to no avail.[222] The core of President Obama's messages was twofold: firstly, that his administration would accept an Iran elevated to a position of regional significance and he would work with Iran to see that happen in a smooth and orderly manner, and secondly, that his administration would not accept a nuclear armed Iran. The fact that the Islamic Republic rejected both calls was a great disappointment for the Administration, but it should have been expected.

When President Bush rejected Khatami's plead for a dialogue among civilizations and opted instead to attack Iran verbally or otherwise, many commentators—such as Kenneth Pollack—criticized him for wrecking a golden opportunity for better ties between the two countries. But from Bush's perspective, his approach seemed perfectly reasonable at the time. Iran had been a long-term and unnecessary problem for the US and in the heyday of Iraq and Afghanistan Wars, when the US military appeared to possess unlimited force, the Bush Administration saw an opportunity to root out the Iranian problem once and for all. Iran had been slow to reconcile with the US even under Khatami. Iranian collaboration with Washington became forthcoming only after 9/11, when the Islamic Republic felt threatened by the presence of US combat forces all around Iran. While in the fifth gear, why should not Bush go all the way to the heart of Tehran? But the plan failed and the Bush Administration was forced to make a humiliating U-turn on Iran. With the U-turn, the table was turned in Iran's favor, and the Islamic Republic could now adopt a similar form of logic as that of the Bush Administration: if the US did not possess unlimited power after all, and if the Islamic Republic had a chance to aim higher and become a regional power, why submit to Obama's plan for Iran? Iran was now in fifth gear. Why should it stop to pick up a hitchhiker from the White House? The Islamic Republic believes or certainly hopes that it can be in power long after President Obama is gone. Who knows if the next US president will honor President Obama's policy vows to Iran? Having burned their fingers amply before, what guarantees would the Iranian leaders see in taking Obama's hand? History has taught the leaders of Iran to graze as long as the grass is green, as tomorrow may bring the dry season.

Three months after the New Year message, there were some cautious signals that Iran would finally embrace Obama's call for talks and improved relations. Ahmadinejad had prepared a letter to his counterpart in expectation of official congratulations from the White House upon his possible reelection to a second term in office. The election was on June 12th 2009, and Ahmadinejad was declared the winner. The opposition claimed election fraud and demanded a recount. Millions of Iranians took to the streets in major cities to protest. After about one week of peaceful gatherings around the country, the police and vigilante groups cracked down the demonstrations violently, killing at least 19 protesters. Ahmadinejad was later sworn in office for a second term. The violent crack-down of demonstrators made it impossible for the Obama Administration to maintain a friendly posture. Once again the US-Iranian relations would take one step forward, but two backwards. Commentators expected Ahmadinejad's letter would contain a reconciliatory language. Many of those who took to the streets opposed Ahmadinejad's uncompromising stance against the West. Some commentators labeled it "the Obama factor." The protestors wanted better relations with the US, but as it is always the case for the Iranian people, they achieved just the opposite of that. This was not President Obama's mistake, nor the mistake of the demonstrators. The problem was the Iranian election process, which inevitably produced the gridlock. Whether or not the election was rigged, it failed to convince many Iranian electorates that the result was fair.

The biggest mistake of the Obama Administration's handling of the Iranian nuclear issue was the adoption of intimidation as a tactic to force the Islamic Republic to the negotiation table. The P5+1—the permanent members of the UN Security Council and Germany—devised a new proliferation-proof proposal for Iran, giving the country only 2 days to respond. On whatever advice President Obama agreed to adopt the two day notice, this was a categorically bad idea, given Iran's proven hard line in the negotiation. It was as if the president was asking for the proposal to be rejected. Every single move Ahmadinejad had made ever since coming to power had reaffirmed that his government would not budge under pressure, not even under the threat of imminent invasion; in fact, the adrenaline rush would make him even more obstinate. Why would President Obama push so hard, when there was so much evidence that it would make even harder for the proposal to be accepted? Did President Obama really think that Ahmadinejad had suddenly changed, or was the two day notice rather designed to boost Obama's domestic image as a tough president? Whatever considerations went through the corridors of White House, one thing remained clear: the harder Obama pushed on the issue, the more determined Tehran became in opposing the president, and the more America looked helpless.

Whether or not the real intention behind the nuclear scheme is the development of WMD, the program is the most important national security issue for Iran at the moment—far greater in significance than, for instance, the healthcare or financial overhaul bill for the United States—and President Obama was giving Iran only 2 days to make a decision.

President Obama's mistake was that he emitted confusing signals. On one hand, he would show respect for the leaders in Tehran, offering to work with them, but on the other his methods of pressuring the government in Tehran appeared to bear little respect for the Iranian leaders; he would paint his image as an advocate of peace and diplomacy, but on the other hand, he would insist on having all options on the table. What went wrong with Obama's stance on the Iranian nuclear issue, as with many other issues under his presidency including many of his domestic issues, was that the president attempted too hard to make everyone happy, but ended up pleasing no one. He offered a hand of friendship to Iran, but never gave it enough time because he wanted to reconcile with Washington's more hard-line voices against Iran too. In his balancing act, he flip-flopped between a soft and a tough stance.[223]

WHAT IS NEXT FOR IRAN?

Morgan Shuster wrote to Iran's defense over a hundred years ago that at the time, the country was "the helpless victim of the wretched game of cards" with the big powers.[224] He had faith that Iranians would be able to grow a full-fledge democracy, if only they were left in peace. But Iran has also fallen victim to its own many mistakes and shortcomings. As Arthur Millspaugh pointed out nearly four decades after Shuster, corruption, lack of willpower, and Iranians' failure to diagnose Iran's problems were the primarily sources for Iran's backwardness. This discussion is still valid today, even after a century. Millspaugh helped set the precedent for the US policy

in the developing world for years to come. He advocated American intervention in the internal affairs of weaker nations, such as Iran, as a measure for
their own good. He worked hard for the Iranian people, while he kept Iranians in low esteem and considered them as children who could not grow up
beyond the intellectual capacity of an eleven year old child.[225] To give from
the bottom of his heart to a people he seemed to deplore says just as much
about his flawed attitude as he said of the attitude of the Iranian people. A
rational person would not intervene, if intervention makes no good—and
the history of foreign intervention in the Middle East demonstrates poor
results.

It cannot be denied that Iran has for the past two centuries been a troubled region, constantly struggling domestically and internationally, abused
not only by foreign powers but also by some of its own people, and often at
the mercy of aid and technology from Britain, America, or other nations. But
Iranians have also proven to be resilient. They have been humiliated in the
past, lived with shame, but made comebacks. Khatami put Iran on a progressive path, which has left a lasting mark on the Iranian society. In spite of the
recent years' retreats to the old ways under Ahmadinejad's presidency, the
Iranian population continues to push for democratic reforms and economic
development. It has often been stated by observers inside and outside Iran
that as long as the highest religious authority—a position currently held
by Ayatollah Khamenei as the Supreme Leader—has absolute power over
all social and political matters, the reform process will be thwarted and no
real progress can ever be made. This statement is based on misguided logic.
The empirical evidence demonstrated that Khatami's reform process was
very often curtailed by the hardliners backed by Khamenei, but that change
was still possible though in slow baby-steps. Even Khatami's election to
office was one of the first examples to that effect. The power structure in
the Iranian politics can best be described as a consortium of different ideological factions, which bitterly compete with one another, but unite in the
face of existential threat to the whole system. There are many hurdles, but
also many opportunities for change in this arrangement. Khatami's ability
to advance in late 1990s and early 2000s suggests that Khamenei either does
not have full control over the Iranian politics, or he is in favor of allowing
small and incremental progressive change towards more democracy even if
he is hiding behind the veil of conservatism.

Politics has a cultural root, and cultural transformations are typically slow and painful. Azar Nafisi wrote in her bestselling book, *Reading Lolita in Tehran*, that she as a young activist in an Iranian communist party and participated in the 1979 Revolution to overthrow the despotic shah, only to see him replaced by a worse authoritarian ruler: Khomeini. Her dream was shattered as Khomeini's men cracked down on people's freedom. As Nafisi wrote, quite correctly, the Islamic Republic was Khomeini's dream, and he forced it upon the Iranian people with violence. But she failed to tell her readers—and her readers did not care to question—that her own dream, that of a communist revolution and the dictatorship of the proletariat, would have equally suppressed the Iranian people—not by the Islamic Sharia law, but by her communist manifesto. In 1979, the royalists, communists, Islamists, and others were vying for power to implement their version of dictatorship, and Khomeini came out the winner. One dream might have been better than the other, one might have been more hideous than the other, but they would all have been the dream of a few enforced on the many.

For democracy to have a real chance, the culture must be ready for it. As a leader, Khomeini had a responsibility to cultivate democracy. He failed to do that, but there was a culture in Iran—and still is—that allowed him to do that. Given this culture, there would be no democracy in Iran, whether Khomeini got his way or Nafisi.

It took over a century for the slavery to be abolished in this country, and the US is still struggling with racial prejudice. It took over a century for women to regain their liberty in the West, and Western women are still struggling with unequal pay and gender prejudice at workplace and at home. It has taken decades for Americans to reform the healthcare system, and the system is still in shambles. Reform process in Iran is not going to be any faster than reforms elsewhere. International pressure makes Iranian leaders more nervous and the reform process slower, not faster. It is unthinkable that a British or French assault on the American healthcare system would enforce reforms any faster. It is unthinkable that a threat of invasion into this country would have made the abolition of slavery or feminist movement any faster. If anything, McCarthyism and 9/11 have proven that foreign threats push democracy into regression rather than vice versa. When Iranians eventually rise from the ashes of their past and current troubles, they will be able to hold their heads high, knowing that, though their record is far from spotless, they have not committed the worst atrocities in the world.

The Bush Administration worked strenuously to isolate Iran from its neighbors. For whatever reason—be it the Administration's desire to find a mighty foe for justifying an invasion, or the Administration's conviction in 2005 and 2006 that Iran was one to two years away from acquiring nuclear weapon—the Bush Administration successfully demonized Iran, as if Iranians had forked tail and horns. The facts of Iran's behavior do not support this view. In the last twenty-one years since the death of Khomeini, Iran has consistently attempted to improve its relations with its neighbors. Rafsanjani, the first Iranian president after the Khomeini's demise, took a pragmatic approach to improving Iran's image abroad. He initiated trade relations with India, China, and other countries. Khatami called for a dialogue among civilizations and worked hard on relationship-building with Iran's neighbors and the West. Even Ahmadinejad, who has been demonized in Western media and who has never hesitated in returning foreign attacks on his government with vitriolic language, has used glimpses of opportunities to reach out to Iran's neighbors. He visited the Saudi prince in his first term; visited Iraq; extended aid to Afghanistan and established trade relations with Baltic, Latin American, and African countries. When Wikileaks recently released secret diplomatic cables, showing that the Saudi king, Abdul, had lobbied the Bush Administration to "cut off the snake's head," meaning militarily attacking Iran to stop its nuclear program, Ahmadinejad rushed to say that the revelations would not affect Iran's "good" relations with its Arab neighbors—he went as far as rejecting the credibility of the cables, calling the release a US plot. Iran's "good" relations with its Arab neighbors is overstated. The Islamic Republic is anxiously aware of the tense Iran–Arab relations, but Ahmadinejad's reaction to the cables, although maybe not totally sincere, at least proves the point here that Iran is not ready for a fight. Ahmadinejad tried to defuse the situation. This is not typical behavior for a mad man.

Neither has Iran ever threatened to stop the flow of its oil to the international market. It is natural and expected that the West is anxious about the prospect of an Iranian initiative to halt its oil in order to harm the West. Iran has the second largest petroleum reserves in the Middle East, and the Western anxiety for the Iranian oil is not unwarranted, but it is exaggerated. The thirty-one years of history of the Islamic Republic has produced no evidence that Iran would ever shut down the production of its crude oil. The Iranian oil has been flowing to the market both during the Iran–Iraq War and after that. In fact, while Saudi Arabia has attempted to limit the production of petroleum to maintain high oil prices, Iran has often defied OPEC to produce more oil. Even when the threat of invasion became imminent under the Bush Administration, Ahmadinejad was careful never to threaten halting its oil production. The Islamic Republic recognizes that the country's economy and the regime's existence depend on income from oil production.

Iran's path forward must be engineered within the country, not in Washington. Only leaders within Iran can mobilize the people, creating the kind of momentum and dynamics necessary for a cultural and structural transformation in Iran over time. It cannot be done hastily and not from 5,000 miles away from its center. The Saban Center for Middle East Policy at the Brookings Institution drafted in 2009 nine different policy options for dealing with Iran. These policies ranged from direct military intervention in the form of full-scale invasion or surgical strike on nuclear sites, containment, regime change through stirring up dissident groups inside Iran, to devising some form of coup d'état to replace the government in Tehran with Iranian dissident figures in exile.[226] The draft is merely a strategic assessment of options. It does not make recommendations; nor does it go into operational details. But, strangely, it highlights Reza Pahlavi, the son of Iran's last shah, as a potential candidate, if a coup d'état becomes the preferred option. If the coup against Mossadegh did not provide Washington with an important lesson, here is a new chance to repeat the mistake. Reza Pahlavi fled to the US as a teenager in 1979, and has lived here ever since. He has neither ever held political office, nor ever gained general professional experience from Iran. Since leaving Iran, he has not had any meaningful relationship with Iranians living inside the country. His approval ratings range from 7% to 12% by his party's own opinion polls. Reza Pahlavi seems genuinely in love with his country, and he is a significant human rights advocate, but he lacks the breadth of knowledge, experience, and support to become the Saban Center's king of Iran. He is simply a guy—a nice guy, I might add—with a bachelor's degree in political science, who most Iranians do not even know if he is making a living in the US other than living off large sums of money that his family smuggled out of Iran in 1979.

It is surprising that the Saban Center would even consider Reza Pahlavi as a candidate for the job, if they were aware of the facts surrounding his qualifications. If they were not aware, it demonstrates a case of Washington's advisors devising foreign policy strategies without proper knowledge.

As if this is not enough to reject Reza Pahlavi's candidacy for the kingdom of Iran, his party's fixation on the Aryan race is disturbing too. Appeal to race began with Reza Shah in 1930s, and the Saltanattalaban—the royalist party—has relied on racial symbols ever since to unite Iranians, although less and less explicitly as time has passed. It must be made clear immediately that the Saltanattalaban is not a racist organization. Quite the contrary, the organization and Reza Pahlavi advocate a foreign policy for Iran that is respectful of all races and nations. Iran has never had a history of racism in the same way as Western Europeans cultivated a racial ideology early in the last century to colonize Africa and Asia. Racial symbols, such as symbol of the Aryan race and Ancient Persian icons, have been used by individual members of the Saltanattalaban more like Americans use American symbols to celebrate America's greatness. But while America refers to a nation, which any race can become a part of through the process of naturalization, the symbols used by Saltanattalaban appeals to race. This is at least an ideological problem, even if the symbols are not used to discriminate other races.

Other groups in exile are even less worthy of being considered, if at all. The leftist party, Tudeh, was a communist party, which was largely destroyed by the Islamic Republic early in 1980s. Traces of the party are scattered all around the world, where Iranians reside, but they hardly constitute anything more than minute social clubs for its nostalgic sympathizers. The Mujahedeen Khalgh has been on the US's list of terrorist organizations for a number of years. They were recently removed from the EU's list of terrorist organizations, yet their journey to the heights of power in Iran seems like an impossible upheaval struggle. The organization alienated the Iranian people by siding with Saddam during the Iran–Iraq War in the 1980s in a hope that Saddam could help them to power, but Saddam did not even get a chance to zip up his pants when the US troops stormed his tiny cellar in December 2003. The Mujahedeen has been foretelling in thirty-one years that the Islamic Republic is only months away from falling, but their predictions have resulted in nothing more than unfulfilled prophecy.

There exists neither a sure dissident group outside Iran, nor inside Iran, which the US can be sure to rely on. The sight of millions of Iranians taking to the streets in June 2009 to protest the alleged rigged reelection of Ahmadinejad and the violent crack-downs of peaceful demonstrators drew international attention and condemnation. The demonstrators believed that Ahmadinejad's rival, Mir-Hossein Mousavi, was the real winner, and sympathetic Westerners quickly threw their lot behind him. Mousavi is a calculated politician, highly educated, and an avid reformist, who has the support of a vast number of Iranian people as well as important figureheads within the Iranian political system. But it is uncertain, if his leadership style is strong enough to pull off the reform process in a country riddled with conservative ideology. Mousavi is more of a quiet man. He served as prime minister of Iran between 1981 and 1988. As prime minister, he eagerly followed Khomeini's politics, and never protested against human rights abuses under his watch. He left the political center stage after his premiership ended and held a low profile for 20 years. In a televised debate with Ahmadinejad days before the June election, Mousavi complained about the damage to Iran's international reputation that had been caused by Ahmadinejad's theatrical behavior in the British Royal Navy incident two years earlier. The incident involved 15 British Royal Navy personnel faring through Persian Gulf and allegedly trespassing into the Iranian waters. The incident occurred during a very hostile atmosphere between Iran and the coalition forces and the Iranian government was keen to show that Iran would not tolerate any assault on its borders. The British crew were arrested by the Iranian coast guards and detained for several days until Ahmadinejad issued a special presidential pardon. Ahmadinejad used the opportunity to stage a high-profile international media circus, where the crews were dressed in suits and he as a clown of the circus with a broad smile on his face would hand them gifts or souvenir before releasing them. The show ridiculed Iran. Iranians around the world watched the event and shook their heads at the absurd behavior of the president of their country. In his election debate with Ahmadinejad, Mousavi criticized the president for his bizarre media stunt, saying that if the British Navy personnel were truly guilty of transgressing into the Iranian waters, they should have been prosecuted and executed, but not used in a circus-like television show. It is doubtful that Mousavi would ever want to execute foreign subjects. The statement was most likely a slip of the tongue. Nonetheless, the words crossed his lips, but they were missed by his sympathetic Western supporters who eagerly desired a regime change in Iran.

The Iranian problem is an evolving story. What solution the future has in store for Iran, we do not know. But, based on what history has taught us, we do know that that solution has a chance of succeeding only if it comes from the Iranians themselves.

APPENDIX TO PART III

An Assessment of the 1953 Coup versus the 1979–1980 Hostage Crisis

In the interest of moving forward, it is important to have an impartial and honest debate about these two incidents. Unfortunately, the incidents are so emotive on both sides that any statement in favor of one side is bound to arouse strong emotions on the other side. Americans were profoundly angered by the hostage crisis. Iranians were angered by the coup. Iranians living abroad were deeply embarrassed or terrified about the repercussions of the hostage-taking for their personal lives. This section attempts to explore the truth of the two regrettable events. If in doing so the reader is made upset, he or she must pause to remember that the objective is not to pass judgment for the judgment's sake but to reach mutual understanding. And this is done with unreserved candor. We make no claim that what is proposed here is necessarily the truth, but it is at least a starting point for further debate.

It is perfectly natural that Americans would recall and be plagued by the memories of the hostage crisis, while ignoring or not even remembering the US involvement in the coup. Every nation would normally view history from its own perspective. There is nothing unusual about this. For this reason many Americans looked down at the Iranian action as barbaric, whereas they ignore the barbarism involved in the CIA's coups, assassinations, and kidnappings around the world. For at least five reasons what the US did to Iran in the 1953 coup was much worse than the hostage crisis:

First, the coup was a bloody event, but the hostage-taking was not. The coup plan involved stirring up a riot in favor and against the government, and then sending in the military to crack down on the riot and seize the opportunity to topple Mossadegh. About 300 people died as the military opened fire. This was a direct casualty of the coup plan.

The US embassy staff and their families were subjected to incredible and unjustifiable anguish, which must not be neglected, but none of them suffered death. The fiasco following the President Carter's rescue plan, where a US helicopter crashed in the Iranian desert killing three members of its crew, was not part of the hostage-taking plan; it was part of Carter's rescue mission. While the death tolls on both sides are, of course deeply disturbing and regrettable, it is important also not to forget that the coup's casualty were about hundred times greater than the casualty following Carter's rescue mission. If bloodshed is an important factor in assessing the severity of two regrettable events, the coup was worse by far than the hostage crisis both in principle and in degree.

Second, the hostage-taking violated the human rights of the American embassy personnel, whereas the coup violated both the human rights of its victims and the principle of the sovereignty of free states. The coup was an act of intervention in the internal affairs of a country which had neither threatened the US nor ever had the power to do so. Kermit Roosevelt attempted first to convince the Shah to dismiss Mossadegh, but the Shah did not have stomach for such action, knowing how popular Mossadegh was. When that plan failed, Roosevelt embarked on his plan B, which was the coup.

Third, the hostage crisis did not alter the American political system. Carter lost the election, but the political system in the US remained intact. The coup was, on the other hand, a major setback for democracy in Iran, as it put the Shah firmly in power for 26 years. The Iranian Revolution in 1979 promised freedom and prosperity, but it turned out worse by far than the Shah's regime. If we were to ask whether the 1953 coup or the 1979 revolution was more detrimental to Iran, the answer is clearly, as has been implied above, the revolution. But in comparing the effect of the coup on the political system in Iran to the effect of the hostage crisis on the political system in the US, the coup was the greater offence. The hostage crisis left Americans with a baggage of strong anti-Iranian emotions, but the coup profoundly altered the Iranian way of life.

The fact that Khomeini was a worse dictator than the US-backed Shah does not mean that putting the Shah in charge as an absolute despot was the right thing to do. A nation's self-harm does not warrant other nations to harm it.

Fourth, the coup was initiated in Washington. It is always much worse when leaders at the very top concoct aggressive and harmful plans than if a group of agitators commit a wrongdoing. The hostage-taking was initiated by a group of radical students, even though Khomeini as the head of the state threw his lot behind it in the end. Khomeini hesitated briefly with his support, but soon decided that he would be on the side of the students and from that moment on the Islamic Republic took ownership of the hostage crisis. By contrast President Eisenhower, who issued the go-ahead for the coup, led a well-established government with a long democratic tradition, but Khomeini's Islamic Republic was still in the experimental stages at the time the hostages were taken. Usually, more is expected of governments that are based on solid foundations than a government which is dealing with post-revolutionary chaos.

Fifth, the coup came first, the hostage crisis second. It is usually the case that the party which delivers a first blow, without proper reason or justification, is more in the wrong or guiltier than the one which hits back in response. The US had left a track record of conspiring policies that suppressed the people of Iran. From the Iranian perspective it was plausible that a second conspiracy could be in the making, and the American Embassy would be a natural base for it. The young and fragile revolutionary government of Iran in 1980 lacked the resources to protect itself. The hostage-taking was their only deterrence against a US advance. Considering the legacy of the Guantanamo Bay detainees without trial, Americans would be very likely to undertake a similar pattern of behavior under extreme national security threats (perhaps not exactly a hostage taking, but something of similar effect). Taking innocent people as hostages for political purposes was regrettable, but the US had set itself up for a strong Iranian reaction. Furthermore, at the time of the hostage-taking, the Iranian students had no way of determining which of the embassy staff were CIA operatives and which ones only innocent diplomats. They had reason to suspect any of the staff as a potential threat to their national security. It became apparent later that the US embassy had no plan of new coup, but even so, as Kenneth Pollack has pointed out, the Carter Administration did indeed send one of its high-ranking generals to Iran to assess the situation and to find out if a coup could possibly be executable just in case. The general had concluded that no such plan could have a chance of succeeding in 1979's Iran. The suspicions of the students who stormed the embassy was heightened when they discovered that the embassy staff had hurriedly destroyed secret documents. The students managed to reconstruct some of the documents by painstakingly taping them back together, but many documents were lost.

On the other hand, Iranians as a nation were in comparison guiltier than Americans in at least one significant respect: Iranian opportunists contributed directly to the execution of the coup, whereas

Americans did not participate in the hostage-taking. The royal court was fully informed about the coup plan, but failed to say no. At first, the Shah rejected the plan, but only because he was scared of a backlash. The royalists and the Iranian military must ultimately bear a great deal of the responsibility for allowing the coup to happen. This fact neither vindicates the US for its involvement in the coup nor alleviates the impact or severity of the coup, but it does highlight the fact that a group of Iranians were guilty too. American commentators sometimes complain that Iranians neglect the role of their own countrymen in this coup. This is not true. Had Iranians neglected the royalist hand in the coup and in other harmful events, the royalists would have been in power today.

A LETTER TO THE IRANIAN LEADERSHIP

The President of Carnegie Corporation, Vartan Gregorian (an Iranian-American), suggested in 2009 that President Obama should send a letter of friendship to Tehran. About the American response to the 1979–1980 hostage crisis he proposed that President Obama should write that "[n]o country, certainly no country in possession of the vast power of the United States, would have failed to act under such circumstances. But we restrained our response, because the powerful have the option not to exercise their power...out of a sense of responsibility."[227]

The draft letter seems to suggest that the US was simply at the liberty to strike Iran if it wanted, but it is doubtful that the US actually did have an option to attack Iran because, firstly, that would have seriously endangered the lives of the American hostages. No use of force could have guaranteed that the hostages would not be killed in the process or that the Iranian students would not harm them in retaliation.

Furthermore, after Carter's rescue mission failed, it looked more and more like the only military option to free hostages would be a full-scale invasion of Iran. The atmosphere in Iran in 1979–1980 was highly revolutionary and nationalistic. About five to ten million people had taken to the streets for one year to oust the shah. The Iranian army was in shambles in 1979, but the revolution had created a huge insurgency force that could resist a US invasion. The hostage crisis occurred only four years after the end of the Vietnam War, and the Carter Administration did not seem to be interested in a new war that would uncomfortably look like that of the Vietnam Conflict—especially considering that Iran had common borders with the Soviet Union at the time. The Soviet Union still appeared strong in 1979, and a US invasion of the Soviet Union's southern neighbor could have involved both of the superpowers in a bloody war.

Finally, the US continued aggressive military interventions—though in smaller scales than that of the Vietnam War—in Latin America throughout 1970s and 1980s. The pattern of the US behavior in this period shows that the US might not have simply restrained itself "out of a sense of responsibility," if it did believe that it could successfully attack Iran and get away with it. In fact, it is not unreasonable to expect that if Washington believed that it could win a war against Iran, it might have welcomed the opportunity as a way of boosting its image after a humiliating withdrawal from Vietnam.

In his proposed letter to the leaders of Tehran for President Obama, Vartan Gregorian attempted to claim moral credit for not attacking Iran under the hostage crisis. But the decision to not attack Iran seems to have been hinged on strategic, not moral, considerations, and furthermore no nation can claim moral credit for the bad things that it did not do, just as no arsonist can claim moral credit for all the fires he did not (yet) set. Why, Iran could claim moral credit for not killing any of the hostages after all. And to be fair, Iran never called for the extradition and punishment of Kermit Roosevelt for his role in the coup, either.

The fact that the US did not attack Iran militarily does not change the equation. Iran was only lucky to escape a US military response, just as the Eisenhower Administration escaped punishment for its coup in Iran.

THE VERDICT

The above presented a comparative assessment of the 1953 coup versus the 1979 hostage crisis. Considering both sides of the argument, the conclusion must clearly be that, although both events were highly unfortunate and devastating for both countries, the coup was comparatively speaking a worse action than the hostage crisis both in degree and principle. Judging by the loss of 300 lives alone, the coup must be condemned far above and beyond the hostage crisis. It was hypocritical of Eisenhower's government that it would topple Mossadegh in the name of freedom, only to install the shah in his place and to put foreign companies in charge of the Iranian oil. For many Americans it comes as a surprise that America comes out looking the worse in this assessment of history; but it is no surprise that the nation with greatest power can do the greatest harm to the weaker nation.

The US provided millions of dollars in financial aid to the Shah after 1953. The Iranian people benefited from this aid, but the bitter memory remained intact. Worst still, the millions of dollars of aid money never translated into any meaningful social transformations in the direction of democracy even when human rights organizations and the Carter Administration pressed the shah years later for democratic reforms. The coup had become possible only because Washington had taken the liberty to play big government and ignored conditions on the ground in Iran. It failed to permanently keep the shah in power, it failed to usher in democracy, and it failed to protect the US interests in the long run. Change coerced from above—via coup or other forms of militaristic actions—would not create a success story for the US or the Iranian people. Kermit Roosevelt was hailed in 1953 at CIA headquarters, but had they known what would happen 26 years later, they might have thought twice.

Just as the coup succeeded as a plot, but failed to produce the intended outcome in the long run, the hostage-taking failed its objectives. It succeeded to cut off the American influence in Iran, but if the purpose was to gain full independence from the US in order to strengthen the country's position in the region, it failed. International sanctions weakened Iran. If it was used to leverage the US extradite the shah and free the Iranian assets, none happened. If it was used to humiliate the world's greatest superpower, Iran itself became the subject of much humiliation and loss of kudos because of that action. But the hostage taking helped Khomeini consolidate his power, just as the coup helped the US consolidate its power in the Middle East. And the immediate costs of these barbaric actions were 300 dead on the Iranian side, and the sufferings of 52 hostages for 444 on the American side—not to mention the crippling sanctions following the hostage crisis and the thousands of individuals who suffered in the shah's prison under the CIA's nose after the coup.

PART IV

THE LESSON FOR FUTURE

9. MILITARIZED DEMOCRACY

The growing international terrorism in the twenty-first century has raised an important question: is democracy the answer in combating the fundamentalist ideologies that inspire terrorism in the Third World, and if democracy is the answer, should the West be actively engaged in democratizing the world? If the answers to both questions are affirmative, how far can or should the West go in its democratization projects? Is the application of military firepower to help press ahead political and cultural change in the world justifiable or even feasible? This book has argued against the idea that military actions and other strongly coercive measures, including crippling sanctions, can transform the world in any meaningful way.

Until the 2003 invasion of Iraq few doubted the power of Western militaries to crush a relatively small group of insurgents with rudimentary weaponry. Things did not turn out as expected and many ask today, if the US military could have acted differently to stifle the insurgency before it got out of hand. In the aftermath of the Iraq invasion few doubts that it is not the sophistication of armaments that counts in militia warfare. To crush the insurgency—it is commonly acknowledged by now—the strategy needs to counter the determination of the enemy and its access to a steady flow of new recruits. But is this undertaking even feasible for US military as an invading force? The evidence on the ground suggests a negative response.

The US and Britain attacked Iraq preemptively on the suspicion that Saddam Hussein was engaged in developing weapons of mass destruction. The war occurred without UN mandate and before weapon inspectors had finished their job in investigating Saddam's alleged WMD program. Britain published a dossier during the run up to the war declaring Saddam as capable of launching missiles to Europe within 45 minutes. The integrity of this dossier was soon brought to question and it became clear that the British government had "sexed up" the dossier to build a case for war. As the UN's chief weapon inspector, Hans Blix, pleaded for more time, the Bush/Blair coalition rather started the war hastily. Many speculated that the allegation of WMD was used as a pretext for invading Iraq, and that the real motives behind the war were something else. If Blix could prove that Saddam neither had WMD nor was engaged in developing WMD, the reason for invading Iraq would have been effectively eliminated. As it turned out, no smoking gun was found after the invasion and both leaders in Washington and London had to tolerate stern criticism.

The US forces have sought to engage in "nation building." The stated aim has been to establish democracy as a counterweight to insurgency. The coalition armies revamped their combat tactics to bring down civilian casualties to a minimum. But the conflict grew inward, giving rise to factional infighting and steadfastly high civilian deaths on the account of it. This was not so much the coalition troops killing Iraqis or Afghanis, but Iraqi and Afghani rebels killing one another. The Operation Iraqi Freedom had dedicated troops to move in quickly from north to gain control over the strategic oil reserves in the Kurdish territory of Iraq, but the Bush administration had gravely underestimated the smoldering factional frictions in the Iraqi society. Saddam's Baath party was rooted in the Sunni Muslim community, which constituted a minority group that ruled over the Iraqi Shia majority and the Kurds. As soon as the US military created a space for groups' rights, tribal skirmishes broke out and got completely out of hand. The Bush administration had not understood the power of internal dynamics. The war had been designed and employed so hastily that no time had been devoted to assessing the internal social and cultural mechanisms in Iraq first. The Bush administration was eager to see Saddam's fall. Saddam's fall threw the country into a state of anarchy while Washington had crafted no plans for restoring order. By the time the Bush/Blair coalition realized their mistake, the dynamics for violence had overtaken the dynamics for social order.

To "win the hearts and minds" of the local population, the coalition forces have attempted to picture themselves as protectors of the Iraqi and the Afghani people. So far the strategy has yielded in disappointing results. Writing in the second half of 2010, the insurgency has incontrovertibly proven a remarkable capability to renew itself. The coalition forces have had multiple strong local showings, only to see other areas under their command slip back into chaos. As soon as the attention was turned into these new areas of conflict, the insurgents regained strongholds in the old ones. Chasing the insurgency has caused the coalition troops to oscillate their attention constantly in the region. In Afghanistan the troubles quickly disseminated over the border to its neighboring Pakistan. A haven for insurgents was founded in northern Pakistan, which soon became frequent target for the US drones. Soon, Sudan was suspected as the next haven and the next possible target for the West's policymakers to engage in a cat-and-mouse-chase. Piles of cash have been handed over to local warlords in exchange for peace. A great portion of the cash has found its way to the deep pockets of insurgents and arm-dealers. As it is typical for any major strife in the world, while the coalition troops and local civilians have been paying a hefty price, many local warlords and some US contractors have earned fat pay checks. The conflict has taken a huge toll on the US military and has also radicalized thousands of youths across Near-Asia and the Arab world—and all of this under the banner of democratization in a volatile region.

Iraq has after seven long years arrived at relative stability. The International Monetary Fund gave recently the go-ahead for a $741 loan to Iraq, praising the country for creating a relative stable environment for economic development.[228]

But the political situation is still capricious. A chance of relapse to the old ways remains strong. No one party won sufficient majority in the March 7th parliamentary election to form a straight government. Negotiations for establishing a coalition government dragged on for eight months at a time when the Iraqi national security dreadfully depended upon a stable political system. To start with, it took nearly three months just to ratify the election on the account of allegations of widespread rigging. The secular Iraqiya headed by former Prime Minister Iyad Allawi came on the top and the National Alliance headed by the incumbent Prime Minister Nouri Maliki and the Shia Cleric's Moqtada Sadr came to second place. Neither parties had enough votes to form a government on its own, nor would them step aside and let the other party form one. A form of agreement reached jus recently after a long battle for power. Yet, as per today, an orderly agreement seems unlikely for some time. Even if Iraq does solidify as a strong democracy in the end, it is dubious whether it was worth the high price the country has paid. The indication that the coalition forces would possibly never again repeat such a war and that the Bush Administration would probably have never gone to war in the first place had it known what difficulties lay ahead, as well as no other developing country in the region voluntarily chose such devastation, should imply that the costs surpassed the prospects of reaping even the sweetest benefits of a potentially blossoming democracy in some distant future. If democracy is supposed to put people's will at its base, the thousands of Iraqis who paid with their lives never got a vote—let alone the survivors who were never asked if they did want the war as a pathway to democracy.

Afghanistan has lived amidst war since 2001 (and a long civil war in the previous century), but is not even close to where Iraq stands today. To sum up the democratic gains for Afghanistan after nine years, it suffices to recall the speech of Hamid Karzai in September 2010—who by the way won a new term in office as the country's president in an allegedly rigged election—in which he had to fight back tears when pleading for an end to growing violence. He expressed anxiety that "our sons might leave this country."

Overall, the West's military effort in the region has been a debacle, given its original objectives of replacing Taliban in Afghanistan and Saddam Hussein in Iraq with advanced democratic models free of turmoil. The advances made have resembled nothing but turmoil. The so-called "war on terror" has bounced back repeatedly to daunt and terrorize the very people that try to put an end to it. The war escalated the atrocities of a limited terrorist group in Afghanistan, the Al Qaeda, to become a worldwide terror network. In a recent interview broadcast by Charlie Rose on PBS the former British Prime Minister and the staunchest European ally of Bush's war on terror, Tony Blair, complained that the problem was not the Islamist extremists only, but the general notion upheld by many moderate Muslims too that the West is at war with Islam. He called on moderate Muslims to declare this notion "nonsense." Tony Blair is correct in his assessment that this interpretation of the war in the Muslim community has created a vibrant breeding ground for Islamist extremism, but he fails to acknowledge his own role in making the war inadvertently a war between the West and Islam. To overcome intense domestic opposition both in Britain and the US, the Bush-Blair coalition carelessly sold the war as a war to protect the "Western values," "our way of life," or the "civilized world." What message does it send to the Muslims, if they are not Westerners, do not live the Western way of life, or are not considered a part of the civilized world? President Bush famously proclaimed that "you are either with us or against us." By ranking the entire world in terms of "us" and "them," the conflict was elevated to a world war. By rendering it a crusade for preserving the West and Western values rather than a limited military operation to take out a terrorist cell, the war was blown up out of proportion and polarized the world into two camps: the West and the Islamic world. Right after 9/11 and before the war on terror gained momentum President Bush reached out to the Muslim community to reassure them that the war was not against Islam. This was an honorable move on the part of the president, but the message fainted piecemeal as the war spread through only Muslim countries: Afghanistan, Iraq, Pakistan, Yemen, nearly Iran and Syria, and so on.

Much has already been written on this conflict and on what, why, and how things went wrong. The purpose of this book was not to become yet another book on this subject. The book studied instead the historical roots of some successful social and cultural transformations over the past two centuries with the view to understand the internal pressure points, internal mobilization, and internal leadership that brought about the desired transformations. It focused on people power rather than on international military operations to democratize and to change the dynamics of a society. If history is to teach a lesson, it should be that for a social transformation to succeed it must be initiated by forces within its system and it must run its internal course to its fullest extent. External pressure and encouragement can sometimes give direction or act as catalyst, but based on the historical evidence they cannot and should not attempt to cut short the process.

THE LESSON FROM ANOTHER WASTED EFFORT

Vietnam is not a perfect society today, but is what the US wanted it to be in 1960s and 1970s: a country that at least economically is moving towards liberalization. In 1986, the country commenced a comprehensive economic reform program, code-named *Doi Moi*. Market orientation and private ownership was encouraged, resulting soon in a booming export-driven economy. Vietnam has been on the path of a remarkable recovery from the inefficiency and corruption of its communist era, and is steadily emerging as a modern liberal economy. The country saw an average annual growth in GDP of about 7 to 8% through 1990s and the early part of this millennium, making it on average the second fastest growing economy in the world after China. In 2007, Vietnam joined World Trade Organization, which reinvigorated its export sector further. The recent years' global economic meltdown has hit the country's export, but government subsidized lending programs and stimulus spending has helped stabilize the economy. Poverty has declined substantially. The percentage of people living on less than $1 a day has fallen below that of China and India. The share of agriculture as a percentage of the overall economy has gone down from 25% in 2000 to 21% in 2009, signifying the contribution of other segments of the economy.[229]

This has all been a promising development, even though the political power remains centralized. It is important to remember that this transformation began from within the system. Reforms were not instigated from outside. An internal leadership for change emerged inside the Socialist republic on the back of dissatisfaction with the status of the economy under the communist model. Internal initiatives were taken to revive commerce. Even though the country officially remains a socialist state, Vietnam today represents no specific threat to the international community. If anything, the country is today an integrated part and a contributor to global trade and prosperity. But the situation looked very different half a century ago. In 1960s, the US military waged a bloody war against the communist revolutionaries in North Vietnam that lasted for about a decade. As with the war on terror, the Vietnam War became a major blow to US forces and a devastating war for Vietnam. The Vietnamese rebels fiercely resisted the US army. By 1968, a total of 550,000 US troops were drawn heavily into the conflict; bogged down in unwinnable guerrilla warfare. The cost of the war had escalated to over $100 billion annually. The images of large-scale destruction and bloodshed on national TV aroused the opposition to the war, which finally led to US withdrawal and a quick communist takeover of all of Vietnam.[230]

More than three decades of communism proved detrimental to the country's economy. The Vietnamese leaders observed and learned from free market economies in the West that the way to achieve economic growth and combat poverty is to free the hands of the market. The success of the

US economy set a clear example for how efficient free market economy is in bringing about prosperity. The American economy became a role model for the rest of the world. In the end, America won the war, not militarily, but by example.

With the benefit of hindsight, one cannot help but wonder how pointless the Vietnam War was. More than thirty years after the end of that conflict, it is clear that a decade of war had produced nothing but substantial desolation and many deaths on both sides, only to witness Vietnam falling into communist hands. A question remains, given that Vietnam is finally opening up its market to the rest of the world on its own terms: what would have happened had we rather waited in 1960s and 1970s than to go to war? The answer is likely to be that Vietnam would have followed the same path, and perhaps even faster. Good relations with the West rather than a devastating war might have speeded up its development sooner. Could we not rather wait for this to happen? The rationale behind Vietnam War was that if communist expansion were not prevented in one country, it could snowball out of control in the rest of the world. The theory was coined "domino-effect," meaning that one communist victory anywhere in the world was a set-back for the "free world" in that it could encourage similar attempts elsewhere. It was therefore, as it was contemplated at the time, vital not to render any vestige to communist expansion. But Vietnam did fall in communist hands, and nothing happened to the free world other than what the free world did to itself. Considering the communist scare of the time, this fear was felt vividly, much in the same way as the fear for Iraqi weapons of mass destruction in post 9/11 era. The same fear was prevalent when dealing with Fidel Castro's Cuba. The CIA contemplated a whole range of attacks on communist Cuba, including the assassination of Castro, but to no avail. Today, however, Cuba is slowly evolving to the West's liking. Again, could we not just wait? Why try to change the world by the bullet, when we can change it by soft power? Why resorting to violence, when we can lead by example?

The fear proved unwarranted in all above cases. The communist triumph in Vietnam or Cuba did not lead to a worldwide communist takeover or the defeat of the "free world," Iraqi WMD proved to be the fantasy of a sort, and Taliban remains as strong as ever and even negotiating its terms with Karzai's government. The irony with the Iraq War is that Saddam Hussein was toppled at the age of 70, and executed at 73. The average life expectancy for male Iraqis is barely 70 years. Had he not been ousted, he would have died a natural death soon anyway. He might have nominated one of his sons or a close aide to continue a dictatorial line of politics even after his death, but as mentioned above, there is no guarantee that Iraq will not retreat into a totalitarian state ten years from now just the same. Judging by the country's acute political gridlock, the direction of Iraqi politics could take any number of turns over the next few years. On the other hand, if Saddam had not been overthrown, his successor might still have liberalized the Iraqi politics. Saddam himself did not want to lose face, but his successor might have changed course and initiated better relationship with the West. History shows ample examples of authoritarian rulers, whose successors abandoned stringent dictatorship in favor of allowing at least some space for dissent and political representation. Iran became gradually a more open society after the death of the revolution's father, though never fully democratic—at least not yet. The same trend seems to be happening in Cuba after Raul Castro took over the control of the state, even if the pace of change is gallingly slow. No meaningful liberalization occurred in the immediate aftermath of Stalin's death, but his successors were less wicked in handling dissent. Real change, however, began in full gear some decades later under Mikhail Gorbachev. There are speculations that the son of North Korea's Eternal President, Kim Jong-il, might follow a liberalization line in the country after his father's demise, but it remains to be seen. The same pattern of smoothening stepwise the grip on power has been prevalent in various shapes and degrees in China after Mao Zedong, Chile after Augusto Pinochet, Spain after Francisco Franco, and other countries. Not all of these countries have become democratic, but they have allowed in varying degrees greater space for political and economic participation. Whether this might have occurred in Iraq too had Saddam's Baath regime not been ousted but replaced by a successor after Saddam's natural death is a matter for pure speculation, but the point is that it is not certain that wars will produce any good, while what is certain is that wars will cost dearly in dollars and human lives. They are costly projects for shortening the terms of dictators by a few years. It feels quite surreal to think that Saddam might not have been here today, even if we had not gone to war against him. But the memory and impacts of the war will be with us for a long time.

The CIA orchestrated coup d'état in Iran in 1953 is another interesting example of a counterproductive intervention. Given the full impact of this action, it was never worth it. Of course, we did not know all the risks in-volved at the time, but the problem is that we do not seem to learn the les-son from it even today. We continue to do more of what does not work. Other than the US engagement in World War II and a few occasional mili-tary actions against ethnic rinsing in Africa or Eastern Europe, none of the recent military operations made great stories. So why cannot we wait? The cost and benefit analyses of past wars have unduly overestimated the short-term benefits while ignoring the resultant backlash over the long run.[231] If the pattern of interventions is such that they frequently fail to hit intended targets, if our fears prove frequently to be unwarranted, if we often learn that we would have been better off acting differently, should we not stop and reassess the calculus of risk?

Absence of proper information married with a misguided sense of pa-triotism accounts for much of the misunderstandings among nations and much of the background that creates support for wars. Military operations are often framed as a necessity to bring freedom to suppressed people. Free-dom is a noble cause. But many of those who perish in combat are individu-als who have fulfilling lives worth living, even if they do not have all the freedoms we enjoy in the West.

The gains in terms of the freedom of expression in Iraq after the 2003 War has been greatly overestimated. Freedom of expression is crucially important for the country's social and cultural development, but as Iraq remains politically stagnant, the benefit of the newly won freedom of ex-pression remains slim for the general public. The fact that Iraqis have today greater freedom to speak out their minds is, of course, valuable in itself, even if the exchange of ideas does not produce meaningful social improvements. But there is usually only a small minority who would benefit directly from the ability to exercise free expression. Even in America, only about 5% of the population can be considered politically active and only up to 2% of the populace is party politicians, labor union executives, senior civil servants, professional political commentators, and public intellectuals. These groups speak out in public, write, and frequently exercise their freedom of expres-sion.[232] For the vast majority of Americans, the freedom of expression is but an untapped reservoir of opportunity. Furthermore, freedom of expression has little value even for some Americans who avidly exercise their right, but whose opinion is largely ignored by mainstream media because their views may deviate radically from the governing social paradigm. The percentage of Iraqis who may directly benefit from the opportunity to speak out their minds may be a little more or a little less than the relevant percentage for Americans, but there is no doubt that freedom of expression benefits only a very limited segment of the Iraqi society. Most Iraqis, just like most Americans, are just interested in living their daily lives, caring for their families, living in peace, and staying alive. It made no sense that so many Iraqis died, so that a few could be able to speak out their minds. We are not suggesting that the freedom of expression is not important, but that the sacrifices made in Iraq were not worth it. After all, saving lives is more important than protecting the right to speak out, as in death there is no freedom. Similar arguments can be made for the status of women in Iraq. Both freedom of expression and the status of women are often used as pretext for military operations or for continued military presence in Third World regions, even though the operations are destabilizing the peace in the region. I remain confident that if the Iraqi women had been asked in 2003, most of them would have chosen peace and the safety of their children before the prospect of having a high-paying job, if that prospect was even possible.

As this book is coming to conclusion, it appears as if a lesson might finally have been learned and America would never again risk its might in a war, such as that in Afghanistan or Iraq. One might ask, if there is a need for this book, if the wisdom has already sunk in. But right after the end of Vietnam War in 1975, many people ardently believed that the lesson was learned back then. Unfortunately, history repeated itself—and this, we cannot let happen again.

10. Afterword — Making a Generation of Peace

It is no coincidence that the words peace and prosperity are often conjoined. No future is going to be better than today, as long as death and destruction lurk on the horizon. For tomorrow to become a better day, peace must indubitably be a part of it. Yet we stubbornly dwell in a mentality of war. We hope that the evolution of human civilization will take humanity to a level free from violence and warfare one day, but we maintain that that day is a distant future.

War is an extension of the human being's natural inclination to exert aggression. But a distinct feature of being a human is its ability to surpass biological constraints in order to advance the civilization.

A creative justification for war is made in the language of self-defense. While there may be legitimate cases in which war can be justified as the only way of defending oneself, there has rarely been an aggressor who has not defined his war in terms of self-preservation. Usually parties on both sides define the aggression as a measure of self-defense. The Roman Empire grew large on the concept of protecting their interests. It invaded territories near its borders to create a buffer zone through which potential enemies could not penetrate. To secure its buffer zones it needed to invade more territories even further out, and so ad infinitum. Other European empires used the same concept to spread their influence worldwide.

Wars are also defined in terms of last-resort. Politicians are too quick to say that war is a necessity only when all other options have been exhausted. In reality, they see war not always as the last option, but as the fastest way to arrive at their objectives. Between 2003 and 2007, the Bush Administration elevated the threat of war against Iran to an imminent level. The Administration stopped short of launching the war at the very last minute in the face of virulent domestic and international opposition and a strong indication that Iran might be mad enough to retaliate. Suddenly the estimated cost of a war on Iran seemed higher than the potential benefits, and the Administration backed down. If a war on Iran was the last resort in dealing with that country, the Administration would have had no other choice, regardless of costs. Last resort means that it has to be done; that no other course of action is possible; that war is a necessity from which the Administration cannot walk away; that not doing it will be a disaster. But the fact that the Administration did back down shows that someone must have initially viewed the war plan as a cost-effective way of dealing with Iran. There were plenty of other options, however.

The most creative justification for war draws from the notion of preemption. If an attack from the enemy is looming, the argument goes, a nation state has a right to respond to that threat preemptively. Avid hawks have masterfully expanded the concept to not only include imminent threats, but also an enemy's capability to attack. With this extension every neighbor can legitimately terminate the existence of another because every neighbor is a potential threat by his or her capacity to kill.

An overly broad definition of self-defense is disturbing because it allows even despots to justify their brutal hands over their people as a measure of self-defense. Consider a country prone to utter chaos, say Iraq between 2003 and 2007, where there is a war of all against all. If the right to self-defense is granted as blank check, would a dictator worse than Saddam not be right in suppressing his people preemptively to safeguard his own existence?

War corrupts the civilization both for those who pay with their blood, and those who brandish the flag of victory in ecstasy. Because it is hard to kill one's brethren, one has to hate him; to demonize him; to fear him; to believe that the world is an awfully dangerous place; one has to feel insecure; one has to ravage one's heart; one has to destroy one's person before one can destroy another person.

The Nobel Committee in Oslo awarded the Peace Prize to Gorbachev in 1990. When a year later the Soviet troops attacked the Vilnius TV Tower in Lithuania killing 15 civilians in an attempt to prevent a Lithuanian secession from the Union, the Norwegian people felt an extraordinary responsibility to protest against Gorbachev's action. The Norwegian public sidelined the Nobel Committee and organized a second special Peace Prize to hand over to the Lithuania's president, Vytautas Landsbergis, on the first anniversary of the Baltic Declaration of Independence. The Middle East has generated such anti-Muslim sentiments in the West and we have become so numb to civilian casualties in Iraq and Afghanistan as a result of incessant violence in that region that no reports of protests hit the news headlines anymore. Civilian casualties are always expected in wars as part of collateral damage, but that we can be completely at ease with it and not feel any discomfort any more represents a loss of human empathy in all of us. Collateral damage is accepted because war is seen as an extraordinary event that requires extraordinary measures. But if the war is too frequent and too widespread, civilian deaths are no longer so extraordinary.

A CHANCE FOR A LASTING PEACE

In exact opposition to the mainstream view that wars are inevitable part of human culture, the mankind is never more than only one single generation away from a culture in which peace is nourished and war is not recognized as a solution. Up until the nineteenth century it was believed that slavery was an inevitable fact of life. They believed that the nature had selected some races as slaves and others as their masters, and that the institution of slavery would always continue to exist. During the period leading up to the Civil War, many in the Democratic Party argued that focusing on the state of the economy was more important than worrying about the abolitionist movement. Fifty years after the emancipation of slaves, slavery was seen entirely as the thing of the past. It became impossible for the new generation to even fantasize about holding slaves, even though racial prejudice persisted long thereafter. The abolition of slavery was a cultural transformation without a reverse gear.

Women were subjugated up until a few decades ago. They were excluded from social life and politically represented only through their fathers or husbands. Women were enfranchised first in 1919, but remained as second-class citizens well into the second half of twentieth century. But things changed for women eventually and they began competing against men in every arena. Fifty years on, it seems impossible to even contemplate restoring a gender division like that practiced by the previous generation. There is no turning back for gender relations.

Europe was torn apart during the World War I, World War II, and during its entire history before the world wars, but 60 years on it seems virtually impossible with any stretch of imagination that the daughters and sons of the old French, British, and German empires would ever again break loose on each other. Europe has irreversibly moved forward.

Today, individuals still kill each other, but the cowboy-style duels seen in Western movies, where peers stand back and watch two contesters shoot one another to death on a count of ten, is no longer part of the Texan culture. Texas is not looking back.

The occasional relapse to the old ways, such as a recent incident involving Brazilian males being forced into sex-slavery in Portugal or the wartime infringements of civil liberties in the US and Europe, have had no lasting effects. It appears that on the whole, once the culture is changed in a fundamental way and there has been general consensus about that change, it only takes one generation to put it beyond reversal. As a rule of thumb, once a generation is used to a new way of life, there is no turning back.

This thesis is highly speculative, I admit. But there are times in history, when only thinking high can move the humanity forward. When the forefathers of this nation proclaimed that all men were equal and that every man had a right to vote, they had no rigorous scientific undertaking to verify these statements. They simply decided to believe in them and they changed history. The notions that all men were equal and that every man had a right to vote were ideological concepts, not a scientific ones. They were two of the least justified concepts at the time, but turned out to be two of the most valuable contributions to the modern civilization. We must likewise believe that we can for ever put the culture of war behind us, or peace shall never come to us. Yet, we swallow the idea that war is an inevitable feature of civilization, not recognizing that what makes war so inevitable is precisely that attitude; just as what made women and blacks second-class citizens was precisely the belief that they were second-class citizens by nature.

The process of making everlasting peace must start from somewhere, and there is no better place to start it from than here in the West. Peace is in the hands of the powerful, not the weak nations, and it is the powerful that must make the first move.

History shows that violence breeds more violence, and ironically greater support for war to curtail violence. A different approach must be invented to ensure peaceful coexistence despite conflicting interests.

The United Nations Educational, Scientific and Cultural Organization (UNESCO) defines the culture of peace as "a set of values, attitudes, modes of behaviour and ways of life that reject violence and prevent conflicts by tackling their root causes to solve problems through dialogue and negotiation...."[233]

To create an environment where peace can flourish, a new culture is required, and a major change of attitude. Many hatchets must be buried, and this chapter pretends by no means to know all the secrets as to how this might be accomplished. Here are only a few suggestions. Neither individually nor collectively will these proposals be sufficient in generating a peace culture, but they are important steps along the way.

First, calculate the real cost of war

Corporate profit is calculated as the difference between gross revenue and the cost of production. Previously, production costs included only the price of raw materials, labor, and overheads costs. Until a couple of decades ago the cost to environment was not included in the equation. The damage to environment was ignored. As a result, manufacturers could show higher profit than they would have had they deducted the cost of cleaning the environment from their profits. It would take decades for politicians and economists to acknowledge that the overall value creation was less when taking into account environmental spoilage, such as the emission of CO_2 into the atmosphere or toxic materials into rivers. Economists began to devise methods to attach a monetary value to environmental damage. Companies would be required to bear the costs to the environment. By incorporating the costs to the environment in the calculus of production, the society could more accurately calculate the value created. It became apparent that the society would be better off in monetary terms, if it produced a little less but maintained a cleaner environment.

The same pattern of calculating corporate profit as was commonplace until a few decades ago is practiced today in assessing the benefits of civilization. The wars that advanced the civilization also left behind much devastation. The civilization is evaluated from the perspective of the survivors, who are not bound by the interests of the victims. The old-fashioned profit calculation did not concern with the environmental cost because that cost was a burden for the future generations who had no choice but to face years of neglected damage to their environment. The cost incurred by the victims of a civilization is a cost not carried by those who benefit from that civilization. A new foundation for the cost-benefit analysis of civilization must take into equation the frustrated dreams of all those who never shared the fruit of civilization. This is not to say that civilization is never worth the sacrifices. Sometimes it is. But it merely means that the push for civilization should not only seek to maximize the gain for those lucky to win the jackpot, but also minimize the pain inflicted upon those people who lose in the process.

Norway never initiated any war or armed conflict anywhere in the world after the Viking incursions. Other than a more or less symbolic participation in NATO coalition forces in conflict regions, such as Iraq and Afghanistan, where the country has maintained for the most part a small peacekeeping force, Norwegians only put up armed resistance against the Nazi occupation during World War II. The resistance amounted to military units committing sabotage operations on Nazi-held infrastructure inside Norway. This was a war initiated by the German Nazi, not Norway. Until oil reserves were found in 1970s, Norway remained a poor and insignificant stretch of land in the northernmost hemisphere. The country was considered rudimentary and backward. On the other hand, the aggressive European empires wore the mantle of civilization for several centuries. There is no doubt that the contribution of the European empires to civilization was considerable. But by changing the cost-benefit calculus of war and civilizations, peacefulness becomes the mark of civilization. Hence, peaceful countries like Norway will be put atop the list of civilizations and other nations will be listed further down in proportion to how much violence they have produced in the making of their civilizations.

Second, Increase tolerance for other cultures.

Being at peace with other cultures means tolerating customs and behavior one does not necessarily like. Tolerance extends as far as accepting something that one considers bad, if efforts to eliminate it will do more harm than good. For instance, Americans heard that the status of Iraqi citizens under Saddam's regime was appalling. In many ways he was brutal and dictatorial, and he is blamed for slaughtering and suppressing whole groups of his people. The ouster of Saddam in 2003 was seen as a major positive achievement, in isolation, but the resulting chaos killed many more Iraqis than Saddam could have ever managed to kill, the nation's infrastructure was destroyed, and the society was torn apart. And that is just counting the cost to Iraq.

Third, do not reward war.

A culture of peace will remain out of reach as long as war is linked to glory. Alexander the Great soared to the heights of international fame already as a young man because he built a mighty army that defeated the Persian king. The price tag was widespread bloodshed, but that seemed a price worth paying for becoming the greatest warrior the world had seen. The Persian kings themselves had gained their reputation through warfare. The daring Mongol warrior, Genghis Khan the Great stormed through Asia, from China to the Mediterranean, crushing whole villages as he went by. What brought glory to the Romans and other imperialist powers was their military might, in other words, their ability to, and tendency to, kill masses of people in cold blood. So far, warfare has been the method by which nations have asserted their superiority and historians have largely focused on glorifying the killers.

It is no wonder that a culture where peace is cultivated does not appear imminent at the present time. In America, for instance, presidents are hardly noticed unless their names have been attached to some form of war or military operations. Without violence, they disappear into obscurity.

The biggest names in history are almost always associated with violence. Some wars look to have been inevitable, but as long as leaders make their names with war and war is glorified, the chances of cultivating a culture of peace are slim. It takes decades of painstaking research to become an Einstein, decades or even centuries of vigorous philosophical debates to build the semblance of Athenian grandeur, a lifetime of struggling with wit and discipline to be known as a Gandhi; but it takes only a few Air Force bombers for a national leader to make his name.

The hawks do not even show guts to attack a mighty rival. They look only for easy scores. After the failure in Vietnam, they targeted small islands and countries like Iraq or Afghanistan with a population a tenth of that of the US. There is nothing glorious about trying to show off military power by attacking small and helpless nations. It is cowardly.

The former British Prime Minister, Tony Blair, won the Liberty Medal 2010, which is awarded annually by National Constitution Center in Philadelphia. Blair was a highly able, intelligent, and likable Prime Minister with a track record of many impressive accomplishments. He redefined the Labor Party under the slogan of New Labor. New Labor became more progressive, focusing on efficiency and economic development. Under Blair's premiership the British economy grew strong. He is credited with reforming the trembling national health system, modernizing the education system, and promoting the country's financial and banking sector. His government strengthened democracy through a host of legislations. The Human Rights and Freedom of Information Acts were passed under his watch. Blair helped devise the Scottish Parliament and regional assemblies in both Ireland and Wales. One of Blair's most admirable contributions to peace and democracy was his successful campaign for peace in Northern Ireland. Any fair assessment of Blair's premiership must take into account these accomplishments, but he also surpassed both his constituency and the UN mandate to take his country to a war on questionable grounds, at a cost of over 150 British lives and hundreds more in injury, not to mention irreparable damage to the integrity of the office. The danger with awarding prizes to people like Blair is the signal it sends out, that world leaders are above the rule of law and that they will be rewarded for the good they produce and simply pardoned for grave mistakes.

Today, Blair travels the world with his head held high as a global celebrity, and every prize is a slap in the face of his victims. He makes millions of dollars every year giving speeches. If humanity is ever to elevate itself above a war mentality and cultivate a peace culture, warfare must not be allowed to become a source of reward and personal approbation.

Fourth, Take a global moral perspective instead of patriotism.

Most wars are fought in the name of patriotism, but what does patriotism really mean? Most often, it seems to mean to fight for one's national interests, even at the cost of unfairly suppressing the national interests of other nations; but that is not patriotism. It is chauvinism. Chauvinism breaks one of the most basic moral principles, that is, "Do not treat others in ways you would not like to be treated." A concept that goes against universal moral norms cannot be valid. If patriotism means to defend one's national interests fairly, while taking into consideration the fair interests of others, then the moral concept will do the job more accurately and the concept of patriotism is redundant.

Patriotism is an invention, not a moral norm. It is a useful tool for the military at times of war, when commanders need to be able to rely 100% on troop loyalty. On the battlefield, there is no time for discussion, no time for pondering moral considerations. When an order is issued to fire at the enemy, the soldier is expected to obey immediately, without question. In this case being "patriotic" means following orders; but that is not patriotism. It is obedience. Obedience is a necessary precondition for the army's success in battlefield, and it will remain a part of the army's culture. But the whole nation cannot be the army, and everywhere cannot be a battlefield. As a nation we have a duty to ponder over right and wrong; to assess pros and cons; and to do only what we feel it can be justified for all parties involved, even for the enemies sometimes.

In an increasingly globalized world, justice and fairness should supersede old conceptions of patriotism. Moral people will stay on the side of virtue whichever side of a border it may be. The old tribal culture was based on patriotism, meaning tribe loyalty. If your brethren had a fight with a member of your rival tribe, you were required to join in the mob and attack any member of the other tribe in retribution, no matter which side was guilty. Modern civilizations have supplanted tribal loyalty with national loyalty. Increasingly, there are efforts to have conflicts judged on a fair basis and resolved through a system of justice rather than by mob reaction. In a world with a growing percentage of educated citizens, unless they are misinformed and misled by the leaders of popular opinion, people follow their moral judgments and instincts rather than blind patriotism. In such a case, being loyal to one's country means precisely to stand up and protest when the country is moving on the wrong path.

Blind patriotism is extremely dangerous for world peace. It forces us to tolerate excessive maltreatment of perceived enemies under the guise of loyalty to our fellow citizens. It also hampers free speech and rational debate, as chauvinists attempt to quell opposition or even questioning, labeling all who hesitate *unpatriotic*. Unchecked "patriotism" is a big hurdle for promoting a culture of peace.

One version of blind "patriotism" has been used in Iran since the inception of the Islamic Republic to protect the regime. Since the Islamic Republic ascribes its success to religion rather than nationalism, the regime's propaganda machine labels those who disagree as "anti-revolutionary" and "the enemy of God." The labels are often used to destroy the opposition. In America, blind "patriotism" is falsely connected with love for one's country. "Love it or leave it," they used to say, as if those who wish to see their country as virtuous were traitors. Chauvinists would rather see America rush down a suicidal path in an unwinnable war than question whether military engagements are valid.

Fifth, Talk with and listen to the "enemy."

Many of the problems in the world derive from one-sided thinking, whether through the lens of prejudices or of a perception of one's own good without regard for the good of others. We have not listened enough to one another. The West pursues its agenda without stopping to talk. The developing countries are fenced in and whatever they say, no one listens. Is it any wonder the anger bursts into violence? If one nation's military outweighs the other's by a factor of 100, is it any wonder the populace resorts to desperate acts? Various currents within Iran and America have cautiously attempted to establish diplomatic channels for talks, but rivalry over resources and strategic positions drown out quiet calls for compromise. Yet one of the costs of not talking is an increase in fear and mistrust, and as fear and mistrust grow, the outcome is often war.

Sixth, Quit language games, propaganda, and political hooliganism.

In an interview at the UN National Assembly in 2010 in New York, the Iranian president Mahmoud Ahmadinejad implied that Washington is hypocritical. He rhetorically asked why Washington interferes in affairs of other nations while ignoring many of its domestic problems. This is an interesting question to ask Ahmadinejad himself. Iran suffers tremendous domestic problems. Poverty is rampant. Unemployment is by public estimates more than twice as that of the United States. The shortage of refined petroleum and electricity in parts of Iran has crippled the economic cycle. Iran also has an acute lack of spare parts as well as high-tech gadgets, in particular for its industrial sector. International sanctions account for many of the shortages in Iran, but the Islamic Republic had ample opportunities in the past to fix its economy but did not do it. Economic and social impediments have created a general despair among the Iranian populace while Ahmadinejad seems to be more concerned about the injustices of the world outside Iran. He speaks frequently in religious terms about the suffering of the poor in the world, but not in Iran. Ahmadinejad is certainly right to claim that Washington should clean its own house before focusing on problems elsewhere, but so must Ahmadinejad too—by his own logic. Ahmadinejad also complained about the overcrowded prisons in the United States. The US does in fact have the largest prison population in the world, both in absolute numbers and as a proportion of the population. On the other hand, Iran keeps the prison population low in part by summarily executing many of would-be prisoners. For example, an explosive device blasted recently in the southeastern province of Iran near the Pakistani border, killing a number of senior clerics and military officials who had assembled in a mosque. The Jundallah, a terrorist and Sunni minority organization with alleged link to Pakistani Islamists, were identified as the perpetrators. Within forty-eight hours of the explosion, two Jundallah members were arrested, prosecuted for terrorism, and executed. This level of efficiency in tackling terrorism is not designed in order to keep the prison population low: Iran is sandwiched between two conflict zones where terrorism is rampant—Iraq to the West and Afghanistan and Pakistan to the East of the country—and the Iranian authorities are anxious to prevent violence spreading through Iran at any cost. Nevertheless, large scale and speedy executions of political dissents, drug addicts, homosexuals, and others convicted of serious crimes or of endangering Islam and Iran's national security helps keep prison population relatively low compared to that of the United States. Of course, the interviewer in New York never confronted Ahmadinejad with these questions. Ahmadinejad is in the business of demonizing Washington, just as the reverse is true.

Washington is an avid player of the language game. War looks ugly on the ground and on the TV screens. With an increasingly politicized constituency, Western governments resort to propaganda and language games to dehumanize the people on the other side and turn the public opinion against the "enemies." A clearly recognizable divide needs to be established between "us," on the right side, and "them," on the wrong side.

Given the atrocities committed by a variety of terrorist groups worldwide, it should be fairly easy to define terrorism, but strangely there is no universally accepted definition of terrorism. The problem is not linguistic but political. The reason that terrorism is not yet clearly defined is neither due to any disagreements about how dreadful terrorist acts are nor due to any mysterious aspect of the word itself. The difficulty with defining "terrorism" is that however we spin the term, the West will likely be implicated in it in some way. The Oxford Dictionary defines terrorism roughly as an act to instigate extreme fear, or "terror," but inciting fear is part of the job of every military in the world. Stating which side of the conflict is in the right is not going to provide a reliable resolution, as enemies on both sides of the divide believe that they, and not the opponent, are in the right. Killing innocent civilians intentionally seems to offer a uniquely clear-cut case. But the problem is that the nuclear assaults on Nagasaki and Hiroshima constitute without a doubt two examples of intentional mass destruction of civilians. The defenders of atomic attacks on these two Japanese cities contend that it was necessary to force Japan surrender. This has been shown to be untrue. Further, in the wake of the 9/11 atrocities, we clearly condemned the killing of innocent people regardless of who the attackers were and whatever motives or justifications the attackers might have had. We would not call the suspected terrorists any less terrorists if they only did it for vengeance, or for political reasons, to make a statement about US foreign policy, or for any other reasons or any combination of the above.

In the struggle to invent a definition that captures the known terrorist organizations but exonerate the Western war mentality, many creative definitions have been proposed. These definitions often include complex components to allow the West maneuver through it legally uninjured. Some highlight the link between terrorism and religion, but there are Spanish or Irish nationalists who perpetuate terrorist acts outside religion. Others point out that terrorist acts are usually expressions of violence without a clear political purpose, but again, would we not call 9/11 a terrorist act regardless of the terrorists' political agenda or lack of it? The more complex a definition becomes the less valuable it becomes; and the more one could ask why exactly certain components should be included in the definition and others left out.

Efficient definitions should be concise and precise. If we call a spade a spade and take its consequences, we must acknowledge that both the West and the Islamic world are implicated in terrorism. Collateral damage can be justified only if absolutely necessary in a war of self-defense. If a war is not necessary, as the Iraq War turned out to be unnecessary, the resulting collateral damage cannot be said to be necessary either and all its innocent victims were victims of a terrorist act.

As long as language games are high on the agenda, chances of overcoming the war mentality in our culture remain minuscule. At the present, both Tehran and Washington have been involved extensively in language games, propaganda, and political hooliganism in recent years. A characteristic of hooligans is that they do not accept defeat. They demand their opponents to play by the rules, but they do not abide by the rules themselves. In the case of Iran and the US, both countries behave in the same way, while condemning the other party. Both countries have been supporting dissident groups and factional infighters in the Middle East. The US supported Taliban against the Soviet invasion in the 1980s. Iran supports Hezbollah and Hamas. The US forces have sandwiched Iran—in Iraq to the west and Afghanistan to the east of the country. Ahmadinejad has sought relations with the US's closest neighbors, Bolivia, Brazil, Venezuela, and so on. The US forces have kidnapped Iranian elements inside the Georgian territory and a group of Iranians operating within Iraq. Iran has taken American hostages. They both meddle in the affairs of Iraq, but they both demand that the other should stop meddling in the Iraqi territory. Both cite national interests to sway the region, and both try to torpedo the influence of the other party. The problem is not just the rivalry between the two nations, but that both sides want only the other side to conform to the rules of the international community, and each side resorts to propaganda to promote its position.

Seventh, Bet your money on homeland security and get out of conflict zones.

Terrorist threat remains high and American people are concerned. Aside from a core group of ardent advocates of war, the overwhelming majority of the American people do not see any value in the last two wars.

A decade of conflict has proven that warfare intensifies the terrorist threat, not diminish it. Both General Petraeus and General McChrystal drew from statistics showing that every time civilians were killed in combat operations, suicide attacks increased (sometimes six fold). The idea that terrorist cells can be taken out and exterminated by a massive army is steadfastly proving to be a fantasy of the twenty first century.

Given the scale of resources poured into war projects and nation building, we might be safer to divert resources from conflict zones to homeland security initiatives instead.

Eighth, Dream the dream.

Every change starts with a dream. Nothing in this chapter unlocks all the secrets we need to know in order to cultivate a culture of peace, but if we are ever going to arrive at a culture where peace replaces war as a path to conflict resolution, we first have to begin dreaming about a peaceful future. We must believe that lasting peace is possible. We live today with an internal contradiction in our culture: the war mentality is deeply rooted in contemporary culture and in our political ideology, while at the same time the ideal of a peaceful world is intimately woven into human moral concept. This contradiction has corrupted the integrity of our culture, but it also represents a promising opportunity for peace in the future. If we decide to opt for peace today, the next generation may already be able to live in a culture of peace. Why not begin the dream today?

BIBLIOGRAPHY

Adam, H. and Giliomee, H., *Ethnic Power Mobilized: Can South Africa Change?*, New Haven and London, 1979, p. 174

Ainslie, G., *Breakdown of Will*, Cambridge University Press, 2001

Alam, A., *Iran and Post-9/11 World Order: Reflections on Iranian Nuclear Programme*, New Century Publications, 2009

An American Profile—Opinions and Behavior, 1972-1989, p. 600, 620, and 623.

Aptheker, H., *Abolitionism: A Revolutionary Movement*, G. K. Hall & Co., 1989

Ash, T. G., *The Magic Lantern – Events in Eastern Europe in 1989*

Aslan, R., *How to Win a Cosmic War*, Random House 2009

Avery, P., *Modern Iran*, Frederick A. Praeger 1965

Beaufre, A., *An Introduction to Strategy*, Faber, 1963

Bialer, S., *Inside Gorbachev's Russia*, Boulder, 1989

Biko, S., *I Write What I Like*, ed. Aelred Stubbs, London, 1979

Boettke, P. J., *Why Perestroika Failed: The Politics and Economics of Socialist Transformation*, Routledge, 1993

Brown, A. and Gray, J., *Political Culture & Political Change in Communist States*, 1979

Brown, A., *The Gorbachev Factor*, Oxford University Press, 1996

Busky, D. F., *Communism in History and Theory: From Utopian Socialism to the Fall of the Soviet Union*, Praeger publishers, 2002

Carwardine, R.J., *Lincoln: Profiles in Power*, Pearson Longman, 2003

Davenport, R. and Saunders, C., *South Africa: A Modern History*, 5th edition, MacMillan Press Ltd, 2000

Desai, P., *Perestroika in Perspective: the Design and Dilemmas of Soviet Reform*, I.B.Tauris & Co. Ltd, 1989

Dillon, M.L., "The Failure of the American Abolitionists," *The Journal of Southern History*, 25, 1959

Donald, D., *Lincoln Reconsidered: Essays on the Civil War Era*, New York, 1956

Doxtader, E., *With Faith in the Works of Words: the Beginnings of Reconciliation in South Africa 1985-1995*, Michigan State University Press & David Philip Publishers

Duby, G. and Goldhammer, A., *A History of Private Life: Revelations of the Medieval World*, The Belknap Press of Harvard University Press, 1988

Esposito, J. L. and Ramazani, R. K., *Iran at the Crossroads*, Palgrave, 2001

Finkelman, P., *Antislavery*, Vol. 14, Garland Publishing, Inc. 1989

George Frederickson, ed., "No Union with Slaveholders," from *William Lloyd Garrison*, Prentice-Hall, Inc., 1968

Freedman, E.B., *No Turning Back: The History of Feminism and the Future of Women*, Ballantine Books, 2002

Gasiorowski, M. J. and Byrne, M., *Mohammad Mosaddeg and the 1953 Coup in Iran*, Syracuse University Press, 2004

Gerteis, L.S., *Morality & Utility in American Antislavery Reform*, The University of North Carolina Press, 1987

Gorbachev, M. S., *On My Country and the World*, Columbia University Press, 2000

Gorbachev's speech in 1990 on Lenin's birthday, Moscow, 1990 – excerpts translated by Kaiser, R. G.

Granin, D., article on "The December 1989 Central Committee Plenum," *Moscow News*, No. 51, 1989

Harris, S., *The End of Faith: Religion, Terror, and the Future of Reason*, W. W. Norton & Company, 2004

Hasanli, J., *At the Dawn of the Cold War: The Soviet-American Crisis over Iranian Azerbaijan, 1941-1946*, Rowman & Littlefield Publishers, Inc. 2006

Headlam, *Papers*, pp. 242-3

Hughes, J. & Sasse, G. *Ethnicity and Territory in the Former Soviet Union: Regions in Conflict*, Frank Cass Publishers, 2002

Hunter, S. T., *Iran and the World: Continuity in a Revolutionary Decade*, Indiana University Press, 1990

Huntington, S., *Reform and Stability in a Modernizing Multi-Ethnic Society*, Politikon 8, no.2, 1981

Iyer, L.A.K., *Devadasis in South India: Their Traditional Origin and Development*, Man in India, Vol. 7, No. 47, 1927

Kaiser, R. G., *Why Gorbachev Happened*, Simon & Schuster, 1991

Kataria, A., *Democracy on Trial, All Rise!*, Algora Publishing, 2010

Keddie, N. R., *Modern Iran*, Yale University Press 2006

Lambton, A. K. S., *Qajar Persia*, University of Texas Press 1988

Lijphart, A., *Democracy in Plural Societies*, Yale University Press, 1977

Litwack, L.F., *The Abolitionist Dilemma: The Antislavery Movement and the Northern Negro*, New England Quarterly, 34, 1961

Louw, P.E., *The Rise, Fall, and Legacy of Apartheid*, Praeger, 2004

Loveland, A.C., *Evangelicalism and 'Immediate Emancipation' in American Antislavery Thought*, Journal of Social History, 1966

Manniche, L., *Sexual Life in Ancient Egypt*, KPI Ltd, 1987, p.65. See also: Wonderly, D.M., *The Quest for a Female Identity*, University Press of America, Inc., 2003

Marais, *Cape Coloured People*, chap. 5

Margolis, J., *O: the Intimate History of the Orgasm*, Grove Press, 2004

Marx, A.W., *Lessons of Struggle: South African Internal Opposition, 1960-1990*, Oxford University Press, 1992, pp. 32-8

McCauley, M. *The Rise and Fall of the Soviet Union*, Pearson Education Limited, 2008

MccGwire, M., *Perestroika and Soviet National Security*, The Brookings Institution, 1991

Medvedev, R. & Chiesa, G., *Time of Change*, New York, 1990

Medvedev, Z., *Gorbachev*, New York, 1986

Millspaugh, A. C., *Americans in Persia*, The Brookings Institution 1946

Mintz, S. & Stauffer, J., *The Problem of Evil: Slavery, Freedom, and the Ambiguities of American Reform*, University of Massachusetts Press, 2007

Mir-Hosseini, Z., *Islam and Democracy in Iran: Eshkevari and the Quest for Reform*, I.B. Tauris, 2006

Mitchell, J. and Oakley, A., *What is Feminism?*, Basil Blackwell, 1986, p. 9

Mui, C.L. and Murphy, J.S., *Gender Struggles: Practical Approaches to Contemporary Feminism*, Rowman & Littlefield Publishers, Inc. 2002

Naji, K., *Ahmadinejad: The Secret History of Iran's Radical Leader*, I.B.Tauris & Co. Ltd., 2008

Perry, L., *Radical Abolitionism: Anarchy and the Government of God in Antislavery Thought*, The University of Tennessee Press, 1996

Platzky, L. and Walker, C., *The Surplus People: Forced Removals in South Africa*, Johannesburg, 1985, p. 65

Pollack, K. M., Byman, D. L., Indyk, M., Maloney, S., O'Hanlon, M. E., Riedel, B., *Which Path to Persia? Options for a New American Strategy toward Iran*, Brookings Institution, 2009

Pollack, K. M., Byman, D. L., Indyk, M., Maloney, S., O'Hanlon, M. E., Riedel, B., *Which Path to Persia? Options for a New American Strategy toward Iran*, Brookings Institution, 2009

Pollack, K. M., *The Persian Puzzle*, Random House 2004

Ryan, B., *Feminism and the Women's Movement: Dynamics of Change in Social Movement, Ideology and Activism*, Routledge, 1992

Schmidt-Häur, C., *Gorbachev: The Path to Power*, I.B.Tauris & Co. Ltd, 1986

Schmittroth, L., *Statistical Record of Women Worldwide*, First Edition, Gale Research Inc., 1991, survey 21

Schumann, C., *Structural Changes and Business Cycles in South Africa 1806-1936*, Westminster, 1938

Sciolino, E., *Persian Mirrors: The Elusive Face of Iran*, The Free Press, 2000

Shakibi, Z., *Khatami and Gorbachev: Politics of Change in the Islamic Republic of Iran and the USSR*, I.B. Tauris Publishers, 2010

Shapiro, A., *Feminists Revision History*, Rutgers University Press, 1994

Shmelyov's Novy Mir article, *Gorbachev & Glasnost*, Isaac J. Tarasulo, 1989 (English translation)

Sklar, K.K., *Women's Rights Emerges within the Antislavery Movement 1830-1870: A Brief History with Documents*, Bedford/St. Martin's, 2000

Smith, H., *The New Russians*, New York, 1990

Sorin, G., *Abolitionism: A New Perspective*, Praeger Publishers, 1972

Stearns, P.N., Adas, M., Schwartz, S.B. and Gilbert, M.J., *World Civilizations: the Global Experience*, Fifth Edition, Pearson Longman, 2007

Survey of Race Relations in South Africa, 1980, p. 85. See also Thompson, p. 202

Taylor, H., *The Ladies Petition*, Westminster Review, January 1867

Tazmini, G., *Khatami's Iran: The Islamic Republic and the Turbulent Path to Reform*, I.B. Tauris Publishers, 2009

Thompson, L., *A History of South Africa*, Revised edition, Yale University Press, 1995

Time Magazine editors, *Mikhail S. Gorbachev: An Intimate Biography*, New York, 1988

Tobias, S., *Faces of Feminism: an Activist's Reflections on the Women's Movement*, Westview Press, 1997

Walters, M., *Feminism: a Very Short Introduction*, Oxford University Press, 2005

Waugh, J.C., *One Man Great Enough: Abraham Lincoln's Road to Civil War*, Harcourt, Inc., 2007

Wonderly, D., *The Quest for a Female Identity*, University Press of America, Inc., 2003

Zogby, J., *Arab Voices: What the Arab World is Saying to Us and Why It Matters*, Palgrave Macmillan, 2010

ENDNOTES

1 Critics often point out that other countries are hypocritical too. It is in fact true that other countries are just as hypocritical and ego-centrist as the US, but they do not try to change America. Ego-centrism only becomes a problem when a state tries to impose its will on other states, in particular when the imposition involves military force.

2 *The Iraq Study Group Report*, p. 29

3 www.guardian.co.uk/politics/2003/feb/11/foreignpolicy.iraq2

4 The former Under Secretary of the State Department from 2001 to 2003, Charlotte Beers, was assigned the task of improving communication with the Arab countries. Beers had a long and successful career as businesswoman and marketing professional. She hoped to utilize her marketing skills to alter the negative image of American foreign policy in the eyes of Arabs. As Zogby recalls, Beers asked his advice before a trip through the region. Zogby's advice was unambiguous and simple. "Listen," he told her. In his latest book *Arab Voices: What the Arab World is Saying to Us and Why It Matters*, Zogby describes how Beers ignored the advice and instead began to sell *at*, rather than trying to sell *to*, the Arabs the American policy and objectives for the region. As he states: "During her stops in Morocco and Egypt, Beers received a warm official welcome. But when the discussion turned to US policy, Arabs repeatedly asked Beers tough questions about Palestine and the double standards America demonstrated in siding with Israel against the Arab states. Though I had warned Beers that these topics would be foremost on the minds of Arabs, I was told this line of questioning frustrated her because it distracted from the message she sought to project: America as a good and tolerant country."

5 BBC News, May 31, 2010: http://www.bbc.co.uk/news/10198036

6 www.bbc.co.uk/news/11932041

7   Apple, R. W., Pentagon Papers: Johnson Administration Had Systematically lied, not only to the Public but also Congress, New York Times, June 23, 1966

8   Riots broke out after an unemployed Tunisian student set himself alight in December 2010 out of frustration with the police, when he was prevented from selling his vegetables because he was unlicensed. The demonstrations ousted the Tunisian President, Ben Ali and triggered a domino-effect throughout the Arab world. Soon democracy movements spread through Jordan, Algeria, Egypt, and Yemen. This had nothing to do with President Obama. Obama is not the galvanizing figure in the Middle East, as the White House is trying to cast him. In fact, the President is viewed in the region as the man who speaks with two tongues.

9   Utilitarianism was developed by Jeremy Bentham and several other British philosophers.

10 Kataria, A., *Democracy on Trial, All Rise!*, Algora Publishing, 2010

11 Kataria, pp. 3-5

12 Kataria pp. 6-8

13 Kataria, pp. 8-9

14 Kataria, pp. 16-9 and 58-61 and 168-72

15 Kataria, p. 172

16 Kataria, pp. 19-25

17 Kataria, p. 148

18 www.electronicsweekly.com/blogs/electronics-legislation/2010/08/new-laws-on-conflict-materials.html

19 This statement is based on an interview with US troops broadcast on radio in 2007 or 2008, as well as the perceived fear of the Islamic culture and influence in the West among some segments of the population.

20 Kataria, p. 148

21 Harris, p. 45

22 Harris, p. 134

23 Harris, p. 15

24 Harris, p. 131

25 Harris, p. 131

26 For instance, the concept of "us" and "them": "you are either with us or against us"; or take Huntington's concept of clash of civilizations in the context of Bush Administration's War on Terror to defend "our way of life."

27 Harris, p. 131

28 Harris, chpt. 5 & 6

29 Kataria, pp. 1-2

30 Mintz & Stauffer, p. 5

31 Mintz & Stauffer, p. 96

32   Mintz & Stauffer, p. 98

33   Sorin, pp. 22-9

34   Mintz & Stauffer, p. 99

35   Sorin, pp. 38-9

36   Dillon, p. 160

37   Sorin, p. 52

38   Sorin, p. 47

39   Sorin, p. 26-9

40   Sorin, p. 48. See also: Finkelman, pp. 511-30

41   Sorin, pp. 49-51

42   Dillon, pp. 160-1. Alternatively see: Finkelman, pp. 166-7

43   Sorin, pp. 42-4

44   Sorin, p. 106

45   Sorin, pp. 53-4

46   Litwack, pp. 51-2

47   Sorin, p. 56

48   Litwack, pp. 52-3

49   Litwack, p. 53

50   Litwack, p. 54

51   Litwack, p. 55

52   Litwack, p. 58

53   Sorin, p. 105

54   Litwack, pp. 72-3

55   Sorin, pp. 90-1

56   Perry, pp. 204-7

57   Perry, p. 158

58   Sorin, p. 85-6

59   Sorin, p. 88

60   Aptheker, p. 119

61   Sorin, pp. 140 & 118

62   Sorin, pp. 140-1

63   Sorin, p. 121

64   Sorin, pp. 121-2

65   Sorin, p. 122

66   Sorin, p. 131

67   Sorin, pp. 131-2

68   Carwardine, p. 145

69   Carwardine, p. 145

70   Carwardine, p. 141

71   Sorin, p. 166

72   Carwardine, p. 141

73   Abraham Lincoln quotes: http://quotationsbook.com/quote/44759/

74   Sorin, p. 142

75   Sorin, pp. 148-54

76   Freedman, p. 20

77   Freedman, p. 46

78   Freedman, pp. 46-7

79   Freedman, pp. 3-4

80   See Sklar for a discussion on this.

81   Mitchell and Oakley, p. 10

82   Mitchell and Oakley, pp. 22-5

83   Tobias, pp. 84-5

84   Tobias, p. 97

85   Tobias, pp. 111-33

86   Wonderly, D., *The Quest for a Female Identity*, University Press of America, Inc., 2003, p. 309

87   Delmar, R. *What is Feminism?*, published in: Mitchell, J. and Oakley, A., *What is Feminism?*, Basil Blackwell, 1986, p. 9

88   Mitchell and Oakley, pp. 12-3

89   Mitchell and Oakley, p. 27

90   Mitchell and Oakley, pp. 20-1

91   Mitchell and Oakley, p. 49

92   Mitchell and Oakley, pp. 18-9

93   Mitchell and Oakley, p. 22

94   Mitchell and Oakley, p. 20. See also: Taylor, H., *The Ladies Petition*, Westminster Review, January 1867, pp. 63-79

95   Cole, pp. 206-7

96   Aslan, p. 24

97   Kengor, pp. 240-1

98   http://wais.stanford.edu//History/history_ussrandreagan.htm

99   Deffeyes, K. S., *Beyond Oil: The View from Hubbert's Peak*, Hill and Wang, 2006

100 Kaiser, R., *Why Gorbachev Happened: His Triumphs and His Failure*

101 Kaiser, p. 177

102 http://articles.baltimoresun.com/1990-12-21/news/1990355075_1_shevardnadze
-dictatorship-gorbachev

103 Kengor, pp. 239-244

104 Ronald Reagan named the Soviet Union "The Evil Empire" and refused to deal
with it until relations were improved following Gorbachev's transformation
initiatives.

105 Kaiser, R., *Why Gorbachev Happened: His Triumphs and His Failure*

106 Kaiser, R., *Why Gorbachev Happened: His Triumphs and His Failure*

107 Louw, p. 190

108 Thompson, L., *A History of South Africa*, Revised edition, Yale University Press,
1995, pp. 31-2

109 Thompson, L., pp. 33-6

110 Thompson, L., pp. 38-9

111 Thompson, L., p. 41

112 Worden, *Slavery*, 143-4

113 Thompson, L., p. 45

114 Thompson, L., p. 56

115 Thomspon, L. p. 53

116 Schumann, C., *Structural Changes and Business Cycles in South Africa 1806-1936*, Westminster, 1938

117 Thompson, L., pp. 52-3

118 Thompson, L. p. 57-60

119 Marais, *Cape Coloured People*, chap. 5

120 Davenport, pp. 49-54

121 The gold deposits in the Witwatersrand province were the largest known
source of gold.

122 Louw, P.E., *The Rise, Fall, and Legacy of Apartheid*, Praeger, 2004, p. 3

123 Thompson, p. 140

124 Louw, p. 18. See also: Headlam, *Papers*, pp. 242-3

125 Thompson, p. 120

126 Louw, p. 22

127 Headlam, p. 459. See also Louw, p. 15

128 Headlam, p. 297. See also Louw, p. 15

129 Louw, p. 19

130 Louw, pp. 29-30

131 Louw, p. 30

132 Louw, p. 37

133 Louw, p. 42

134 Louw, pp. 41-3

135 Thompson, p. 121

136 Louw, pp. 22 and 25, and Thompson, p. 157

137 Thompson, p. 156

138 Louw, p. 25

139 Thompson, p. 135

140 He was assassinated on September 6th 1966 after entering the House of Assembly in Cape Town.

141 Louw, pp. 28-9

142 Louw, pp. 32-5

143 Adam, H. and Giliomee, H., *Ethnic Power Mobilized: Can South Africa Change?*, New Haven and London, 1979, p. 174

144 Thompson, p. 201

145 *Survey of Race Relations in South Africa*, 1980, p. 85. See also Thompson, p. 202

146 Thompson, pp. 202-4

147 Thompson, p. 197-8

148 Thompson, p. 190

149 Thompson, pp. 190-1

150 Platzky and Walker, p. 10

151 The Bantu people consist of several hundred African ethnic groups in South Africa practicing Bantu languages and cultures.

152 Platzky, L. and Walker, C., *The Surplus People: Forced Removals in South Africa*, Johannesbur, 1985, p. 65

153 Thompson, p. 206

154 * Do not confuse him with Louis Botha who was mentioned earlier in this chapter.

155 Louw, p. 88

156 Lijphart, A., *Democracy in Plural Societies*, Yale University Press, 1977

157 Louw, p. 89

158 Huntington, S., *Reform and Stability in a Modernizing Multi-Ethnic Society*, Politikon 8, no.2, 1981

159 Beaufre, A., *An Introduction to Strategy*, Faber, 1963

160 Louw, pp. 91-3

161 Thompson, pp. 224-5

162 Thompson, pp. 226-7

163 Marx, A.W., *Lessons of Struggle: South African Internal Opposition, 1960-1990*, Oxford University Press, 1992, pp. 32-8

164 Black Consciousness is usually abbreviated to BC.

165 Biko, S., I Write What I like, ed. Aelred Stubbs, London, 1979, p. 49. See also Thompson, p. 212

166 He was beaten severely by the police, then transported naked in the back of a van for 750 miles the night before he died. He died of brain injuries. (Thompson, p. 213)

167 Thompson, pp. 212-3

168 Thompson, p. 228-9

169 Doxtader, E., *With Faith in the Works of Words: the Beginnings of Reconciliation in South Africa 1985-1995*, Michigan State University Press & David Philip Publishers, chp. 2

170 Louw, p. 164

171 Thompson, pp. 232-3

172 Louw, p. 165

173 Thompson, p. 247

174 Low, p. 162

175 Known as the Convention for a Democratic South Africa (CODESA).

76 Louw, p. 163

177 Thompson, p. 247

178 Thompson, p. 248

179 Thompson, p. 248

180 Louw, p. 172

181 Known as the Bisho Massacre

182 Louw, pp. 166-7

183 Louw, p. 165

184 Louw, p. 163

185 Louw, p. 172

186 Thompson, 278

187 Louw, p. 173

188 Keddie, p. 23

189 Keddie, pp. 23-25 & 37-39

190 The company was expected to generate an annual profit in excess of one million US dollars. The Iranian treasury was to receive £15,000 (less than 30,000 US dollars) per annum and a quarter of the net profit.

191 Aslan, p. 24

192 Lambton, p. 249

193 Pollack, p. 20

194 Avery, p. 128

195 Avery, p. 134

196 Nasir al-Din Shah was assassinated by one of Al-Afghani's disciples in 1896. Mozaffir al-Din Shah assumed the power after his father's death. It was Mozaffir al-Din Shah who signed the Constitution. Mohammad Ali Shah was the son of Mozaffir al-Din Shah.

197 Ramazani, p. 106

198 Shuster, p. 182

199 Shuster, pp. 188-89

200 Shuster, p. 191

201 Ramazani, p. 106

202 Keddie, pp. 73-5

The word *jangal* and the English term *jungle* are related.

203 Keddie, p. 76

204 Keddie, p. 78

205 Millspaugh, pp. 27-8

206 Millspaugh, p. 28

207 Millspaugh, pp. 27-8

208 Shuster, p. 204

209 Millspaugh, p. 243

210 Millspaugh, pp. 242-3

211 Naji, p. 143

212 Naji, p. 142

213 The Council on Foreign Relations: www.cfr.org/publication/12806/timeline. html

214 Shakibi, pp. 292-3

215 Naji, Forward

216 Naji, p. 207

217 Naji, p. 157

218 Sympathy for Iran ran high on the Arab Street even before the election of Ahmadinejad thanks to President Bush's numerous verbal attacks on the country. In January 2005, a friend of mine and I visited the airport tax free shop in Hurgata, a tourist destination on the Red Sea in Egypt, to purchase a bottle of wine each before our departure. As we queued up at the end of a very long line waiting to be served, an Egyptian airport security agent recognized that we were Iranians. He rushed to us and said "follow me," taking us to the very front of the queue bypassing 15 or 20 other customers while he shouted to the cashier in Arabic, "Iranians, Iranians...." The special service made us realize how the West's biased media campaign against Iran had made Iranians so popular on Arab street.

219 Naji, p. 140

220 Naji, pp. 122-3

221 Naji, p. 133

222 A copy of President Obama's letter to the Iranian leaders in 2009 can be found on: www.carnegiecouncil.org/resources/articles_papers_reports/0020.html

223 He flip flopped on many other issues too: one minute he would attack the Israeli leader, the next he would reaffirm the US-Israeli relations and pressure the Palestinian leader to soften his stance; he would say that the principle of religious freedom should be unbreakable, when the Muslims wanted to build a mosque near the Ground Zero, but he would back down the next day, saying he was not talking about the wisdom of the mosque being built there; he ran on a platform of creating a universal healthcare system, but he budged too fast to Republican demands, even though the Republicans never accepted his watered down healthcare bill anyway. In his defense, he came to power in one of toughest periods of American history and it is not sure, if a different president would have accomplished any better results, but his flip flopping has not been helping him much.

224 Shuster, p. 204

225 Millspaugh, p. 74 (footnote)

226 The policy options were published in: Pollack, K. M., Byman, D. L., Indyk, M., Maloney, S., O'Hanlon, M. E., Riedel, B., *Which Path to Persia? Options for a New American Strategy toward Iran*, Brookings Institution, 2009

227 A copy of the letter Vartan Gregorian proposed President Obama should send to the Iranian leaders in 2009 can be found on: www.carnegiecouncil.org/resources/articles_papers_reports/0020.html

228 BBC News, October 13, 2010: http://www.bbc.co.uk/news/business-11457074

229 CIA – The World Factbook: https://www.cia.gov/library/publications-the-world-factbook/geos/vm.html

230 Stearns, P. N., Adas, M., Schwartz, S. B., and Gilbert, M. J., p. 855

231 Cognitive discounting was studied in depth by the American psychiatrist, George Ainslie. He developed the theory of hyperbolic discounting, which claimed that people devalue an expected future event at different rates, depending upon how far away it is. The farther away the future, the more its value is discounted, while the values of events immediately present are magnified in comparison. Mathematically, the discounting takes the path of a hyperbole, Ainslie argues. He devised the hyperbolic discounting theory to explain self-harming behavior, such as addiction, gambling, akrasia, etc., where immediate satisfaction distorts an individual's assessment of harm that is expected to materialize at a point in the future (Ainslie, chps 1–4).

In our analysis, the short term successes in the battlefield are nearer to us and their benefits inflated, while the longer term failures are discounted hyperbolically.

232 Russett, B., Starr, H., Kinsella, D., *World Politics: The Menu for Choice*, Ninth Edition, Wadsworth Cengage Learning, 2010, p. 146

233 http://portal.unesco.org

INDEX